SCHAUM'S OUTLI

THEORY AND P

of

MACROECONOMIC THEORY

•

by

EUGENE A. DIULIO, Ph. D.

Associate Professor of Economics
Fordham University

SCHAUM'S OUTLINE SERIES

McGRAW-HILL BOOK COMPANY

New York   St. Louis   San Francisco   Auckland   Düsseldorf   Johannesburg
Kuala Lumpur   London   Mexico   Montreal   New Delhi   Panama
Paris   São Paulo   Singapore   Sydney   Tokyo   Toronto

07-017049-5

1 2 3 4 5 6 7 8 9 10 11 12 13 14 15 16 17 18 19 20   SH SH   7 9 8 7 6 5 4

Library of Congress Cataloging in Publication Data

Diulio, Eugene A
    Schaum's outline of theory and problems of macro-
economic theory.

    (Schaum's outline series)
    1. Macroeconomics — Problems, exercises, etc.

I. Title.   II. Title: Theory and problems of
macroeconomic theory.
[HB171.5.D545]   339'.01   74-20611
ISBN 0-07-017049-5

Preface

Macroeconomics seeks to explain the level of employment, output and prices in a decentralized economic system. Over the past thirty years, the study of macroeconomics has become increasingly important as governments have committed themselves to promoting "maximum employment, production and purchasing power."

The purpose of this book is to present in a clear and systematic way the theoretical core of macroeconomics found in most intermediate macroeconomics texts. The book can be used by undergraduates or graduate business students as a supplement to current standard texts or by instructors as an independent text supplemented by empirical or policy readings. The book should also prove useful to graduate economics students as a review of the analytical core of macroeconomic theory.

Each chapter begins with definitions and a concise presentation of theory supported by illustrative material. This is followed by multiple-choice review questions with answers. Solved problems further illustrate and amplify the material and aid in refining the theory. The solved problems are both graphical and numerical; the learning-by-doing methodology involves the student in macroeconomic analysis and provides repetition of the analytical core which is imperative to the learning of economic theory.

The approach is traditional, presenting the Keynesian spending model first and integrating the money and labor markets into the model in subsequent chapters. The theories of consumption and investment demand and the demand for money are also included. In using the book, it is possible to omit entire chapters without impairing the development of later analysis. For example, Chapters 5 and 6 on the international sector and multipliers for a four-sector model are not essential for the analysis of commodity equilibrium in Chapter 11. Similarly, Chapter 12 on money and the level of income and Chapter 15 on the contemporary theory of the demand for money are not necessary for the analysis of money market equilibrium in Chapter 14 and the effectiveness of monetary and fiscal policy in Chapter 17.

Portions of this book have been used in preliminary form by graduate business and undergraduate economics students at Fordham University. I am deeply grateful for their suggestions as well as the valuable comments of my colleague, Professor Dominick Salvatore. I would also like to express my sincere gratitude to the entire Schaum staff of McGraw-Hill for their patient assistance, to Mrs. Ruth Rubin for her excellent typing and to my wife Rosemary for her continuous encouragement and support.

EUGENE A. DIULIO

New York
November 1974

CONTENTS

CONTENTS

CONTENTS

Chapter 1

An Introduction to Macroeconomic Analysis

1.1 MACROECONOMICS

Macroeconomics is the study of aggregate economic behavior. In macroeconomics, we analyze the principal determinants of an economy's *level of income, general level of prices* and *growth of income*. This can be contrasted to microeconomics, where the behavior of individual units is analyzed.

1.2 MODEL BUILDING

A model of individual or aggregate economic behavior represents a simplification of real-world economic complexities. In constructing such models, economists concentrate on what they consider the most important determinant(s) of the phenomenon under consideration. For instance, in analyzing the level of aggregate output, it has been useful to divide the economy into the following spending sectors: *household, business, government* and *international*. Once the spending behavior for each sector is specified, the economist is able to predict the level of aggregate output.

EXAMPLE 1. Spending by the household, business, government and international sectors determines the value of goods and services produced.

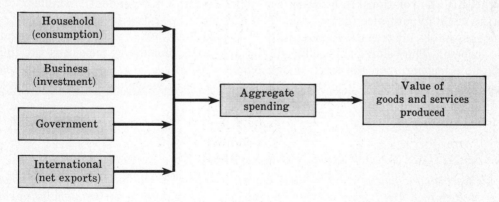

Fig. 1-1

1.3 FUNCTIONS, EQUATIONS AND GRAPHS

Economists generally link the volume of consumption by the household sector to the receipt of disposable income. Such behavior is specified by saying that consumption C is a function f of disposable income Yd, or $C = f(Yd)$, meaning that aggregate consumption depends systematically upon the amount of aggregate disposable income.

1

Functional notation is both a concise and convenient way of presenting hypothesized economic behavior. Furthermore, it defines the economic relationship under study (i.e., which is the dependent and which is the independent variable). The expression $C = f(Yd)$ shows that aggregate consumption depends on the receipt of disposable income. Thus, consumption is the dependent variable and disposable income is the independent variable.

If the relationship between aggregate consumption and aggregate disposable income has been statistically established, it is possible to specify consumption behavior through an equation, graph or table.

EXAMPLE 2. Suppose that the measured relationship of consumption and disposable income is given by the equation $C = \$40 + 0.80\,Yd$. This measured relationship of aggregate consumption and aggregate disposable income is shown in Table 1 and Fig. 1-2.

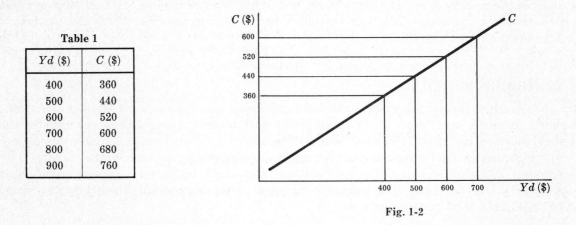

Table 1

Yd (\$)	C (\$)
400	360
500	440
600	520
700	600
800	680
900	760

Fig. 1-2

In the absence of statistical measurement, it is possible to specify the form of the function (i.e., to specify the relationship between the dependent and independent variables). For instance, we could hypothesize that $C = a_1 + a_2 Yd$, where a_1 and a_2 have values greater than zero. Accordingly, aggregate consumption is a positive, linear function of aggregate disposable income. The behavioral coefficient for disposable income a_2 measures the influence of disposable income upon the level of aggregate consumption. (a_2 is in effect the slope of the consumption function.) The parameter a_1 has a positive value and is independent of disposable income.

1.4 ENDOGENOUS AND EXOGENOUS VARIABLES

A variable is *endogenous* if its value is determined within the model and *exogenous* if its value is determined by forces outside the model. A change in an exogenous variable is classified as an *autonomous* change.

EXAMPLE 3. The consumption equation is specified by $C = \$40 + 0.80\,Yd$. In macroeconomics, the level of income is determined by the model, thereby making $0.80\,Yd$ an endogenous variable. The constant \$40 represents exogenous forces since the effect of nonincome forces upon consumption is not specified. If outside forces change the consumption function from $C = \$40 + 0.80\,Yd$ to $C = \$50 + 0.80\,Yd$, there is a \$10 autonomous increase in consumption spending.

The economist assumes that the parameters of the equations are constant (i.e., that endogenous relationships are constant and exogenous forces do not change unless specified). This assumption is noted by *ceteris paribus*, meaning other things held constant.

1.5 EQUILIBRIUM

Equilibrium exists in economics when the intentions of diverse forces are in balance. Disequilibrium therefore indicates imbalance and change from a current position.

EXAMPLE 4. Businesses produce goods and services with the expectation of selling these goods and services at specified prices. If consumers do not wish to buy at the expected prices, there is disequilibrium and prices and/or output will change. If consumers purchase output at the expected price, there is equilibrium and therefore no change in output or price.

1.6 MONEY AND REAL VALUE OF OUTPUT

The value of aggregate output is the dollar value of final goods and services produced in an economy during a specified period of time. This value is derived by summing the price times quantity ($\Sigma \, p \times q$) of all final output. Obviously the value of output changes if there is a change in price and/or quantity. A change in price and/or quantity is classified as a change in the money value of output. Changes in the real value of output occur only from changes in the quantity of output. Money values are denoted by capital letters while real values carry small letters.

1.7 AGGREGATE ECONOMIC BEHAVIOR

Aggregate economic behavior is the sum of individual behavior.

EXAMPLE 5. An economy is composed of five households. The spending behavior of each household is specified in Table 2.

Suppose that each household has the same level of disposable income. The aggregate consumption function is the sum of the exogenous variables plus the sum of the behavioral coefficients of the endogenous variable divided by 5. Thus,

$$\text{Aggregate Consumption} = \$25 + \frac{4.50 \, Yd}{5}$$

$$= \$25 + 0.90 \, Yd$$

Table 2

Household	Consumption Function
A	$C_A = \qquad\quad 1.00 \, Yd$
B	$C_B = \$10 + 0.90 \, Yd$
C	$C_C = \quad 10 + 0.80 \, Yd$
D	$C_D = \qquad 5 + 0.85 \, Yd$
E	$C_E = \qquad\quad 0.95 \, Yd$

Alternatively, if disposable income is not evenly distributed, weights are assigned to the behavioral coefficients according to the given distribution. The sum of these weights will be the denominator of the endogenous variable in the summing process. We shall assume that the disposable income of households B and C is twice that of A, D and E. A weight of one is attached to the behavioral coefficients of A, D and E and two to the behavioral coefficients of B and C. Thus,

$$\text{Aggregate Consumption} = \$25 + \frac{6.20 \, Yd}{7}$$

$$= \$25 + 0.8857 \, Yd$$

Example 5 shows that aggregate consumption depends not only upon the behavior of individual units but upon the importance of each behavioral unit. To theorize about aggregate economic behavior, we assume that the behavior of individual units is stable and that the composition of the aggregate is constant or changing in some predictable way. In making the latter assumption, we assume that income changes are dispersed among and not concentrated within individual household units.

Review Questions

1. Macroeconomics is concerned with (a) the level of output of goods and services, (b) the general level of prices, (c) the growth of income or (d) all of the above.

2. The equation $C = \$20 + 0.90\,Yd$ predicts that consumption is (a) \$90 when disposable income is \$100, (b) \$100 when disposable income is \$90, (c) \$110 when disposable income is \$100 or (d) \$180 when disposable income is \$200.

3. The level of money income increases (a) if there is an increase in the price level, (b) if there is an increase in the output of goods and services, (c) if there is an increase in the price level or the output of goods and services or (d) all of the above.

4. In the equation $C = C_0 + bYd$, the behavioral coefficient is (a) C_0, (b) Yd, (c) b or (d) all of the above.

5. *Ceteris paribus* means that (a) other factors are held constant, (b) no other variable affects the dependent variable, (c) there is no other model that can explain the dependent variable or (d) the model is logical.

6. In the equation $C = C_0 + bYd$, C_0 is (a) a parameter helping to determine the level of consumption, (b) a parameter whose value depends upon the level of disposable income, (c) a behavioral coefficient or (d) a dependent variable.

7. The equation $I = jY + vi$, where $j > 0$ and $v < 0$, indicates that I is (a) positively related to Y and i, (b) negatively related to Y and i, (c) positively related to Y and negatively related to i or (d) negatively related to Y and positively related to i.

8. Which of the following statements is *correct*?
   (a) A variable is endogenous if its value is determined by forces outside the model.
   (b) A change in an exogenous variable is classified as an autonomous change.
   (c) A variable is exogenous if its value is determined by forces within the model.
   (d) There is imbalance and therefore disequilibrium if there are diverse forces within a model.

9. In stating that $C = f(Yd, W)$,
   (a) it is hypothesized that Yd is a more important determinant of C than W,
   (b) it is hypothesized that W is a more important determinant of C than Yd,
   (c) W and Yd are dependent variables explaining C or
   (d) Yd and W are independent variables explaining C.

10. Which of the following statements is *not* correct?
   (a) An increase in the real value of output indicates an increase in the quantity of output.
   (b) In constructing a theory of aggregate behavior, we assume that the composition of the aggregate is relatively constant.
   (c) Empirical fact is the basis for model construction in macroeconomic theory.
   (d) Equilibrium occurs when the intentions of diverse forces are in balance.

Answers to Review Questions

1. (d) Review Section 1.1.

2. (c) Review Section 1.3.

3. (d) Review Section 1.6.

4. (c) Review Section 1.3.

5. (a) Review Section 1.4.

6. (a) Review Section 1.3.

7. (c) Review Section 1.3.

8. (b) Review Sections 1.4 and 1.5.

9. (d) Review Section 1.3.

10. (c) Review Sections 1.2, 1.5, 1.6 and 1.7.

Solved Problems

1.1. Explain the following functions and establish the dependent and independent variables for (a) $I = f(i)$ and (b) $I = f(Y_{t+1} - Y_t)$.

(a) Investment I is a function of (depends upon) the rate of interest i. Investment is the dependent variable; the rate of interest is the independent variable.

(b) Investment I is dependent upon the change in income Y between periods $t+1$ and t. Investment is the dependent variable; the change in income is the independent variable.

1.2. For the following equations, state the (a) dependent variables, (b) independent variables, (c) parameters and (d) behavioral coefficients.

$$(1) \quad z = a + by$$

$$(2) \quad m = an + by$$

$$(3) \quad d = aj - by$$

(a) Dependent variables: (1) z, (2) m, (3) d.

(b) Independent variables: (1) y, (2) n and y, (3) j and y.

(c) Parameters: (1) a and b, (2) a and b, (3) a and b.

(d) Behavioral coefficients: (1) b, (2) a and b, (3) a and b.

1.3. Are the variables in Problem 1.2 positively or negatively related?

(1) z is positively related to y.

(2) m is positively related to both n and y.

(3) d is positively related to j and negatively related to y.

1.4. Explain the following statement: Aggregate consumption is explained by the receipt of disposable income, *ceteris paribus*.

Aggregate consumption is systematically related to (is a function of) disposable income. Other factors that influence consumption are held constant so that a precise statement can be made about the dependency of consumption upon disposable income.

1.5. What is the importance of the *ceteris paribus* assumption in economic theory?

Ceteris paribus allows the economist to make precise statements about the theoretical relationship between an independent and a dependent variable. For example, if consumption is assumed to be a function of disposable income, one is able to specify in the model how a change in aggregate disposable income affects aggregate consumption.

1.6. Explain the components of the equation $C = C_0 + bYd$.

C_0 represents other factors that are assumed constant. The behavioral coefficient b measures the relationship between disposable income and consumption. Since b is positive, consumption moves in the same direction as disposable income.

1.7. Explain the components of the equation $C = \$20 + 0.90\,Yd$.

> There is $20 of consumption regardless of the level of disposable income. Consumption changes by 90¢ for every $1 change in disposable income. Consumption changes in the same direction as disposable income.

1.8. Using the equation $C = \$20 + 0.90\,Yd$, construct a schedule for consumption when disposable income is $200, $250, $300, $350 and $400.

> The schedule for consumption is shown in Table 3.

Table 3

Yd ($)	200	250	300	350	400
C ($)	200	245	290	335	380

1.9. Is there a difference between a graph, a schedule and an equation?

> Graphs, schedules and equations are alternate ways of presenting relationships between variables. When only two variables are being related, each method has individual merits. Graphs and schedules become cumbersome when a number of variables are being related.

1.10. Construct an equation from the straight-line consumption function in Fig. 1-3.

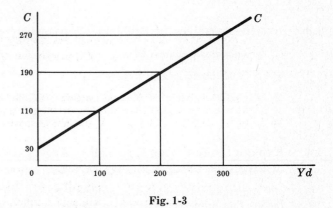

> Consumption is $30 when disposable income is zero. Consumption increases $80 for each $100 increase in disposable income. Thus the behavioral coefficient of the equation is 0.80. The linear consumption function is
>
> $$C = \$30 + 0.80\,Yd$$

(see Example 2).

Fig. 1-3

1.11. Suppose that the business sector intends to produce goods valued at $380 while households plan to spend $330 and save $50 and businessmen plan to borrow $30 from households in order to invest $30 in new plant and equipment. Does this situation represent equilibrium or disequilibrium?

> There is disequilibrium since the intentions of diverse parties are not in balance. In this situation, businessmen produce goods at a value exceeding the spending intentions of households and businesses.

1.12. Would there still be disequilibrium in Problem 1.11 if businessmen intended to invest $50 in new plant and equipment?

> There would be equilibrium since plans to purchase would be equal to intentions to produce.

1.13. Table 4 gives the consumption functions for five households. Identify the households in which there have been autonomous changes in consumption demand between periods t and $t+1$.

Table 4

Household	Period t	Period $t+1$
A	$C_A = \$10 + 0.90\,Yd$	$C_A = \$20 + 0.90\,Yd$
B	$C_B = \quad 5 + 0.95\,Yd$	$C_B = \quad 5 + 0.95\,Yd$
C	$C_C = \quad 30 + 0.80\,Yd$	$C_C = \quad 30 + 0.80\,Yd$
D	$C_D = \quad 15 + 0.85\,Yd$	$C_D = \quad 10 + 0.85\,Yd$
E	$C_E = \quad 10 + 0.80\,Yd$	$C_E = \quad 10 + 0.80\,Yd$

Household A had a \$10 autonomous increase in consumption demand. Household D had a \$5 decrease in autonomous consumption demand.

1.14. Identify the exogenous and endogenous variables in the investment demand equation $I = I_0 + aY - vi$.

The value of an exogenous variable is determined by forces outside the model while the value of an endogenous variable is determined within the model. I_0 is obviously an exogenous variable. In the model of income determination Y is an endogenous variable. The variable i is an endogenous variable if the level of interest rates is determined in the model of income determination and exogenous if not. (See Section 1.4.)

1.15. An economy has a 2% increase in its money level of income in period t, 4% in period $t+1$ and 6% in period $t+2$. What are the possible explanations for the growth in the money level of income?

In this economy, growth in the money level of income may be due to (1) real output increasing at an increasing rate, (2) real output remaining constant, while the price level rises 2% in period t, 4% in $t+1$ and 6% in $t+2$ or (3) combinations of (1) and (2).

1.16. Given the data in Table 5, construct aggregate consumption functions assuming (a) that there is equal distribution of disposable income, (b) that households A and C have three times the level of disposable income of B and D respectively and (c) that household A has four times the disposable income of B and D while C has twice the disposable income of B and D.

Table 5

Household	Consumption Function
A	$C_A = \$50 + 0.80\,Yd$
B	$C_B = \quad 5 + 0.90\,Yd$
C	$C_C = \quad 25 + 0.85\,Yd$
D	$C_D = \quad 4 + 0.95\,Yd$

(a) Aggregate consumption $= \$84 + \dfrac{3.50\,Yd}{4} = \$84 + 0.875\,Yd.$

(b) Aggregate consumption $= \$84 + \dfrac{6.80\,Yd}{8} = \$84 + 0.85\,Yd.$

(c) Aggregate consumption $= \$84 + \dfrac{6.75\,Yd}{8} = \$84 + 0.84375\,Yd.$

(See Example 5.)

Chapter 2

The Level of Income in a Two-Sector Model of the Economy

In this chapter we will analyze the circular flow of income in a two-sector model of the economy. Then, assuming specific behavior for productive and spending units, we will determine the equilibrium level of income in the two-sector model.

2.1 THE CIRCULAR FLOW IN A TWO-SECTOR, NO SAVING ECONOMY

Initially, we assume that the economy is composed of only two sectors: *business* and *household*. In this hypothetical economy, the business sector is the sole producer of goods and services and production occurs by hiring the factors of production (land, labor and capital) owned by the household sector. We further assume that households are the sole buyers of goods and services and that they spend their entire income. These assumptions are presented in Fig. 2-1 as a circular flow. Households receive money income by selling services of productive factors to the business sector. The household sector uses its entire money income to purchase the output of the business sector.

Figure 2-2 presents two identities implicit in the circular flow of Fig. 2-1. Households' receipt of money income equals the value of output for the business sector. The revenues for the business sector equal households' spending.

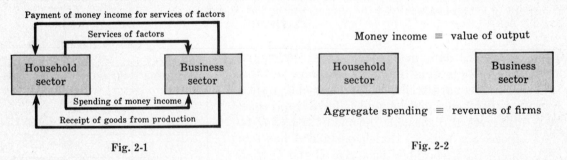

Fig. 2-1   Fig. 2-2

By introducing a behavioral assumption into the circular flow, we devise a theory of money income. Suppose that the business sector produces only as long as it receives revenues equal to its disbursement of money income. By assumption, the level of money income (and therefore the value of output) depends upon aggregate spending.

EXAMPLE 1. If the revenues of firms equal the disbursement of money income, the business sector continues to produce at its current rate. If revenues are less than the payment of money income, output is reduced. Output is increased when revenues exceed the value of output.

2.2   THE CIRCULAR FLOW IN A TWO-SECTOR, SAVING ECONOMY

Household saving is a leakage in the circular flow (i.e., a saving leakage). The circular flow in Fig. 2-3 shows that household saving does not have to result in a reduction of aggregate spending if it is loaned to the business sector to finance investment spending. If production depends upon the relationship of revenues of firms and the disbursement of money income, it follows that the value of output depends upon households' decisions to consume and save and the business sector's intentions to invest.

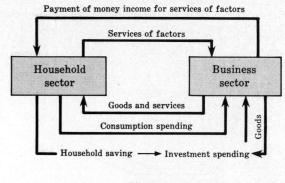

Fig. 2-3

EXAMPLE 2.   The level of money income in a two-sector model depends upon the planned volume of aggregate spending *or* alternatively upon the plans to save and invest. If households intend to save more than businesses intend to invest, the revenues of firms are less than their disbursement of money income and output falls. That is, the value of output is greater than planned aggregate spending. Output increases when intended investment exceeds intended saving (when planned aggregate spending is greater than the value of output) and remains the same when planned saving equals planned investment.

2.3   A GRAPHICAL ANALYSIS OF THE LEVEL OF INCOME IN A TWO-SECTOR MODEL

Prediction of the level of money income necessitates determination of planned consumption, saving and investment. We assume that (1) there is a constant level of planned investment I, regardless of the level of money income Y and (2) household spending (aggregate consumption C) is a positive linear function of the level of aggregate disposable income Yd. Since household saving equals disposable income less consumption, aggregate saving S is also a positive, linear function of aggregate disposable income. If the household sector receives the total value of output, aggregate disposable income Yd equals the level of money income Y.

EXAMPLE 3.   The assumed behavior of consumption, investment and saving is presented in Fig. 2-4. In Fig. 2-4(a), aggregate consumption is $450 when disposable income is $500 and $530 when disposable income is $600. Aggregate saving S equals $Yd - C$. Thus, aggregate saving, read from either Fig. 2-4(a) or 2-4(b), is $50 when disposable income is $500 and $70 when disposable income is $600. Intended investment in Fig. 2-4(c) is $50 regardless of the level of income.

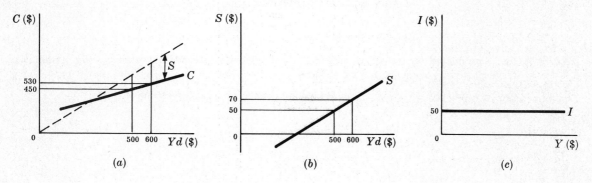

Fig. 2-4

Given the specified behavior of consumption, saving and investment, there is only one value of output where the revenues of firms equal the level of money income. This equilibrium level of income occurs when planned aggregate spending $C + I$ equals the value of output Y or alternately where households' intended saving S equals intended investment I.

EXAMPLE 4. In Fig. 2-5(a), equilibrium exists at a $500 level of income where planned aggregate spending (C of $450 plus I of $50) equals the $500 value of output. We see in Fig. 2-5(b) that intended investment equals intended saving at this $500 value of output.

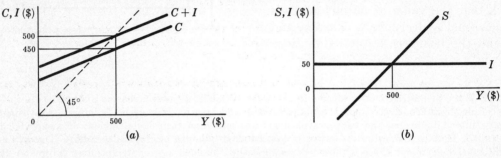

Fig. 2-5

2.4 AN ALGEBRAIC SOLUTION TO THE EQUILIBRIUM LEVEL OF INCOME

We have assumed that consumption is a positive, linear function of disposable income. Thus, the consumption function in Fig. 2-4 can be presented in equation form as $C = \$50 + 0.80\,Yd$. Given a constant level of intended investment, we can determine the equilibrium level of income by equating planned aggregate spending and the value of output (Example 5) or by equating intended saving and intended investment (Example 6).

EXAMPLE 5. Equilibrium income occurs where planned aggregate spending equals the value of output. By assumption, the value of output equals households' disposable income ($Y = Yd$). Household spending is represented by the equation $C = \$50 + 0.80\,Yd$. Intended investment I is $50.

Equilibrium condition: Value of output equals planned aggregate spending

$$
\begin{aligned}
Y &= C + I \\
Y &= \$50 + 0.80\,Y + \$50 \\
Y - 0.80\,Y &= \$100 \\
Y(1 - 0.80) &= \$100 \\
Y(0.20) &= \$100 \\
Y &= \$100/0.20 \\
Y &= \$500
\end{aligned}
$$

EXAMPLE 6. Equilibrium occurs where intended saving equals intended investment. By assumption, $Yd = Y$. Intended saving S equals $Y - C$. Therefore $S = -\$50 + 0.20\,Y$. Intended investment is $50.

Equilibrium condition: Intended saving equals intended investment

$$
\begin{aligned}
S &= I \\
-\$50 + 0.20\,Y &= \$50 \\
0.20\,Y &= \$100 \\
Y &= \$100/0.20 \\
Y &= \$500
\end{aligned}
$$

Review Questions

1. The circular flow of income for a two-sector model shows
   (a) the flow of income between the household and business sectors,
   (b) the amount of money held by the household and business sectors,
   (c) whether the household sector is satisfied with the output of the business sector   or
   (d) whether the business sector is satisfied with the spending of the household sector.

2. The circular flow of income for a two-sector model shows that saving leakages (a) always equal investment spending, (b) sometimes equal investment spending, (c) are always less than investment spending   or   (d) are always greater than investment spending.

3. Equilibrium occurs in a two-sector model when (a) saving equals investment, (b) consumption plus investment equals the value of output, (c) planned saving equals planned investment   or   (d) aggregate spending equals the revenues of business firms.

4. An economy is in equilibrium when (a) planned consumption exceeds planned saving, (b) planned consumption exceeds planned investment, (c) planned spending equals the value of output   or   (d) planned spending equals the revenue of the business sector.

5. If planned saving is greater than planned investment, (a) output should increase, (b) output should decrease, (c) output will not change   or   (d) none of the above.

6. If the value of output exceeds planned spending, (a) there is unsold output and the level of income will fall, (b) there is unsold output and the level of income will rise, (c) there is no unsold output and the level of income does not change   or   (d) none of the above.

7. If planned consumption equals $40 + 0.90\,Yd$ and planned investment is $50, the equilibrium level of income is (a) $90, (b) $400, (c) $500   or   (d) $900.

8. If planned saving equals $-$40 + 0.20\,Yd$ and planned investment is $60, the equilibrium level of income is (a) $100, (b) $400, (c) $500   or   (d) $1000.

Answers to Review Questions

1. (a) Review Section 2.1.
2. (a) See Problem 2.2.
3. (c) Review Section 2.2.
4. (c) Review Section 2.1.

5. (b) Review Section 2.2.
6. (a) Review Section 2.3.
7. (d) Review Section 2.4.
8. (c) Review Section 2.4.

Solved Problems

2.1. What is the relationship between the value of output and the level of income in a two-sector model of the economy?

   If households receive the entire value of output, their receipt of money income is by definition equal to the value of output. Thus, value of output and level of income measure the dollar value of production.

2.2. Suppose that the business sector produces $500 in goods for the household sector and $60 for business investment. If households plan to save $70 of their $560 income and planned investment is $60, does saving equal investment?

Households consume $490 of the $500 produced for the household sector. Thus the business sector has $10 of unsold inventory. Planned investment plus unplanned inventory investment equals $70, which is the sum of household saving. Thus, if planned saving and planned investment are not equal, the saving-investment equality is reached through the holding of inventory by the business sector.

2.3. **Does the situation in Problem 2.2 represent an equilibrium level of income?**

There is disequilibrium since there is unplanned inventory investment. Equilibrium exists when the plans of all sectors are fulfilled.

2.4. **Why does the equality of planned spending and the value of output signify equilibrium?**

Equilibrium means an absence of forces for change. If businessmen sell output at prices they expect and buyers achieve their desired level of spending, there are no forces present for changing the value of output.

2.5. **In a two-sector model, $40 is saved when household disposable income is $500 and $60 is saved when disposable income is $550. If planned investment is $60, what is the equilibrium level of income?**

The equilibrium level of income is $550, where planned saving equals planned investment. Saving leakages are replaced by an equal amount of planned investment.

2.6. **What is meant by a saving leakage?**

If households do not spend their entire income, they are not purchasing the entire output they helped create. That is, there is a saving leakage. Investment must fill the void created by saving if the level of income is to be maintained.

2.7. **If planned saving is greater than planned investment, will the income level expand or contract?**

The income level contracts since saving leakages are not replaced by an equal amount of planned investment spending.

2.8. **Will the income level expand or contract if planned spending is greater than the value of output?**

The level of money income will expand since buyers wish to purchase more than has been produced. If output cannot expand, prices will increase.

2.9. **From Fig. 2-6 (page 13), determine the levels of consumption and saving at income levels (a) OY_1, (b) OY_2 and (c) OY_3.**

(a) For OY_1, consumption is OA and saving is zero.

(b) For OY_2, consumption is OB and saving is $OD - OB$.

(c) For OY_3, consumption is OC and saving is $OE - OC$.

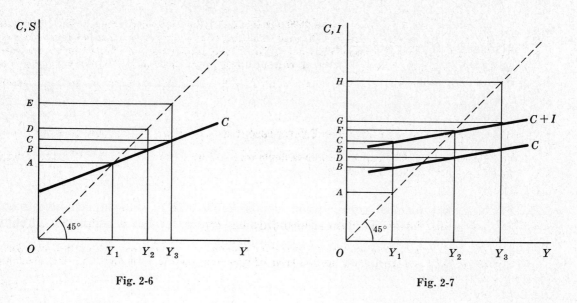

Fig. 2-6   Fig. 2-7

2.10. From Fig. 2-7 above, determine the levels of *planned* saving and *planned* investment at income levels (*a*) OY_1, (*b*) OY_2 and (*c*) OY_3.

(*a*) For OY_1, planned investment is $OC - OB$ and planned dissaving is $OB - OA$.

(*b*) For OY_2, planned investment is $OF - OD$ and planned saving is $OF - OD$.

(*c*) For OY_3, planned investment is $OG - OE$ and planned saving is $OH - OE$.

2.11. What is the equilibrium level of income in Problem 2.10?

Equilibrium occurs at income level OY_2 where (1) planned spending OF equals the value of output OY_2 and (2) where planned saving $OF - OD$ equals planned investment $OF - OD$.

2.12. From Fig. 2-8, define the relationship between planned spending and the value of output at points *A*, *B* and *C*. Do these points represent equilibrium or disequilibrium?

Point *A* is a position of disequilibrium since planned spending is greater than the value of output.

Point *B* is an equilibrium position since planned spending equals the value of output.

Point *C* represents disequilibrium since planned spending is less than the value of output.

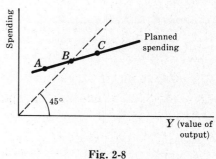

Fig. 2-8

2.13. Why does equilibrium occur when planned consumption plus planned investment intersect the 45° line?

The 45° line is equidistant from the output (income) and spending axes. Anywhere on the 45° line income equals spending. Since the planned spending function is upward sloping, it intersects the 45° line at only one point, this point being the position where planned spending equals the value of output.

2.14. In Fig. 2-9, (a) what are the levels of planned saving for income levels OY_1, OY_2 and OY_3 and (b) what is the equilibrium level of income?

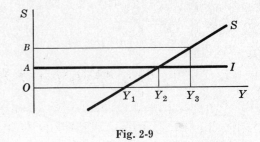

Fig. 2-9

(a) Saving is zero when income is OY_1, OA when income is OY_2 and OB when income is OY_3.

(b) The equilibrium level of income is OY_2 where planned saving equals planned investment.

2.15. Suppose that planned consumption equals $\$40 + 0.75\,Y$ and planned investment is $\$60$. Find (a) the equilibrium level of income, (b) the level of consumption at equilibrium and (c) the level of saving at equilibrium.

(a) The equilibrium condition is given by $Y = C + I$. Thus,

$$Y = \$40 + 0.75\,Y + \$60$$

$$Y - 0.75\,Y = \$100$$

$$Y = \$400 \quad \text{the equilibrium level of income}$$

(b) When $Y = \$400$, $C = \$40 + 0.75(\$400) = \$340$.

(c) The saving equation is $S = Y - C$. Thus,

$$S = Y - (\$40 + 0.75\,Y)$$

$$S = -\$40 + 0.25\,Y$$

When $Y = \$400$, $S = -\$40 + 0.25(\$400) = \$60$.

2.16. Using the answers to Problem 2.15, show that at equilibrium (a) planned spending equals the value of output and (b) planned saving equals planned investment.

(a) Planned spending equals the value of output.

$$C + I = Y$$

$$\$340 + \$60 = \$400$$

(b) Planned saving equals planned investment

$$S = I$$

$$\$60 = \$60$$

Chapter 3

The Multiplier for a Two-Sector Model

In this chapter we find that an autonomous change in aggregate spending causes a multiple change in the equilibrium level of income because consumption spending is related to the receipt of disposable income.

3.1 THE MARGINAL PROPENSITY TO CONSUME

In Chapter 2 we assumed that aggregate consumption is a positive, linear function of disposable income. In equation form, this assumption is written $C = C_0 + bYd$, where b is the behavioral coefficient relating disposable income to consumption. In economics, the behavioral coefficient b is called the marginal propensity to consume.

The marginal propensity to consume (MPC) *measures the change in consumption resulting from a change in disposable income* (i.e., $\Delta C/\Delta Yd$). As presented in Fig. 3-1, the MPC has a value less than one since the change in consumption is less than the change in disposable income.

Since households use their income to consume or save, *the marginal propensity to save* (MPS) equals $1 - $ MPC.

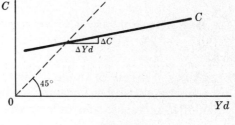

Fig. 3-1

EXAMPLE 1. Suppose that for every $100 increase in disposable income, consumption spending increases $80. The marginal propensity to consume equals 0.80 and the marginal propensity to save equals 0.20.

3.2 THE MULTIPLYING EFFECT OF AUTONOMOUS CHANGES IN AGGREGATE SPENDING

We return to the model of income determination developed in Sections 2.3 and 2.4 to establish the effect of spending changes upon the equilibrium level of income. Spending changes originate with exogenous variables and therefore represent autonomous changes in spending.

A multiple change in income occurs because of the dependency of consumption spending upon disposable income. Changes in autonomous spending alter the level of income and thereby induce changes in consumption spending.

EXAMPLE 2. We initially assume an equilibrium income level of $500 with investment and consumption spending totaling $50 and $450 respectively. The spending schedule in Fig. 3-2 shifts from $(C+I)_0$ to $(C+I)_1$ as a result of a $10 increase in investment spending. The new equilibrium income level is $550 with investment spending totaling $60 and consumption spending totaling $490. Thus, a $10 increase in investment induces an additional $40 of spending by the household sector.

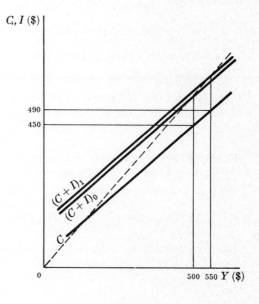

Fig. 3-2

15

3.3 THE VALUE OF THE MULTIPLIER

We derive a multiplier value for the multiplying effect of autonomous changes in spending by dividing the resulting change in income by the autonomous change in spending. In Fig. 3-2, a \$10 increase in investment spending caused income to increase \$50. Thus, the value of the multiplier k_e equals $\Delta Y / \Delta I = 50/10 = \$5$.

EXAMPLE 3. Assume that investment spending equals I_0, consumption spending is presented by the equation $C = C_0 + bYd$ and the value of output is paid to the household sector so that $Yd = Y$.

Equilibrium condition: The value of output Y equals aggregate spending $C + I$.

$$Y = C + I$$
$$Y = C_0 + bY + I$$
$$Y = \frac{C_0 + I_0}{1 - b} \tag{1}$$

If there is an autonomous change in investment, *ceteris paribus*, the change in the equilibrium level of income is

$$\Delta Y = \frac{\Delta I}{1 - b} \tag{2}$$

The value of the multiplier is derived by dividing ΔY by ΔI. Thus,

$$\frac{\Delta Y}{\Delta I} = \frac{1}{1 - b} = k_e \tag{3}$$

Equation (*3*) in Example 3 shows that the value of the multiplier depends upon b, the marginal propensity to consume. This dependency is positive. As the MPC increases, the value of k_e increases and falls as the MPC decreases in value. (See Problems 3.4 and 3.5.)

EXAMPLE 4. The value of the multiplier can be used as a short-cut method for determining the equillibrium level of income.

Equilibrium occurs where $Y = \dfrac{C_0 + I_0}{1 - b}$ or where $Y = \dfrac{1}{1 - b}(C_0 + I_0)$.

Since $k_e = \dfrac{1}{1 - b}$, equilibrium occurs where

$$Y = k_e(C_0 + I_0)$$

3.4 DYNAMIC MULTIPLIERS

In this section we analyze the multiplier under dynamic rather than comparative static conditions. In dynamics, the focus is on time and therefore on the process of change. There must be a lag structure between a dependent and independent variable for there to be a "dynamic process of change."

EXAMPLE 5. In a dynamic process, there is a *lagged* (Situation II) rather than simultaneous (Situation I) relationship between consumption and disposable income.

Given: An equilibrium income level of \$450 in period t. Consumption and investment spending are given as $C = \$40 + 0.80\,Yd$ and $I = \$50$ respectively. The value of output is paid to the household sector so that $Yd = Y$. The value of output for each period equals aggregate spending for that period.

Situation I: There is no lag between consumption spending and disposable income. Thus, $C_{t+1} = \$40 + 0.80\,Yd_{t+1}$. In period $t + 1$, there is a \$10 increase in investment spending.

Period $t + 1$:
$$Y_{t+1} = C_{t+1} + I_{t+1}$$
$$Y_{t+1} = \$40 + 0.80\,Y_{t+1} + \$60$$
$$Y_{t+1} = \$500$$

Assuming no other changes, the level of income reaches a new equilibrium position in the same period that investment increased.

Situation II: Consumption spending lags disposable income by one period. Thus, $C_{t+1} = \$40 + 0.80\,Yd_t$. In period $t+1$ there is a \$10 increase in investment spending.

Period $t+1$:
$$Y_{t+1} \;=\; C_{t+1} + I_{t+1}$$
$$Y_{t+1} \;=\; \$40 + 0.80\,Y_t + \$60$$

Since $Y_t = \$450$,
$$Y_{t+1} \;=\; \$460$$

Period $t+2$:
$$Y_{t+2} \;=\; C_{t+2} + I_{t+2}$$
$$Y_{t+2} \;=\; \$40 + 0.80\,Y_{t+1} + \$60$$

Since $Y_{t+1} = \$460$,
$$Y_{t+2} \;=\; \$468$$

Period $t+3$:
$$Y_{t+3} \;=\; C_{t+3} + I_{t+3}$$
$$Y_{t+3} \;=\; \$40 + 0.80\,Y_{t+2} + \$60$$

Since $Y_{t+2} = \$468$,
$$Y_{t+3} \;=\; \$474.40$$

In each succeeding period, the income level moves closer to the equilibrium \$500 level of income.

Figure 3-3 presents graphically the multiplier process described in Example 5.

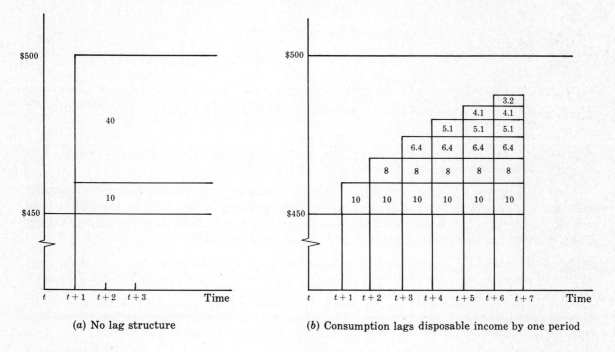

(a) No lag structure   (b) Consumption lags disposable income by one period

Fig. 3-3

The dynamic multiplier process of Fig. 3-3(b) can be presented as a decreasing geometric series where the change in income after n periods is

$$\Delta Y \;=\; \Delta I(1 + b + b^2 + \cdots + b^n) \tag{3.1}$$

Using the change in investment and the MPC from Example 5, the change in income after three periods is

$$\Delta Y \;=\; \$10(1 + 0.80 + 0.80^2)$$
$$\Delta Y \;=\; \$24.40$$

Given the dynamic multiplier process in (*3.1*), it follows that the dynamic expenditure multiplier k_{de} after n periods is

$$\Delta Y/\Delta I \;=\; k_{de} \;=\; (1 + b + b^2 + \cdots + b^n) \tag{3.2}$$

EXAMPLE 6. If we compare the dynamic and static multipliers, we find that a major portion of the multiplier effect is realized in fewer periods when there is a smaller marginal propensity to consume.

Situation I: The MPC equals 0.90.

$$k_e = \frac{1}{1-b} = \frac{1}{1-0.90} = 10$$

$$k_{de} \text{ for 3 periods} = (1+b+b^2) = (1+0.9+0.81) = 2.71$$

$$\frac{k_{de} \text{ for 3 periods}}{k_e} = \frac{2.71}{10} = 0.271$$

After three periods, 27.1% of the multiplier effect is realized.

Situation II: The MPC equals 0.80.

$$k_e = \frac{1}{1-b} = \frac{1}{1-0.80} = 5$$

$$k_{de} \text{ for 3 periods} = (1+b+b^2) = (1+0.8+0.64) = 2.44$$

$$\frac{k_{de} \text{ for 3 periods}}{k_e} = \frac{2.44}{5} = 0.488$$

After three periods, 48.8% of the multiplier effect is realized.

Situation III: The MPC equals 0.50.

$$k_e = \frac{1}{1-b} = \frac{1}{1-0.50} = 2$$

$$k_{de} \text{ for 3 periods} = (1+b+b^2) = (1+0.5+0.25) = 1.75$$

$$\frac{k_{de} \text{ for 3 periods}}{k_e} = \frac{1.75}{2} = 0.875$$

After three periods, 87.5% of the multiplier effect is realized.

Previous analysis of the dynamic multiplier assumed that the increase in investment spending was permanent. If increased investment spending occurs only in the initial time period, the increase in income equals the one-period increase in investment spending, falling slowly back to the income level prior to the change in investment.

EXAMPLE 7. Suppose that a $10 increase in investment occurs only during period $t+1$. If the MPC equals 0.80 and there is no lag structure, a $10 increase in investment spending in Fig. 3-4(a) increases income in period $t+1$ by $50 with income in period $t+2$ returning to its previous level. In Fig. 3-4(b), consumption lags disposable income and the income level increases $10 in period $t+1$, declining in successive periods to the income level in period t. When there is a lag in consumption spending, induced consumption is dispersed over numerous periods rather than being concentrated in one period.

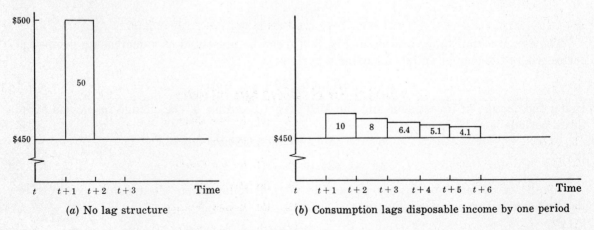

(a) No lag structure   (b) Consumption lags disposable income by one period

Fig. 3-4

Review Questions

1. By definition, the marginal propensity to consume   (a) equals $\Delta C/\Delta Yd$,   (b) is the behavioral coefficient b in the equation $C = C_0 + bYd$,   (c) is the slope of the consumption function   or   (d) all of the above.

2. The marginal propensity to consume has a value   (a) greater than one but less than two,   (b) equal to one,   (c) less than one but greater than zero   or   (d) none of the above.

3. The value of the spending multiplier derived in Chapter 3 equals   (a) $1/(1 - \text{MPC})$,   (b) $1/(1 - \text{MPS})$,   (c) $1/\text{MPC}$ or   (d) $1/(1 + \text{MPC})$.

4. The value of the spending multiplier relates
   (a) the change in income to the change in autonomous spending,
   (b) the change in autonomous spending to the change in income,
   (c) the change in consumption to the change in income   or
   (d) the change in income to the change in consumption.

5. If $C_t = f(Yd_{t-1})$,
   (a) there is an imperfect relationship between consumption and disposable income,
   (b) there is no relationship between consumption and disposable income,
   (c) consumption spending lags the receipt of disposable income by one period   or
   (d) the receipt of disposable income lags consumption spending by one period.

6. Dynamic multipliers occur when   (a) we drop the assumption of *ceteris paribus*,   (b) the economy is not in equilibrium,   (c) consumption is unrelated to disposable income   or   (d) there is a lagged response between consumption and disposable income.

7. If the marginal propensity to consume is 0.75, the multiplier has a value of   (a) 5,   (b) 4,   (c) 3   or   (d) 2.

8. Multiplier analysis shows that
   (a) an increase in saving causes a shift in the investment line,
   (b) an increase in investment causes a shift in the saving line,
   (c) an increase in saving causes movement along the investment line until a higher income level is achieved   or
   (d) an increase in investment causes movement along the saving line until a higher income level is achieved.

9. If consumption spending lags the receipt of disposable income by one period, there is
   (a) no change in the income level if there is a one-period change in investment,
   (b) only a relatively small change in the income level if there is a one-period change in investment,
   (c) a relatively small change in the income level if there is a permanent change in investment   or
   (d) no change in the income level if there is a permanent change in investment.

10. An autonomous change in spending is represented by   (a) a movement along a spending line,   (b) a shift of a spending line,   (c) a change in a behavioral coefficient   or   (d) none of the above.

11. If the marginal propensity to consume is 0.50, the dynamic multiplier for three periods is   (a) 2,   (b) 1.75,   (c) 1.50   or   (d) 1.0.

12. A major portion of the dynamic multiplier is realized in two periods if the MPC is   (a) 0.90,   (b) 0.80,   (c) 0.75   or   (d) 0.50.

Answers to Review Questions

1. (d) Review Section 3.1.
2. (c) Review Section 3.1.
3. (a) Review Example 3.
4. (a) Review Section 3.3.
5. (c) Review Section 3.4.
6. (d) Review Section 3.4.

7. (b) Review Example 3.
8. (d) Review Example 2.
9. (b) Review Section 3.4.
10. (b) Review Section 3.2.
11. (b) Review Example 5.
12. (d) Review Section 3.4.

Solved Problems

3.1. What does the marginal propensity to consume measure?

The marginal propensity to consume measures households' willingness to change consumption spending as a result of a change in disposable income. It is generally assumed that households consume part of, but not the entire, change in disposable income. That is, $\Delta C < \Delta Yd$.

3.2. What is the relationship between the marginal propensity to consume and the marginal propensity to save?

Disposable income that is not consumed is saved. Thus, $MPC + MPS = 1$.

3.3. Given the equilibrium condition $Y = (C_0 + I_0)/(1 - b)$, determine (a) the change in income that results from an autonomous change in C_0 and (b) the value of the multiplier.

(a) $\Delta Y = \Delta C/(1 - b)$. (See Example 3.)

(b) The value of the multiplier indicates the change in income that results from an autonomous change in spending. Thus, $\Delta Y/\Delta C = k_e = 1/(1 - b)$.

3.4. Derive the static multiplier when the MPC is (1) 0.90, (2) 0.80, (3) 0.75 and (4) 0.50.

The multiplier equals $1/(1 - b)$. Thus, in (1) $1/(1 - 0.90) = 1/0.10 = 10$, (2) 5, (3) 4 and (4) 2.

3.5. What is the relationship between the marginal propensity to consume and the value of the multiplier?

There is a multiplier effect because consumption spending is dependent upon the level of disposable income. As shown in Problem 3.4, the value of the multiplier is directly related to the magnitude of the marginal propensity to consume.

3.6. (a) Derive the multiplier when the MPS is (1) 0.10, (2) 0.20, (3) 0.25 and (4) 0.50. (b) Using these multiplier values, find the change in the equilibrium level of income that results from a $20 decrease in investment.

(a) The multipliers equal (1) 10, (2) 5, (3) 4 and (4) 2.

(b) The decline in income equals $\Delta I(k_e)$. Thus, the decrease in income is (1) $200, (2) $100, (3) $80 and (4) $40.

3.7. Explain in terms of the saving/investment equality why the decrease in the equilibrium level of income is greater than the decrease in planned investment.

In a two-sector model, equilibrium income exists where planned saving equals planned investment. If planned investment falls, there exists an abundance of planned saving at the former level of income. Income must fall until planned investment equals planned saving. Since only a portion of any change in income is saved, income must fall by a multiple of the decline in investment to equate planned saving and planned investment.

3.8. Two spending functions are given in Fig. 3-5. In which one would the larger change in equilibrium income occur as a result of an autonomous change in spending?

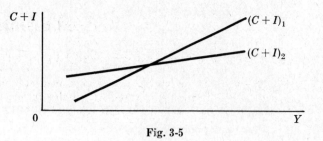

Fig. 3-5

$(C+I)_1$, since it has the larger marginal propensity to spend.

3.9. If investment falls $20 and the marginal propensity to consume is 0.60, what are (a) the change in the equilibrium level of income, (b) the autonomous change in spending and (c) the induced change in consumption spending?

(a) The change in the equilibrium level of income equals $k_e \Delta I$. Since $k_e = 2.5$, $\Delta Y = -\$50$.

(b) The $20 decline in investment is the autonomous change in spending.

(c) The induced change in spending is the difference between the change in the level of income and the change in autonomous spending. That is, $\Delta Y - \Delta I = \Delta C$. Induced spending falls $30.

3.10. The equilibrium level of income is $500 when $C = \$40 + 0.80\,Yd$ and $I = \$60$. Exogenous forces change the spending equations so that $C = \$30 + 0.80\,Yd$ and $I = \$70$. What is the new equilibrium level of income? The autonomous change in spending? The induced change in spending?

Equilibrium exists where $Y = k_e(C_0 + I_0)$. Since the total of C_0 plus I_0 does not change, there is no change in the equilibrium level of income. Therefore, there is no net change in autonomous or induced spending.

3.11. Explain the function $C_t = f(Yd_{t-1})$.

The function $C_t = f(Yd_{t-1})$ indicates that consumption spending is a function of disposable income lagged by one period. That is, consumption is a function of disposable income but disposable income received in period $t - 1$ is not consumed until period t.

3.12. The MPC b is equal to 0.90. Consumption is a function of disposable income lagged by one period. In period $t + 1$, there is a permanent $20 fall in investment. For periods $t + 1$ to $t + 3$, calculate (a) the decrease in the level of income and (b) the expenditure multiplier.

(a) For a one-period lag structure, the change in the level of income for each period is

$$\Delta Y_{t+1} = \Delta I(1)$$
$$\Delta Y_{t+2} = \Delta I(1 + b)$$
$$\Delta Y_{t+3} = \Delta I(1 + b + b^2)$$
$$\Delta Y_{t+n} = \Delta I(1 + b + b^2 + \cdots + b^{n-1})$$

Thus, the declines in income for periods $t + 1$ to $t + 3$ are

$$\Delta Y_{t+1} = -\$20$$
$$\Delta Y_{t+2} = -\$38$$
$$\Delta Y_{t+3} = -\$54.20$$

(b) The expenditure multiplier equals $\Delta Y/\Delta I$.   Thus,

$$\text{for period } t+1, \quad \Delta Y/\Delta I = -\$20/(-\$20) = 1$$
$$\text{for period } t+2, \quad \Delta Y/\Delta I = -\$38/(-\$20) = 1.9 = 1 + b$$
$$\text{for period } t+3, \quad \Delta Y/\Delta I = -\$54.20/(-\$20) = 2.71 = 1 + b + b^2$$

3.13. Differentiate between the static and dynamic multipliers.

The static multiplier establishes the change in the level of income from an autonomous change in spending, given no lag in induced spending.   The dynamic multiplier establishes the change in the level of income for a specified number of periods, given a lag in induced spending.   (See Example 5, Situations I and II.)

3.14. If consumption is a function of disposable income lagged by one period, derive the dynamic multiplier for four periods when the marginal propensity to consume is (1) 0.50, (2) 0.80 and (3) 0.90.

For four periods, k_{de} equals $1 + b + b^2 + b^3$.   Thus,

$$(1) \quad k_{de} = 1 + 0.50 + 0.25 + 0.125 = 1.875$$
$$(2) \quad k_{de} = 1 + 0.80 + 0.64 + 0.512 = 2.952$$
$$(3) \quad k_{de} = 1 + 0.90 + 0.81 + 0.729 = 3.439$$

3.15. Assume that consumption is a function of disposable income lagged by one period and that there is a permanent increase in investment.   How many periods will it take to realize 50% of the eventual change in the level of income if the marginal propensity to consume is (a) 0.50? (b) 0.90?

(a) Since we want to determine 50% of the eventual change in the level of income, k_{de}/k_e must equal 0.5. $k_e = 1/(1 - \text{MPC}) = 2$.   Since k_{de}/k_e must equal 0.5, k_{de} must have a value of 1.   Time: one period.

(b) $k_e = 1/(1 - \text{MPC}) = 10$.   Since k_{de}/k_e must equal 0.5, k_{de} must have a value of 5.   Time: during the seventh period.

3.16. Suppose that the marginal propensity to consume b is 0.90 and investment increases $10 in period $t+1$ and then returns to its previous level in $t+2$.   Calculate the increases in the levels of income for periods $t+1$, $t+2$ and $t+3$.

Given a one-period lag structure, the changes in the levels of income for one period change in investment are

$$\Delta Y_{t+1} = \Delta I(1) = \$10(1) = \$10.00$$
$$\Delta Y_{t+2} = \Delta I(b) = \$10(0.90) = \$9.00$$
$$\Delta Y_{t+3} = \Delta I(b^2) = \$10(0.81) = \$8.10$$

(See Example 7.)

3.17. Assume that (1) the equilibrium level of income is currently $500, (2) the marginal propensity to consume is 0.80 and (3) consumption is a function of disposable income lagged by one period (one period equals three months).   (a) What permanent increase in investment is needed to bring the income level to $559 within one year? (b) What is the eventual change in the equilibrium level of income?

(a) The dynamic multiplier for four periods is 2.95.

$$2.95\,\Delta I = \$59$$
$$\Delta I = \$20$$

(b) The eventual change in the equilibrium level of income is $100.

Chapter 4

Government and the Level of Income

In introducing a government into the model, we move from a two-sector to a three-sector model. With the addition of this third sector, the level of income is affected by the actions of government (federal, state and local) as well as by the behavior of the private $(C+I)$ sector.

4.1 THE CIRCULAR FLOW IN A THREE-SECTOR ECONOMY

The government can tax and spend. In Fig. 4-1 we see that taxes upon the value of output reduce the money flow to the household sector. We also see that tax receipts, if not spent, are leakages in the circular flow. The circular flow of money income and therefore the value of output depend upon households' intentions to consume, businesses' intentions to invest and government's plans to tax and spend.

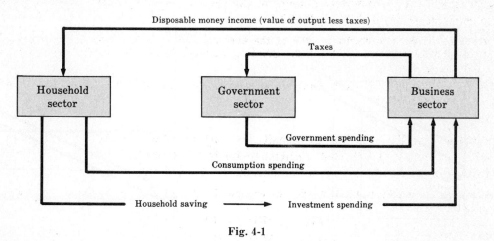

Fig. 4-1

EXAMPLE 1. The value of output falls if aggregate spending $(C+I+G)$ is less than the value of goods produced by the business sector and increases if aggregate spending is greater than the value of output. Thus, the value of output falls when saving leakages (taxes plus household savings) exceed intended investment plus government spending and increases when saving leakages are less than the sum of intended investment and government spending.

4.2 GOVERNMENT SPENDING, TAXES AND THE LEVEL OF INCOME

In a three-sector model, equilibrium income occurs where $Y = C+I+G$ in the aggregate spending approach and $Tx + S = I + G$ in the saving/investment approach to income determination.

EXAMPLE 2. The addition of government spending, *ceteris paribus*, increases the equilibrium level of income in Fig. 4-2(a) from Y_0 to Y_1. The saving/investment approach in Fig. 4-2(b) shows that the deficit caused by government spending must be financed by increased private saving of $S_1 - S_0$.

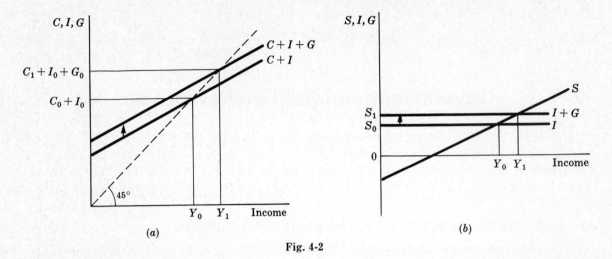

(a)   (b)

Fig. 4-2

An increase in taxes, *ceteris paribus*, lowers the level of income. Taxes are a saving leakage. In Fig. 4-3(a), the introduction of taxes, *ceteris paribus*, lowers aggregate spending since the government is receiving revenue that it is not spending. In Fig. 4-3(b), taxes that are not spent are a government saving and analytically can be added to private saving.

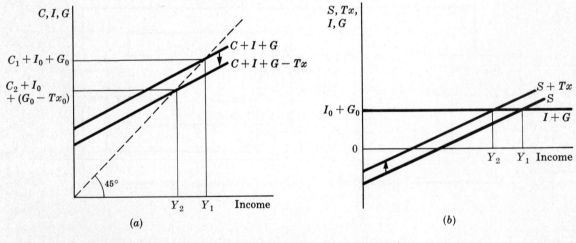

(a)   (b)

Fig. 4-3

EXAMPLE 3. Suppose that $C = \$40 + 0.80\,Yd$ and $I = \$60$; $S = Y - \$40 - 0.80\,Y$ since $S = Yd - C$ and $Yd = Y$ when there are no taxes. Equilibrium income equals \$500.

Situation I: Government spending of \$10 is added to the model. There is no other parameter change.

The Spending Equation	The Saving/Investment Equation
$Y = C + I + G$	$S = I + G$
$Y = \$40 + 0.80\,Y + \$60 + 10$	$0.20\,Y - \$40 = \$60 + \$10$
$Y = 0.80\,Y + \$110$	$0.20\,Y = \$110$
$Y = \$550$	$Y = \$550$

The multiplier effect upon income from government spending is of the same magnitude as the effect from autonomous changes in investment.

Situation II: To equate government receipts and spending, $10 in taxes is added to the model. With taxes, $Yd = Y - Tx$.

The Spending Equation	The Saving/Investment Equation

The Spending Equation

$$Y = C + I + G$$
$$Y = \$40 + 0.80(Y - 10) + \$60 + \$10$$
$$Y - 0.80Y = \$110 - \$8$$
$$Y = \$510$$

The Saving/Investment Equation

$$S + T_x = I + G$$
$$Y - \$10 - \$40 - 0.80(Y - \$10) + \$10 = \$60 + \$10$$
$$Y - \$10 - \$40 - 0.80Y + \$8 + \$10 = \$60 + \$10$$
$$0.20Y - \$32 = \$70$$
$$Y = \$510$$

A $10 increase in taxes lowers income by $40. Note that income falls by $40 when taxes are raised $10 while income increases $50 when government spending is increased $10.

4.3 BALANCED BUDGETS IN THE PUBLIC SECTOR AND THE LEVEL OF INCOME

An equal increase in government taxes and spending raises the equilibrium level of income while a decrease lowers it (see Example 3, Situation II). The effect of equal changes in government spending and taxes is called *the balanced budget multiplier*. There is a balanced budget multiplier since a change in taxes affects aggregate saving less than a change in government spending affects aggregate spending.

4.4 GOVERNMENT TRANSFERS

Government transfers (e.g., social security payments, unemployment benefits) are the return of government receipts to the private sector. As shown in Example 4, increased government transfers reduce tax leakages originating from the public sector in the same manner as a direct reduction in taxes. Hence, transfers Tr can be viewed as a negative tax.

EXAMPLE 4. The income level equals $510 when $C = \$40 + 0.80Yd$, $I = \$60$, $G = \$10$, $Tx = \$10$ and $Yd = Y - Tx$.

Situation I: If the government increases transfers by $5, disposable income now equals $Y - Tx + Tr$ and

$$Y = C + I + G$$
$$Y = \$40 + 0.80(Y - \$10 + \$5) + \$60 + \$10$$
$$Y = \$530$$

Situation II: Now assume instead that taxes are reduced $5.

$$Y = C + I + G$$
$$Y = \$40 + 0.80(Y - \$5) + \$60 + \$10$$

so that once again

$$Y = \$530$$

Thus, an increase in transfers or a decrease in taxes has the same effect upon the equilibrium level of income.

4.5 GOVERNMENT SECTOR MULTIPLIERS

Once a government sector is added to the model, there are tax, transfer and balanced budget multipliers as well as an expenditure multiplier. These multipliers are presented in Example 5.

EXAMPLE 5. Given: $C = C_0 + bYd$, $Yd = Y - Tx + Tr$, $I = I_0$, $G = G_0$, $Tx = Tx_0$ and $Tr = Tr_0$. For equilibrium,

$$Y = C + I + G$$
$$Y = C_0 + b(Y - Tx_0 + Tr_0) + I_0 + G_0$$
$$Y - bY = C_0 + bTr_0 - bTx_0 + I_0 + G_0$$
$$Y = \frac{C_0 + I_0 + G_0 - bTx_0 + bTr_0}{1 - b}$$

$$(1)$$

The Expenditure Multiplier. Assume an autonomous change in G_0, *ceteris paribus.* The corresponding change in the equilibrium level of income is given by equation (1) as

$$\Delta Y = \frac{\Delta G}{1 - b}$$

The expenditure multiplier is then

$$k_e = \frac{\Delta Y}{\Delta G} = \frac{1}{1 - b}$$

The Tax or Transfer Multiplier. The change in the equilibrium level of income in equation (1) for an autonomous change in Tx_0 is

$$\Delta Y = \frac{-b\Delta Tx}{1 - b}$$

The tax multiplier is then

$$k_{tx} = \frac{\Delta Y}{\Delta Tx} = \frac{-b}{1 - b}$$

The same value is derived for the transfer multiplier k_{tr} but the sign is positive. Thus,

$$k_{tr} = \frac{\Delta Y}{\Delta Tr} = \frac{b}{1 - b}$$

The Balanced Budget Multiplier. Assuming equal changes in G_0 and Tx_0, the change in the equilibrium level of income would read

$$\Delta Y = \frac{\Delta G - b\Delta Tx}{1 - b}$$

Assuming a balanced budget where $\Delta G = \Delta Tx$,

$$\Delta Y = \frac{\Delta G - b\Delta G}{1 - b}$$

$$\Delta Y = \frac{\Delta G(1 - b)}{1 - b}$$

$$\Delta Y = \Delta G$$

Hence, the multiplier for equal changes in G and Tx is

$$k_b = \Delta Y/\Delta G = 1$$

4.6   TAXES RELATED TO THE LEVEL OF INCOME

Taxes are a flat sum or are related to the level of earned income. Thus, taxes equal $Tx_0 + tY$, where Tx_0 represents an administered tax (such as property taxes) and t is a tax tied to earned income. For ease of analysis, we shall assume that t is a proportional income tax and is constant. (If there is a progressive income tax, the value of t increases with aggregate income.)

EXAMPLE 6.   An income tax moderates the multiplier effect of autonomous changes in spending upon equilibrium income. When $C = \$40 + 0.80\,Yd$, $I = \$60$, $G = \$40$ and $Yd = Y - tY$ where $t = 0.10$, then the equilibrium income level is $500 and taxes equal $50. Assume a $20 increase in investment. Equilibrium income is then

$$Y = C + I + G$$
$$Y = \$40 + 0.80(Y - 0.10\,Y) + \$80 + \$40$$
$$Y = \$571.43$$

and taxes increase to $57.14.

If taxes are unrelated to income and remain at $50 while investment increases $20, equilibrium income will be

$$Y = C + I + G$$
$$Y = \$40 + 0.80(Y - \$50) + \$80 + \$40$$
$$Y = \$600$$

4.7 GOVERNMENT SECTOR MULTIPLIERS WHEN TAXES ARE RELATED TO INCOME

When tax receipts are linked to the level of income, there is an induced saving leakage which alters the multiplier effect of autonomous changes in spending.

EXAMPLE 7. The multipliers for a model with income taxes are derived below, given the parameters $C = C_0 + bYd$, $Yd = Y - Tx + Tr$, $Tx = Tx_0 + tY$, $Tr = Tr_0$, $I = I_0$ and $G = G_0$. For equilibrium,

$$Y = C + I + G$$

$$Y = C_0 + b(Y - Tx_0 - tY + Tr_0) + I_0 + G_0$$

$$Y = \frac{C_0 + I_0 + G_0 - bTx_0 + bTr_0}{1 - b + bt} \tag{1}$$

The Expenditure Multiplier. Assume an autonomous change in G_0. The change in the equilibrium level of income from equation (1) is

$$\Delta Y = \frac{\Delta G}{1 - b + bt} \quad \text{or} \quad k_e = \frac{\Delta Y}{\Delta G} = \frac{1}{1 - b + bt}$$

The Tax or Transfer Multiplier. Assume an autonomous change in Tr_0. From equation (1), the change in the equilibrium level of income is

$$\Delta Y = \frac{b\Delta Tr}{1 - b + bt} \quad \text{or} \quad k_{tr} = \frac{\Delta Y}{\Delta Tr} = \frac{b}{1 - b + bt}$$

The tax multiplier holds the same value but is negative.

$$k_{tx} = \frac{\Delta Y}{\Delta Tx} = \frac{-b}{1 - b + bt}$$

The Balanced Budget Multiplier. For an equal autonomous change in Tx_0 and G_0, the change in the equilibrium level of income from equation (1) is

$$\Delta Y = \frac{\Delta G - b\Delta Tx}{1 - b + bt}$$

Assuming a balanced budget where $\Delta G = \Delta Tx$,

$$\Delta Y = \frac{\Delta G - b\Delta G}{1 - b + bt}$$

and

$$k_b = \frac{\Delta Y}{\Delta G} = \frac{1 - b}{1 - b + bt}$$

which takes a value of less than one.

4.8 FISCAL POLICY AND *CETERIS PARIBUS*

So far, the results of various fiscal measures have been analyzed under the assumption of *ceteris paribus*. As we shall see in Chapter 16, other factors might change as a result of a fiscal action so that the fiscal measure is partially or totally offset by other parameter changes. It is important, therefore, to keep in mind the methodological observations in Section 1.4. Simple models allow us to analyze *with precision* the result of a single parameter change. Whether we can approximate reality with this model depends upon the importance of and possible change in other factors.

Review Questions

1. Given a proportional income tax structure and a government budget that is currently in balance, an autonomous increase in investment will increase the level of equilibrium income and the budget (*a*) will still be in balance, (*b*) will have a surplus or (*c*) will have a deficit.

2. If the federal government lowers taxes and spending by $10, then with a MPC of 0.90 the income level will fall by (*a*) $9, (*b*) $80 or (*c*) $10.

3. Given a three-sector ($C + I + G$) model, equilibrium income occurs where (*a*) $I + S = Tx + G$, (*b*) $I + G = S + Tx$, (*c*) $I + Tx = S + G$ or (*d*) $S = I + Tx + G$.

4. The tax multiplier is (*a*) greater than the government expenditure multiplier, (*b*) equal to the government expenditure multiplier, (*c*) less than the government expenditure multiplier or (*d*) equal to the investment expenditure multiplier.

5. If taxes are proportional to the income level rather than a constant sum,
   (*a*) the balanced budget multiplier has a zero value,
   (*b*) the value of the government expenditure multiplier is increased,
   (*c*) the transfer multiplier has an increased value or
   (*d*) the value of the government expenditure multiplier is reduced.

6. If the investment expenditure multiplier is 5 and taxes are proportional to the income level, (*a*) the tax multiplier equals 4, (*b*) the government expenditure multiplier equals 4, (*c*) the tax multiplier is less than 4 or (*d*) the tax multiplier is greater than 4.

7. Given a MPC equal to b and a flat sum tax, the multiplier for government transfer payments is (*a*) $-b/(1-b)$, (*b*) $b/(1-b)$, (*c*) $-b/(1-b-bt)$ or (*d*) $b/(1-b-bt)$.

8. If there is full employment with price stability and taxes and government spending are increased by an equal amount, the economy (*a*) will remain at full employment and price stability, (*b*) will be at less than full employment or (*c*) will experience inflation.

9. If the decrease in government spending is matched by an increase in transfer payments, the income level will (*a*) stay the same, (*b*) rise or (*c*) fall.

10. The only difference between the tax and transfer multipliers is that
    (*a*) the transfer multiplier is one more than the tax multiplier,
    (*b*) the tax multiplier is one more than the transfer multiplier,
    (*c*) one affects disposable income while the other affects the MPC or
    (*d*) one is positive while the other is negative.

11. If there is an increase in taxes and government spending, then
    (*a*) the $S + Tx$ schedule shifts upward and $I + G$ schedule shifts upward,
    (*b*) the $S + Tx$ schedule shifts downward and the $I + G$ schedule shifts downward,
    (*c*) the $S + Tx$ schedule shifts downward and the $I + G$ schedule shifts upward or
    (*d*) the $S + Tx$ schedule shifts upward and the $I + G$ schedule shifts downward.

12. If there is an equal increase in taxes and government spending, (*a*) $C + I + G$ is shifting upward, (*b*) $C + I + G$ is shifting downward or (*c*) $C + I + G$ does not shift.

Answers to Review Questions

1. (*b*) Review Section 4.6.
2. (*c*) Review Section 4.3.
3. (*b*) Review Section 4.2.
4. (*c*) Review Section 4.5.
5. (*d*) Review Section 4.7.
6. (*d*) Review Section 4.7.

7. (*b*) Review Section 4.5.
8. (*c*) Review Section 4.3.
9. (*c*) Review Sections 4.3 and 4.4.
10. (*d*) Review Section 4.4.
11. (*a*) Review Section 4.2.
12. (*a*) Review Section 4.3.

Solved Problems

4.1. Rank the following proposals in terms of their ability to increase the equilibrium level of income. (1) Government spending and taxes increase by x. (2) Government spending and taxes decrease by x. (3) Government spending increases by x. (4) Taxes increase by x.

Proposal (3) increases the equilibrium level of income by k_e times x; proposal (1), an example of the balanced budget multiplier, increases equilibrium income by x; proposals (2) and (4) both result in a reduction in the equilibrium level of income.

4.2. Assuming that the marginal propensity to consume equals 0.75, find the change in the equilibrium level of income if (a) government spending increases \$10, (b) taxes increase \$15 and (c) transfers increase \$10.

(a) $k_e = 1/(1-b) = 4$. The equilibrium level of income increases \$40.

(b) $k_{tx} = -b/(1-b) = -3$. The equilibrium level of income falls \$45.

(c) $k_{tr} = b/(1-b) = 3$. The equilibrium level of income increases \$30.

4.3. Using the situations in Problem 4.2, establish the change in the equilibrium level of income if there is a proportional income tax of 20%.

(a) $k_e = 1/(1-b+bt) = 2.5$. The equilibrium level of income increases \$25.

(b) $k_{tx} = -b/(1-b+bt) = -1.875$. The equilibrium level of income falls \$28.12.

(c) $k_{tr} = b/(1-b+bt) = 1.875$. The equilibrium level of income increases \$18.75.

4.4. Why is a progressive income tax considered a "built-in" stabilizer?

A progressive income tax is an automatic or built-in stabilizer since tax receipts change proportionately more than the level of income. As the economy expands, proportionately more taxes are collected, dampening the expansion. As the economy contracts, tax receipts automatically fall proportionately more than income, slowing the contraction.

4.5. Why do income taxes reduce the value of the expenditure multiplier?

The multiplier derives its value from induced expenditures (i.e., induced consumption). As a result of relating taxes to income, there is less induced consumption for income level changes.

4.6. If the current level of income is \$500, the marginal propensity to consume is 0.50 and taxes are unrelated to income, what is the new equilibrium level of income if government spending increases \$10?

Since $k_e = 1/(1-0.50) = 1/0.50 = 2$, the new equilibrium level of income is $\$500 + 2(\$10) = \$520$.

4.7. If the current level of income is \$500, the marginal propensity to consume is 0.80 and taxes are unrelated to income, what is the new equilibrium level of income if taxes are cut \$5?

$k_{tx} = 4$. The new equilibrium level of income is \$520. (See Example 5.)

4.8. Given $C = \$20 + 0.50\,Yd$, $I = \$40$, $G = \$10$, $Yd = Y - Tx$ and $Tx = \$5$, determine (a) the equilibrium level of income, (b) the levels of consumption and saving and (c) the equality of saving and investment.

(a)
$$Y = \$20 + 0.50(Y - \$5) + \$40 + \$10$$
$$Y = \$135$$

(b)
$$C = \$85, \quad S = \$45$$

(c)
$$S + Tx = I + G$$
$$\$45 + \$5 = \$40 + \$10$$

4.9. If $C = \$40 + 0.80\,Yd$, $Yd = Y - Tx$, $I = \$60$, $G = \$20$ and $Tx = \$20$, calculate (a) the equilibrium level of income and (b) the new equilibrium income level if investment falls \$10 and as a result of a falling income level unemployment insurance increases \$5. (c) Given the income level in (b), what change in government spending is needed to bring the income level back to its position in (a)?

(a)
$$Y = \$40 + 0.80(Y - \$20) + \$60 + 20$$
$$Y = \$520$$

(b)
$$Y = \$40 + 0.80(Y - \$20 + \$5) + \$50 + \$20$$
$$Y = \$490$$

(c) Since ΔY equals \$30 and k_e equals 5, ΔG must equal \$6.

4.10. The current equilibrium level of income is \$500. Full employment is defined as \$550. If taxes are unrelated to income and the marginal propensity to consume is 0.80, how much of an increase in government spending is needed to move the economy to full employment if the government is committed to operating with a balanced budget?

The income level must be increased \$50. With the balanced budget multiplier, $\Delta G = \Delta Tx = \$50$.

4.11. Assume in Problem 4.10 that the government is willing to operate with a deficit. What change in (a) taxes or (b) government spending must be made to bring the economy to full employment?

(a) The income level must be increased \$50. Since $k_{tx} = -4$, $\Delta Tx = -\$12.50$.

(b) Since $k_e = 5$, $\Delta G = \$10$.

4.12. The current level of income is \$500. Full employment is defined as \$550. If the marginal propensity to consume is 0.80 and there is a proportional income tax of 10%, (a) how much must government spending increase to bring about full employment? (b) What change in taxes will result from the increased equilibrium level of income?

(a) The income level must increase \$50. Since $\Delta Y = \Delta G/(1 - b + bt)$, $\Delta G = \$14$.

(b) Since the change in income is \$50 and income taxes equal 0.10(Y), the change in taxes equals 0.10(50) = \$5.

4.13. There are increased government expenditures of $20 in a full employment economy with an annual growth rate of 4%. The current level of income is $500, the marginal propensity to consume is 0.50 and taxes are unrelated to income. Must the government increase taxes to meet the higher level of government spending?

The change in potential capacity ΔY is $20. Since $\Delta Y \neq k_e \Delta G$, taxes must increase $20 ($\Delta Y = k_e \Delta G - k_{tx} \Delta T_x$).

4.14. Government expenditures increase $20 in a full employment economy. The current level of income is $500, the marginal propensity to consume is 0.50 and taxes are unrelated to income. How much must taxes increase to maintain price stability?

To maintain price stability, the stimulative effect of increased government spending must be completely offset by an increase in taxes. Thus, $k_e \Delta G = k_{tx} \Delta Tx$. Since $k_e = 2$, $k_{tx} = 1$ and $\Delta G = \$20$, $\Delta Tx = \$40$.

4.15. The economy is currently at full employment. Assuming a lump-sum tax, if the government sector decreases its level of spending but does not want this policy to be deflationary, what reduction in taxes is required to maintain price stability?

Suppose that the equilibrium condition is given by

$$Y = \frac{C_0 + I_0 + G_0 - bTx_0 + bTr_0}{1 - b}$$

If there is an equal reduction of G and Tx and $\Delta Y = 0$, $\Delta C = 0$, $\Delta I = 0$, $\Delta Tr = 0$, we have

$$0 = \frac{\Delta G - b\Delta Tx}{1 - b}$$

$$\Delta G = b\Delta Tx$$

$$\frac{\Delta G}{b} = \Delta Tx \quad \text{the required decrease in taxes}$$

4.16. Full employment is defined at an income level of $600. The behavior of consumption is given by $C = \$10 + 0.90\,Yd$, investment is set at $60, government expenditures total $35 while tax receipts equal $5 + 0.10\,Y$. (a) What is the current equilibrium level of income? (b) What are the levels of consumption, investment and taxes at this income level? (c) Is this income level inflationary or deflationary? (d) How much must government spending be changed to achieve the goal of full employment and price stability?

(a) $Y = \$528.95$.

(b) $C = \$433.95$, $Tx = \$57.89$, $I = \$60$.

(c) This income level is deflationary since it is below the $600 income level defined as full employment.

(d) $\Delta Y = \$71.05$. Since $\Delta Y = \Delta G/(1 - b + bt)$, $\Delta G = \$13.50$.

4.17. The current level of income is $500. Full employment is defined as $560. If taxes are unrelated to income and the marginal propensity to consume is 0.80, what tax or transfer policy could be used to bring about full employment?

$\Delta Y = k_{tx} \Delta Tx$ and $Y = k_{tr} \Delta Tr$. Since $k_{tx} = -4$ and $k_{tr} = +4$, full employment can be achieved by a $15 decrease in taxes or a $15 increase in transfers.

4.18. Full employment is defined at an income level of $800. The behavior of consumption is given by $C = \$10 + 0.90\,Yd$. Investment is $60, government expenditures total $15 and tax receipts which are unrelated to income total $12. (a) Establish the equilibrium level of income. (b) Is this income level inflationary or deflationary? (c) Using government expenditures as the policy variable, establish the required change to achieve an income level of $800. (d) Is the government budget still in deficit?

(a) $Y = \$742$.

(b) The income level is deflationary since it is below the one defined as full employment.

(c) The government must increase spending by $5.80.   ($\Delta Y = k_e \Delta G$.)

(d) The government's deficit has increased from $3 to $8.80.

4.19. Assume that taxes are the policy variable for Problem 4.18. (a) What change in taxes is needed to achieve full employment? (b) What is the size of the government's deficit after the cut in taxes?

(a) $\Delta Y = k_{tx} \Delta Tx$. $\$58 = 9(\Delta Tx)$.   Taxes must be reduced $6.44.

(b) The government's deficit will increase to $9.44.

4.20. All government sectors are currently operating with a balanced budget. At the local level, expenditures are increased $50. Households in this locality increase saving $50 to repay the debt issue at a future period. (a) Has the MPC or the constant of the consumption function changed? (b) What impact will these additional local expenditures have upon the income level, assuming a marginal propensity to consume of 0.90?

(a) A change in saving indicates a shift in the aggregate saving function. Thus, the constant of the consumption equation has changed.

(b) The $50 decrease in C_0 is equal to the $50 increase in G_0 so that there is no change in the level of income.

Chapter 5

The International Sector and the Level of Income

We have dealt thus far with a closed economy (i.e., an economy that has not traded with other nations). This chapter analyzes the impact of international trade upon a country's equilibrium level of income. To simplify the presentation, we have eliminated the government sector.

5.1 IMPORTS AND EXPORTS AS AUTONOMOUS VARIABLES

A country exports domestic goods and services and imports foreign-made goods and services. Thus, an increase in exports increases the demand for domestic goods and services while an increase in imports reduces it. As indicated in Figs. 5-1 and 5-2, changes in exports X and imports Z, like other autonomous changes in spending, cause a multiple change in the equilibrium level of income.

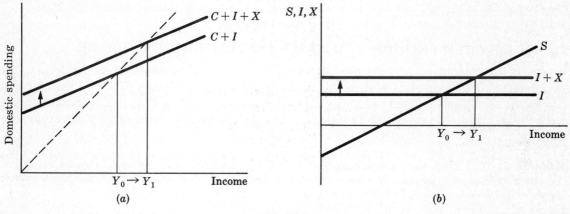

Fig. 5-1

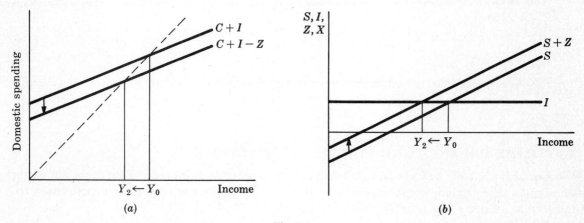

Fig. 5-2

EXAMPLE 1. With respect to the equilibrium level of income, the multiplier effects associated with autonomous changes in exports and imports are similar but have opposite signs. Thus, equal changes in exports and imports have no effect upon the equilibrium level of income.

Given: $C = \$40 + 0.80\,Yd$ and $I = \$60$. $Yd = Y$ since there is no government sector. The equilibrium level of income is \$500.

Situation I: Exports of \$10 are added to the model.

The Spending Equation	The Saving/Investment Equation
$Y = C + I + X$	$I + X = S$
$Y = \$40 + 0.80\,Y + \$60 + \$10$	$\$60 + \$10 = -\$40 + 0.20\,Y$
$0.20\,Y = \$110$	$\$110 = 0.20\,Y$
$Y = \$550$	$\$550 = Y$

When $Y = \$550$, $I = \$60$, $X = \$10$ and $S = \$70$.

Situation II: Imports of \$10 are added to the model.

The Spending Equation	The Saving/Investment Equation
$Y + Z = C + I + X$	$I + X = S + Z$
$Y + \$10 = \$40 + 0.80\,Y + \$60 + \$10$	$\$60 + \$10 = -\$40 + 0.20\,Y + \$10$
$0.20\,Y = \$100$	$\$100 = 0.20\,Y$
$Y = \$500$	$\$500 = Y$

When $Y = \$500$, $I = \$60$, $X = \$10$, $S = \$60$ and $Z = \$10$.

The \$10 increase in imports and exports leaves the equilibrium level of income unchanged at \$500.

5.2 AN IMPORT FUNCTION AND THE EXPENDITURE MULTIPLIER

As income increases, consumption of domestic and foreign goods rises. Further, the need for imported materials is directly related to production levels. Thus we assume that imports are positively related to income with $Z = Z_0 + zY$, where Z_0 is autonomous imports and z is the marginal propensity to import. Exports, by assumption, remain an exogenous variable.

EXAMPLE 2. It follows that autonomous changes in aggregate spending influence a nation's imports. The endogenous import function also changes the expenditure multiplier since the marginal propensity to import is an additional saving leakage.

Given: $C = C_0 + bYd$, $Yd = Y$, $I = I_0$, $X = X_0$ and $Z = Z_0 + zY$.

For equilibrium,

$$Y = \frac{C_0 + I_0 + X_0 - Z_0}{1 - b + z}$$

For autonomous changes in C, I and X, the expenditure multiplier is

$$k_e = \frac{1}{1 - b + z}$$

For autonomous changes in Z, the expenditure multiplier is

$$k_e = \frac{-1}{1 - b + z}$$

5.3 TRADE BALANCE AND THE LEVEL OF INCOME

A country's *trade balance* is its net balance of exports and imports. There is a net export or surplus trade balance when exports exceed imports and a net import or deficit trade balance when imports are greater than exports.

If exports and imports are exogenous variables, a country's income level is positively related to its net export balance, *ceteris paribus*. This means that a country at less than full employment would seek an expanding net export balance.

EXAMPLE 3.   A rising income level may be associated with either a net export or net import balance when imports are a function of the level of income.

Given: $C = \$40 + 0.80\,Yd$, $I = \$60$, $Z = \$15 + 0.05\,Y$ and $X = \$40$. $Yd = Y$ since there is no government sector. The equilibrium level of income is \$500. The net export balance is zero since exports equal imports.

Situation I: Assume a \$10 increase in autonomous investment. The equilibrium level of income now equals \$540. There is a net import balance of \$2 since exports remain at \$40 while imports increase to \$42 $[Z = \$15 + 0.05(\$540)]$.

Situation II: Assume a \$10 increase in autonomous exports. The equilibrium level of income increases to \$580. A net export balance of \$6 develops since exports are now \$50 while imports increase to \$44.

If imports are a function of income and exports are exogenously determined, a trade deficit develops when the rise in income is attributed to autonomous increases in private $(C + I)$ spending. A trade surplus occurs if increased domestic output is due to an autonomous increase in exports.

5.4   AN IMPORT AND EXPORT FUNCTION

So far we have assumed that the level of exports is independent of changes in the domestic level of income. Domestic exports could be related to domestic imports and therefore income through changes in a second country's level of income.

EXAMPLE 4.   A linkage model of income levels demonstrates that domestic imports affect the level of domestic exports through a "feedback" effect.

Given: $C = C_0 + bYd$, $Yd = Y$, $I = I_0$, $X = X_0$ and $Z = Z_0 + zY$.

Equilibrium exists where

$$Y = \frac{C_0 + I_0 + X_0 - Z_0}{1 - b + z} \tag{1}$$

Assume that all of country A's exports are sent to B, which represents the rest of the world. Assume further that the rest of the world's imports from A can be presented by the linear function $H = H_0 + hY_B$, where H_0 represents exogenous imports and h is B's marginal propensity to import from A. Since A is exporting to B,

$$X_0 = H_0 + hY_B$$

Substituting into the equilibrium condition in (1) above,

$$Y = \frac{C_0 + I_0 + H_0 + hY_B - Z_0}{1 - b + z} \tag{2}$$

The equilibrium equation in (2) shows, *ceteris paribus*, the linkage of income in country A to income in B.

We now consider how *changes* in domestic imports affect domestic exports. An autonomous increase in aggregate spending in country A results in increased imports from B (which we assume represents the rest of the world). Higher imports from B are, in effect, increased exports for B. As B's exports rise, so does its level of income. However, a rise in B's income level, given the assumed marginal propensity to import from A, also increases B's imports from A, and therefore A's exports. Hence, an autonomous increase in aggregate spending in country A raises both its level of imports and exports, the latter as a result of the feedback effect of A's increased imports.

The strength of the feedback effect depends upon the magnitude of B's marginal propensity to import from A. If B's marginal propensity to import from A is extremely small, the equilibrium equation for A is best presented by equation (1) in Example 4 rather than the feedback model [equation (2)] since the small value for h allows the term hY_B to be dropped from the model.

A strong feedback effect shows how inflationary and deflationary conditions may spread through the economies of the world. Given a general condition of full employment and price stability, a substantial increase in aggregate spending in one country, *ceteris paribus*, would result in world inflation. Likewise, a substantial decrease in aggregate spending, *ceteris paribus*, would cause generally depressed economies.

Review Questions

1. If the increase in exports exceeds the increase in imports, *ceteris paribus*, the level of income will (*a*) fall, (*b*) rise or (*c*) stay the same.

2. An autonomous increase in exports will result in
   (*a*) an equal increase in imports if imports are a function of income,
   (*b*) imports increasing more than exports if imports are a function of income   or
   (*c*) imports increasing less than exports if imports are a function of income.

3. If imports increase, *ceteris paribus*, (*a*) the domestic spending schedule shifts upward, (*b*) the domestic spending schedule shifts downward, (*c*) there is a movement along the domestic spending schedule or (*d*) there is no change in domestic spending.

4. The value of the multiplier (*a*) is unaffected by changes in the marginal propensity to import, (*b*) increases as the marginal propensity to import increases or (*c*) falls as the marginal propensity to import increases.

5. If there is an increase in imports, *ceteris paribus*, (*a*) the investment schedule shifts upward, (*b*) the investment schedule shifts downward, (*c*) the saving schedule shifts upward or (*d*) the saving schedule shifts downward.

6. In a two-country model of trade where imports in both countries are a function of their domestic levels of income, an increase in A's imports (*a*) causes B's exports to decrease, (*b*) causes B's exports to increase, (*c*) has no effect on B's exports or (*d*) causes B's income level to fall.

7. In a two-country model of trade where imports in both countries are a function of their domestic levels of income, an increase in investment in country A (*a*) causes the income level in country B to fall, (*b*) has no effect upon the income level in country B, (*c*) causes the income level in country B to rise or (*d*) causes the imports of country A to fall.

8. If imports equal exports and the import function reads $Z = Z_0 + zY$,
   (*a*) imports will exceed exports if the income level rises and exports are exogenously determined,
   (*b*) imports will exceed exports if the income level falls and exports are exogenously determined,
   (*c*) exports will exceed imports if the income level rises and exports are exogenously determined or
   (*d*) exports will exceed imports if there is an autonomous increase in investment and exports are exogenously determined.

9. In a two-country model of trade where imports in both countries are a function of their domestic levels of income, a tax cut in country A (*a*) will cause a tax cut in country B, (*b*) will cause the income level in country B to fall, (*c*) will have no effect on the income level in country B or (*d*) will cause the income level in country B to rise.

10. If exports equal imports and the import function reads $Z = Z_0 + zY$, a tax cut will (*a*) increase imports, (*b*) decrease imports, (*c*) have no effect upon the level of imports or (*d*) cause the income level to fall.

Answers to Review Questions

1. (*b*) Review Section 5.1.
2. (*c*) Review Section 5.3.
3. (*b*) Review Section 5.1.
4. (*c*) Review Section 5.2.
5. (*c*) Review Section 5.1.

6. (*b*) Review Section 5.4.
7. (*c*) Review Section 5.4.
8. (*a*) Review Section 5.3.
9. (*d*) Review Section 5.4.
10. (*a*) Review Section 5.2.

Solved Problems

5.1. Assuming that country A's exports equal imports, establish the direction of change in A's income and balance of trade when (a) the change in imports equals the change in exports, *ceteris paribus*, (b) the increase in imports exceeds the increase in exports, *ceteris paribus*, and (c) the increase in exports exceeds the increase in imports, *ceteris paribus*.

(a) The income level remains the same. There is no change in A's trade balance.

(b) The income level falls and a trade deficit develops.

(c) The income level rises and a trade surplus develops.

5.2. Suppose that (1) the marginal propensity to consume is 0.80, (2) both exports and imports are exogenously determined and (3) exports currently equal imports. Establish the change in income and the trade balance if (a) imports increase $10 while exports increase $10, (b) imports decrease $10 while exports decrease $12 and (c) imports decrease $10 while exports decrease $7.

(a) There is no change in the income level since $k_e \Delta Z$ is equal to $k_e \Delta X$. There is no change in the trade balance since ΔZ is equal to ΔX.

(b) The income level falls $10. There is a net import balance of $2.

(c) The income level increases $15. There is a net export balance of $3.

5.3. Country A's exports currently equal imports and are exogenously determined. The marginal propensity to import is 0.10. The marginal propensity to consume is 0.60. What happens to A's trade balance and income level if (a) government spending increases $10, (b) exports fall $10 or (c) investment falls $10.

(a) Since the expenditure multiplier is 2, the equilibrium income level increases $20. A trade deficit develops since imports increase $2 and there is no change in exports.

(b) The equilibrium income level falls $20. A trade deficit develops since imports fall $2 while exports decrease by $10.

(c) The equilibrium income level falls $20. A trade surplus develops since imports fall $2 while there is no change in exports.

5.4. Calculate the expenditure multipliers (a) with and (b) without a marginal propensity to import when (1) MPC = 0.90, MPZ = 0.10; (2) MPC = 0.80, MPZ = 0.20 and (3) MPC = 0.80, MPZ = 0.05.

(a) The multiplier without the marginal propensity to import equals $1/(1 - b)$. The multipliers are (1) 10, (2) 5 and (3) 5.

(b) The multiplier with the marginal propensity to import equals $1/(1 - b + z)$. The multipliers are (1) 5, (2) 2.5 and (3) 4.

5.5. If the marginal propensity to consume is 0.90, the marginal propensity to import is 0.10 and we assume an autonomous increase in exports of $10, calculate (a) the value of the multiplier, (b) the change in the level of income and (c) the change in the level of imports.

(a) $k_e = 1/(1 - \text{MPC} + \text{MPZ}) = 5$.

(b) $k_e \Delta X = 5 \times \$10 = \$50$.

(c) The change in the level of imports equals $\text{MPZ}(\Delta Y) = 0.10(\$50) = \$5$.

5.6. Suppose that the marginal propensity to consume is 0.90, the marginal propensity to import is 0.10 and we assume an autonomous increase in investment of $10. Calculate (a) the value of the multiplier, (b) the change in the level of income and (c) the change in the level of imports.

(a) $k_e = 1/(1 - \text{MPC} + \text{MPZ}) = 5$.

(b) $k_e \Delta I = 5 \times \$10 = \$50$.

(c) The change in the level of imports equals $\text{MPZ}(\Delta Y) = 0.10(\$50) = \$5$.

5.7. In Problems 5.5 and 5.6, an increase in exports causes the same change in the level of income and the level of imports as does a similar increase in investment. Does it matter, then, whether investment or exports causes the increase in income?

There is no difference if one is only interested in the change in income. There *is* a difference if one is concerned with a country's balance of trade. In Problem 5.5, the $10 increase in exports exceeds the $5 increase in imports. In Problem 5.6, there is no change in exports while imports increase $5.

5.8. Suppose that exports currently equal imports and that imports are a function of the level of income while exports are exogenously determined. What happens to the level of income and the country's trade balance if (a) government expenditures increase, (b) taxes decrease or (c) exports decrease.

(a) The income level increases. A deficit trade balance develops since exports are unchanged while imports increase.

(b) The income level increases. A deficit trade balance occurs as imports increase while exports are unchanged.

(c) The income level falls. The decrease in exports exceeds the induced decrease in imports. A deficit trade balance develops.

5.9. Full employment is defined as an income level of $600. The current income level is $550. The marginal propensity to consume is 0.90 while the marginal propensity to import is 0.10. What increase in government spending is needed to bring the income level to full employment?

The expenditure multiplier equals $1/(1 - 0.90 + 0.10) = 5$. Government spending must increase $10. (Full employment income is discussed in Section 18.5.)

5.10. Assume a zero marginal propensity to import in Problem 5.9. What increase in government spending is needed to bring the economy to full employment?

The expenditure multiplier equals $1/(1 - 0.90) = 10$. Government spending must increase $5 rather than $10.

5.11. Is the increase in government spending in Problem 5.9 equal to the increase in personal saving?

No. The $10 increase in government spending is financed through increased personal saving and import leakages. $(\Delta Z + \Delta S = \Delta G.)$ The change in imports is $5 $(0.10 \times \$50)$ while the change in personal saving is $5 $(0.10 \times \$50)$.

5.12. Why does an increase in imports represent a saving leakage?

When country A imports, it is buying goods from another country. We shall assume that these goods are paid for with A's currency. A foreign party now owns A's currency, and by assumption, does not use it to buy goods from A. Thus, by not using these receipts, the foreign seller is saving in country A. That is, demand for A's goods has fallen since the foreign country has elected not to spend its receipts from A. If the foreign seller elects to spend its receipts in A, then exports increase and offset the import leakage.

5.13. What is meant by a feedback effect in a two-country model of trade?

If country A increases its imports from B, B's exports and income level rise. With a higher income level, country B imports more goods from A. Thus, a change in imports in country A has a feedback effect on its exports.

5.14. If there is a minimal feedback effect, what happens to a country's balance of trade as its income level expands, assuming that the causes of expansion are forces other than increased exports?

Imports are increasing with little change in exports. The country's trading position is deteriorating. Thus, it is in or moving toward a deficit trade balance.

5.15. Countries A and B each have a marginal propensity to consume of 0.75. A's marginal propensity to import is 0.15, B's is 0.25. If there is increased investment in country A, which country has the greater increase in its level of income?

Country A has the greater increase in its income level since it has a smaller import leakage than does country B. (See Section 5.3.)

5.16. In Problem 5.15, which country develops a trade deficit if exports equal imports prior to this change in investment?

Country B develops a deficit trade balance since it has the greater marginal propensity to import. (See Section 5.3.)

5.17. The MPC and the MPZ are the same for two countries in a two-country trade model. If there is an autonomous increase in investment in country A, will the increase in income be the same for both countries?

The induced change in spending will be the same for both countries. Since country A also experiences the autonomous increase in investment demand, A's income level increases more than B's.

Chapter 6

Multipliers for a Four-Sector Model of the Economy

In Chapters 4 and 5, the value of the multiplier decreased as an income tax and an import function were introduced into the model of the economy. Additional functions are introduced in this chapter and the multipliers are re-evaluated. The dynamic multiplier, introduced in Chapter 3, is also analyzed here for the effect upon income of variant lags in marginal saving and spending.

6.1 HOUSEHOLD SECTOR FUNCTIONS

We retain the consumption function $C = C_0 + bYd$ introduced in Section 2.3, where the marginal propensity to consume b takes a value greater than zero but less than one. Given a two-sector model of the economy, equilibrium income equals

$$Y = \frac{C_0 + I_0}{1 - b}$$

and the expenditure multiplier for autonomous changes in C_0 and I_0 equals

$$k_e = \frac{1}{1 - b} \qquad (6.1)$$

The expenditure multiplier in (6.1) shows that induced consumption is the reason that autonomous changes in C_0 and I_0 result in a multiple change in the equilibrium level of income.

6.2 BUSINESS SECTOR FUNCTIONS

An Investment Function. Investment appears to be influenced by the level of profits, the cost and availability of labor and other factors. Rising profits generate optimism about future profit levels and therefore stimulate new investment outlays. Labor shortages and impending higher wage rates depress profit prospects but they too generate investment outlays as businessmen move to adopt labor-saving production methods. Since profits and labor availability are, in general, positively related to the level of economic activity, it is reasonable to hypothesize that investment is a positive function of the level of income (i.e., $I = I_0 + aY$, where a is the marginal propensity to invest and I_0 represents other investment forces).

EXAMPLE 1. If investment function $I = I_0 + aY$ is added to the two-sector model in Section 6.1, equilibrium income is now

$$Y = \frac{C_0 + I_0}{1 - b - a}$$

and the expenditure multiplier for autonomous changes in C_0 and I_0 is

$$k_e = \frac{1}{1 - b - a} \qquad (1)$$

The value of the expenditure multiplier in (1) is larger than in (6.1) since there is both induced consumption and investment for autonomous changes in aggregate spending.

A Business Saving Function. Corporations generally retain a portion of their profits. Thus, personal disposable income for a two-sector model with business saving is $Y - U$, where U represents undistributed corporate profits.

Higher corporate profits do not immediately result in increased dividends since most corporations will not increase dividend disbursements unless they can be maintained. Given such behavior, we can hypothesize a short-run undistributed profits function where undistributed profits are positively related to profit levels. Since profit levels are generally positively related to income, the undistributed profit function can be presented as $U = U_0 + uY$, where u represents the marginal propensity to retain earnings.

EXAMPLE 2. If the business saving function $U = U_0 + uY$ is added to the two-sector model in Example 1, equilibrium income becomes

$$Y = \frac{C_0 + I_0 - bU_0}{1 - b - a + bu}$$

and the expenditure multiplier for autonomous changes in C_0 and I_0 is

$$k_e = \frac{1}{1 - b - a + bu} \tag{2}$$

In (2) we see that the positive relationship between business saving and income lowers the value of the expenditure multiplier.

6.3 GOVERNMENT SECTOR FUNCTIONS

Tax function. We retain the tax function $Tx = Tx_0 + tY$ introduced in Section 4.6. Tx_0 represents administered taxes and t is a proportional tax upon income, taking a value greater than zero but less than one.

Transfer Function. The majority of government transfers are exogenous. Unemployment payments, however, are negatively related to income at income levels below full employment. For example, in Fig. 6-1 government transfers to the unemployed fall as the income level approaches Y_f, the full employment level of income. Beyond Y_f, transfers are an administered sum and as such are unrelated to the level of income.

Transfers equal $Tr_0 - rY$. Tr_0 is the sum of exogenous government transfers and r represents marginal unemployment payments. As long as there is less than full employment of the labor force, r has a value greater than zero but less than one.

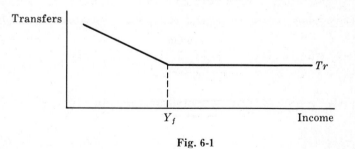

Fig. 6-1

Government Spending Function. While Congress authorizes federal expenditures, the President has a degree of discretion in administering the timing of these expenditures. Thus, government spending can be accelerated or decelerated as economic activity expands or falls. We would expect, then, that some federal spending is negatively related to income, similar to the behavior of the transfer function in Fig. 6-1.

The government spending function is given as $G = G_0 - gY$, where g represents marginal federal spending and has a value greater than zero but less than one.

EXAMPLE 3. If government sector functions $Tx = Tx_0 + tY$, $Tr = Tr_0 - rY$ and $G = G_0 - gY$ are added to the model in Example 2, equilibrium income now equals

$$Y = \frac{C_0 + I_0 + G_0 - bU_0 + bTr_0 - bTx_0}{1 - b - a + bu + bt + br + g}$$

and the expenditure multiplier for autonomous changes in C_0, I_0 and G_0 is

$$k_e = \frac{1}{1 - b - a + bu + bt + br + g} \qquad (3)$$

The government sector functions reduce the value of the expenditure multiplier. The tax function is a saving function. The transfer and government spending functions are negative spending functions where induced transfers and government spending fall as income expands and increase as income falls.

6.4 INTERNATIONAL SECTOR FUNCTIONS

We retain the import and export functions introduced in Section 5.2. Imports equal $Z_0 + zY$ while exports equal X_0.

6.5 MULTIPLIERS FOR A FOUR-SECTOR MODEL

Combining the various saving and spending functions of Sections 6.1 through 6.4, the equation for the equilibrium level of income for a four-sector model of the economy is

$$Y = \frac{C_0 + I_0 + G_0 + X_0 - Z_0 - bU_0 - bTx_0 + bTr_0}{1 - b - a + bu + bt + br + g + z} \qquad (6.2)$$

Letting λ (lambda) equal $bu + bt + br + g + z$, equation (6.2) is rewritten as

$$Y = \frac{C_0 + I_0 + G_0 + X_0 - Z_0 - bU_0 - bTx_0 + bTr_0}{1 - b - a + \lambda} \qquad (6.3)$$

λ represents the various saving and spending functions that negatively affect the level of spending. Thus, it represents the forces that reduce the magnitude of the multipliers.

The multipliers for a four-sector model of the economy derived from equation (6.3) are

$$k_e = \frac{1}{1 - b - a + \lambda} \qquad \text{for autonomous changes in } C_0, I_0, G_0 \text{ and } X_0 \qquad (6.4)$$

$$k_e = \frac{-1}{1 - b - a + \lambda} \qquad \text{for autonomous changes in } Z_0 \qquad (6.5)$$

$$k_{tx} = \frac{-b}{1 - b - a + \lambda} \qquad \text{for autonomous changes in } U_0 \text{ and } Tx_0 \qquad (6.6)$$

$$k_{tr} = \frac{b}{1 - b - a + \lambda} \qquad \text{for autonomous changes in } Tr_0 \qquad (6.7)$$

$$k_b = \frac{1 - b}{1 - b - a + \lambda} \qquad \text{for equal autonomous changes in } G_0 \text{ and } Tx_0 \qquad (6.8)$$

The values of the multipliers derived from the equilibrium condition in (6.3) depend upon the magnitudes of b, a and λ. We shall assume that b is always greater than λ. Thus, autonomous changes in spending, taxes, etc. always have the sign assigned in equations (6.4)-(6.8). The value of the balanced budget multiplier depends upon the relationship between a and λ. (See Problem 6.13 for examples of various relationships.) If the value of a exceeds that of λ, then k_b has a value greater than one. If a equals λ, k_b equals one; when a is less than λ, k_b has a value less than one.

The values of a, b, and λ may vary with economic conditions, thereby altering the value of the multiplier over time. For instance, the marginal propensity to consume may be lower in a contraction than during an expansion. Marginal federal spending depends upon the nearness of the economy to full employment as well as upon the ability and willingness of government agencies to use discretion in spending. With the value of the multiplier subject to change, the volume of fiscal action needed to stabilize income is not as easily prescribed as our examples might suggest.

6.6 DYNAMIC MULTIPLIERS

In Section 3.4, we analyzed the multiplier process whereby the multiplier effect is realized over time because of a lag in induced consumption. Example 4 expands upon this earlier analysis, showing the effect that two different lag structures have upon the level of income after four periods.

EXAMPLE 4.   Suppose that the income level equals \$400 in period t, given $I_t = \$80$, $G_t = \$70$, and $C_t = \$10 + 0.75\,Yd_{t-1}$, where $Yd_{t-1} = Y_{t-1} - 0.20\,Y_{t-1}$. Y in $t-1$ equals \$400.

Situation I: If there is a permanent \$20 increase in investment, *ceteris paribus*, the income level *eventually* reaches \$450, regardless of the lag structure of induced consumption and taxes.

Situation II: Given the established lag structure and a \$20 increase in investment in period $t+1$, the income levels in periods $t+1$ to $t+4$ are

Period $t+1$: $C_{t+1} = \$10 + 0.75(Y_t - 0.20\,Y_t)$, $I_{t+1} = \$100$ and $G_{t+1} = \$70$.

$$\begin{aligned} Y_{t+1} &= C_{t+1} + I_{t+1} + G_{t+1} \\ &= \$10 + 0.75(\$400 - 0.20 \times \$400) + \$100 + \$70 \\ &= \$420 \end{aligned}$$

Period $t+2$: $C_{t+2} = \$10 + 0.75(Y_{t+1} - 0.20\,Y_{t+1})$, $I_{t+2} = \$100$ and $G_{t+2} = \$70$.

$$\begin{aligned} Y_{t+2} &= C_{t+2} + I_{t+2} + G_{t+2} \\ &= \$10 + 0.75(\$420 - 0.20 \times \$420) + \$100 + \$70 \\ &= \$432 \end{aligned}$$

Period $t+3$: $Y_{t+3} = \$439.20$ Period $t+4$: $Y_{t+4} = \$443.52$

Situation III: We now assume a different lag structure whereby taxes are collected in the period earned. Then, although $C_t = \$10 + 0.75\,Yd_{t-1}$, Yd in period $t-1$ equals $Y_{t-1} - 0.20\,Y_t$. We continue to assume that income in Y_t is \$400 and that investment in $t+1$ increases \$20. The income level in periods $t+1$ to $t+4$ are

Period $t+1$: $C_{t+1} = \$10 + 0.75(Y_t - 0.20\,Y_{t+1})$, $I_{t+1} = \$100$ and $G_{t+1} = \$70$.

$$\begin{aligned} Y_{t+1} &= C_{t+1} + I_{t+1} + G_{t+1} \\ &= \$10 + 0.75(\$400 - 0.20\,Y_{t+1}) + \$100 + \$70 \\ &= \$417.39 \end{aligned}$$

Period $t+2$: $C_{t+2} = \$10 + 0.75(Y_{t+1} - 0.20\,Y_{t+2})$, $I_{t+2} = \$100$ and $G_{t+2} = \$70$.

$$\begin{aligned} Y_{t+2} &= C_{t+2} + I_{t+2} + G_{t+2} \\ &= \$10 + 0.75(\$417.39 - 0.20\,Y_{t+2}) + \$100 + \$70 \\ &= \$428.73 \end{aligned}$$

Period $t+3$: $Y_{t+3} = \$436.13$ Period $t+4$: $Y_{t+4} = \$440.96$

We can see that income after four periods is larger when the consumption and tax functions have a similar lag structure than when consumption lags disposable income by one period and taxes are collected as income is earned. Thus, if induced saving has a shorter lag than induced spending, income changes are more gradual and the dynamic multiplier after four periods is smaller. When induced saving has the longer lag, income level changes are greater in earlier periods and a larger proportion of the eventual change in income is realized in fewer periods.

Review Questions

1. If a saving function such as $U = U_0 + uY$ is introduced into a model of the economy, the value of the expenditure multiplier (a) falls, (b) increases or (c) stays the same.

2. If a spending function such as $G = G_0 - gY$ is introduced into a model of the economy, the value of the expenditure multiplier (a) falls, (b) increases or (c) stays the same.

3. In the equation for the expenditure multiplier, $k_e = 1/(1 - b - a + \lambda)$, the value of $a + b$ is (a) always equal to the value of λ, (b) always greater than the value of λ or (c) always less than the value of λ.

4. In the equation for the expenditure multiplier, $k_e = 1/(1 - b - a + \lambda)$, the value of the multiplier
   (a) increases as the value of λ increases *ceteris paribus*,
   (b) decreases as the value of λ increases, *ceteris paribus*,
   (c) decreases as the value of $a + b$ increases or
   (d) increases as the value of $a + b$ decreases.

5. In the spending equation $I = I_0 + aY$, (a) k_e increases as income increases, (b) k_e decreases as income increases, (c) spending increases as income increases or (d) spending decreases as income increases.

6. In the saving equation $U = U_0 + uY$, (a) saving increases as income decreases, (b) saving is negatively related to income or (c) saving is positively related to income.

7. If 0.60 is a positive spending coefficient and 0.10 is a negative spending coefficient, the spending multiplier for these two coefficients equals (a) 4, (b) 3.3, (c) 2.5 or (d) 2.

8. The balanced budget multiplier $k_b = (1 - b)/(1 - b - a + \lambda)$
   (a) has a value less than zero if the sum of $b + a$ exceeds the value of λ,
   (b) has a value equal to zero if the sum of $b + a$ exceeds the value of λ,
   (c) has a value of one if the value of a equals the value of λ or
   (d) has a value greater than one if the value of λ exceeds the value of a.

9. If induced spending lags induced saving,
   (a) it takes more periods for a major portion of the multiplier to be realized,
   (b) it takes less periods for a major portion of the multiplier to be realized,
   (c) induced spending occurs before any induced saving or
   (d) there is a reduction in the static multiplier.

10. The function that does not add a measure of built-in stability to the economy is
    (a) $U = U_0 + uY$, (b) $Tr = Tr_0 - rY$, (c) $Tx = Tx_0 + tY$ or (d) $I = I_0 + aY$.

Answers to Review Questions

1. (a) Review Section 6.2.
2. (a) Review Section 6.3.
3. (b) Review Section 6.5.
4. (b) Review Section 6.5.
5. (c) Review Section 6.2.

6. (c) Review Section 6.2.
7. (d) Review Section 6.5.
8. (c) Review Section 6.5.
9. (a) Review Section 6.6.
10. (d) Review Section 6.5.

Solved Problems

6.1. What determines the value of the expenditure multiplier in a four-sector model of the economy?

The value of the expenditure multiplier depends upon spending and saving that is related to the level of income.

6.2. What effect do the following spending and saving functions have upon the value of the expenditure multiplier? What is the sign of the behavioral coefficient in the multiplier formula?

   (*a*) Marginal spending is positively related to income.

   (*b*) Marginal spending is negatively related to income.

   (*c*) Marginal saving is positively related to income.

   (*d*) Marginal saving is negatively related to income.

   (*a*) The value of the expenditure multiplier increases when spending is positively related to income. The spending coefficient has a negative sign in the formula for the multiplier.

   (*b*) The value of the expenditure multiplier decreases when spending is negatively related to income. The spending coefficient has a positive sign in the formula for the multiplier.

   (*c*) The value of the expenditure multiplier decreases when saving is positively related to income. The saving coefficient has a positive sign in the formula for the multiplier.

   (*d*) The value of the expenditure multiplier increases when saving is negatively related to income. The saving coefficient has a negative sign in the formula for the multiplier.

   (See Section 6.5.)

6.3. Assuming that the following behavioral coefficients are positively related to income, what happens to the value of the expenditure multiplier if (*a*) the marginal propensity to invest increases, (*b*) the marginal propensity to import increases or (*c*) the marginal propensity to retain earnings decreases?

   (*a*) The value of the expenditure multiplier increases.

   (*b*) The value of the expenditure multiplier decreases.

   (*c*) The value of the expenditure multiplier increases.

6.4. Why are imports and corporate retained earnings classified as saving leakages?

   Imports represent a saving leakage since the purchase of foreign-made goods reduces the demand for domestic goods. Retained earnings are a saving leakage because, by not spending, the corporation is withholding money income from the circular flow.

6.5. Calculate the value of the expenditure multiplier if consumption and investment are positively related to income and the marginal propensity to consume *b* is 0.80 while the marginal propensity to invest *a* is 0.10.

   The value of the expenditure multiplier is

$$k_e = \frac{1}{1 - b - a} = 10$$

6.6. Find (*a*) the equilibrium level of income and (*b*) the expenditure multiplier given the following economic behavior.

   (1) Investment is positively related to income and other forces.

   (2) Consumption is positively related to disposable income and other forces.

   (3) Taxes are an administered sum unrelated to the level of income.

   (4) Government spending is exogenously determined.

   (5) Exports are exogenously determined.

   (6) Imports are positively related to the level of income and other forces.

(a) The behavioral relationships in equation form are

$$\begin{array}{rll}
(1) & I & = aY + I_0 \\
(2) & C & = bYd + C_0 \\
(3) & Tx & = Tx_0 \\
(4) & G & = G_0 \\
(5) & X & = X_0 \\
(6) & Z & = zY + Z_0
\end{array}$$

Equilibrium occurs where $Y = C + I + G + X - Z$. Thus,

$$Y = \frac{I_0 + C_0 + G_0 + X_0 - Z_0 - bTx_0}{1 - b - a + z}$$

(b) The expenditure multiplier is

$$k_e = \frac{1}{1 - b - a + z}$$

6.7. (a) Derive the equilibrium level of income for a model with the following behavioral equations: $C = C_0 + bYd$, $Yd = Y - Tx$, $Tx = Tx_0 + tY$, $I = I_0 + aY$ and $G = G_0$. (b) What are the expenditure, tax and balanced budget multipliers for this model?

(a) Equilibrium occurs where $Y = C + I + G$.

$$Y = C_0 + b(Y - Tx_0 - tY) + I_0 + aY + G_0$$

$$Y = \frac{C_0 + I_0 + G_0 - bTx_0}{1 - b - a + bt}$$

(b) The expenditure multiplier measures the change in income from an autonomous change in spending. Thus,

$$\frac{\Delta Y}{\Delta I} = k_e = \frac{1}{1 - b - a + bt}$$

The tax multiplier measures the change in income from an autonomous change in Tx_0. Thus,

$$\frac{\Delta Y}{\Delta Tx} = k_{tx} = \frac{-b}{1 - b - a + bt}$$

The balanced budget multiplier measures the change in income from equal autonomous changes in government spending and taxes. Thus,

$$k_e + k_{tx} = k_b$$

Substituting,

$$k_b = \frac{1 - b}{1 - b - a + bt}$$

6.8. Find the values of the (a) expenditure, (b) tax and (c) balanced budget multipliers in Problem 6.7 if the marginal propensity to consume is 0.75, the marginal propensity to invest is 0.15 and the income tax rate is 0.20.

(a) The expenditure multiplier is

$$k_e = \frac{1}{1 - b - a + bt} = 4$$

(b) The tax multiplier is

$$k_{tx} = \frac{-b}{1 - b - a + bt} = -3$$

(c) The balanced budget multiplier is

$$k_b = \frac{1 - b}{1 - b - a + bt} = 1$$

6.9. Why are income taxes, retained earnings and unemployment insurance classified as built-in stabilizers?

Both income taxes and retained earnings are positively related to the income level, while unemployment insurance is negatively related to the income level. Income taxes, retained earnings and unemployment insurance reduce the value of k_e since their coefficients have positive signs in the equation for the multiplier. With a lower value for the expenditure multiplier, autonomous changes in demand produce smaller changes in the equilibrium level of income. As a result, the income level is less sensitive to autonomous changes and is therefore more stable.

6.10. (a) Derive the expenditure multiplier for the following behavioral equations: $C = C_0 + bYd$, $Yd = Y - Tx$, $Tx = Tx_0 + tY$, $G = G_0$, $I = I_0 + aY$, $a > 0$ when unemployment is less than 5% and $a = 0$ when the unemployment rate exceeds 5%. (b) Is the expenditure multiplier larger when the economy is near full employment or when it is in the midst of a recession?

(a) Equilibrium occurs where $Y = C + I + G$.

$$Y = \frac{C_0 + I_0 + G_0 - bTx_0}{1 - b - a + bt}$$

$$k_e = \frac{1}{1 - b - a + bt}$$

(b) Since $a = 0$ when there is a recession, the expenditure multiplier has its larger value when the economy is near full employment.

6.11. Prior to a contraction, the sum of the marginal propensity to consume and the marginal propensity to invest is +0.93, while the value of λ (other saving and spending coefficients) is −0.18. During the contraction, the value of λ falls to −0.13. (a) What happens to the value of the expenditure multiplier during the contraction? (b) What change in government spending is needed during the contraction to increase the equilibrium level of income $50?

(a) Prior to the contraction, k_e is 4. During the contraction, k_e is 5.

(b) Government spending must increase $10 during the contraction to increase the income level $50.

6.12. From Problem 6.11, assume further that during the contraction the sum of the MPC and MPI falls from +0.93 to +0.73. (a) What is the value of the expenditure multiplier during the contraction? (b) What change in government spending is now needed during the contraction to increase the income level $50?

(a) The expenditure multiplier k_e now equals 2.5.

(b) Increased government spending must be $20.

6.13. If a is the marginal propensity to invest, b is the marginal propensity to consume and λ is the value of the other saving and spending coefficients, find the values of the (a) expenditure, (b) tax and (c) balanced budget multipliers for each of the following situations.

$$(1) \quad a = +0.10, \ b = +0.70 \ \text{and} \ \lambda = -0.30$$

$$(2) \quad a = +0.25, \ b = +0.75 \ \text{and} \ \lambda = -0.25$$

$$(3) \quad a = +0.25, \ b = +0.50 \ \text{and} \ \lambda = -0.15$$

(a) Since $k_e = \dfrac{1}{1 - b - a + \lambda}$, in

$$(1) \quad k_e = 2$$
$$(2) \quad k_e = 4$$
$$(3) \quad k_e = 2.5$$

(b) Since $k_{tx} = \dfrac{-b}{1 - b - a + \lambda}$, in

$$(1) \quad k_{tx} = -1.4$$
$$(2) \quad k_{tx} = -3$$
$$(3) \quad k_{tx} = -1.25$$

(c) Since $k_b = k_e + k_{tx}$,

$$k_b = \frac{1 - b}{1 - b - a + \lambda}$$

Therefore, in

$$(1) \quad k_b = 0.6$$
$$(2) \quad k_b = 1.0$$
$$(3) \quad k_b = 1.25$$

6.14. The current equilibrium level of income is \$500 given the following behavioral equations: $C = \$10 + 0.75\,Yd$, $I = \$20 + 0.20\,Y$, $Tx = 0.20\,Y$ and $G = \$70$. (a) What is the new equilibrium level of income if there is a \$10 increase in government spending? (b) What is the level of income in period $t + 3$ if there is a permanent increase in government spending in $t + 1$ and consumption, investment and taxes lag income by one period.

(a) $k_e = 1/(1 - b - a + bt) = 5$. Since $k_e \Delta G = \$50$, the new equilibrium level of income is \$550.

(b) If there is a one-period lag in induced consumption, investment and taxes, the change in the level of income for each period is

$$\Delta Y_{t+1} = \Delta G(1)$$
$$\Delta Y_{t+2} = \Delta G[1 + (b - bt + a)]$$
$$\Delta Y_{t+3} = \Delta G[1 + (b - bt + a) + (b - bt + a)^2]$$

Thus, the increases in income for periods $t + 1$ to $t + 3$ are

$$\Delta Y_{t+1} = +\$10.00$$
$$\Delta Y_{t+2} = +\$18.00$$
$$\Delta Y_{t+3} = +\$24.40$$

6.15. Derive the dynamic expenditure multipliers for periods $t + 1$ to $t + 3$ in Problem 6.14.

The dynamic multiplier for each period is $\Delta Y / \Delta G$. Thus, for period $t + 1$,

$$k_{de} = 1.0$$

for period $t + 2$,

$$k_{de} = 1.8$$

for period $t + 3$,

$$k_{de} = 2.44$$

6.16. What are the changes in the income levels for periods $t+1$ to $t+3$ if the $10 increase in government spending in Problem 6.14 occurs only during period $t+1$, returning to its previous level in periods $t+2$ and $t+3$?

If there is a one-period lag in marginal saving and spending, the change in the level of income for a one-period change in government spending is

$$\Delta Y_{t+1} = \Delta G(1)$$

$$\Delta Y_{t+2} = \Delta G(b - bt + a)$$

$$\Delta Y_{t+3} = \Delta G(b - bt + a)^2$$

Thus, the increases in the levels of income for periods $t+1$ to $t+3$ are

$$\Delta Y_{t+1} = +\$10.00$$

$$\Delta Y_{t+2} = +\$ 8.00$$

$$\Delta Y_{t+3} = +\$ 6.40$$

6.17. Retain the parameters of Problem 6.14 and the $10 increase in government spending but assume that the lag structure is as follows: $C_t = f(Yd_{t-1})$, $I_t = f(Y_{t-1})$ and $Tx = f(Y_t)$. What are the levels of income in periods $t+1$ to $t+3$?

For this lag structure, the changes in the levels of income for periods $t+1$ to $t+3$ are

$$\Delta Y_{t+1} = \Delta G\left(\frac{1}{1+bt}\right)$$

$$\Delta Y_{t+2} = \Delta G\left[\frac{1}{1+bt} + \frac{b+a}{(1+bt)^2}\right]$$

$$\Delta Y_{t+3} = \Delta G\left[\frac{1}{1+bt} + \frac{b+a}{(1+bt)^2} + \frac{(b+a)^2}{(1+bt)^3}\right]$$

Thus, the increases in income for periods $t+1$ to $t+3$ are

$$\Delta Y_{t+1} = +\$ 8.70$$

$$\Delta Y_{t+2} = +\$15.88$$

$$\Delta Y_{t+3} = +\$21.81$$

6.18. Explain why the income levels in periods $t+1$ through $t+3$ differ for Problems 6.14 and 6.17 although there is no difference in the parameters of the model.

There is a difference in income levels as a result of the collection of taxes upon earned income. In Problem 6.14, taxes are collected from income earned in the previous period whereas taxes are collected during the period earned in Problem 6.17. By eliminating the lag in collecting taxes, there are increased saving leakages in the earlier periods in Problem 6.17 which in turn reduce the stimulative effect of increased government spending. Eventually in both problems, the $10 increase in government spending results in a $50 increase in the level of income.

Chapter 7

The Keynesian Theory of Consumption Demand

7.1 CONSUMPTION AND DISPOSABLE INCOME

As formulated by Keynes, *the consumption function* is the schedule of planned consumption for various levels of disposable income. Keynes believed that this schedule of planned consumption was subject to a "fundamental psychological law" whereby the change in consumption is less than the change in disposable income. Accordingly, the consumption function presented in Fig. 7-1 has a slope that is less than one.

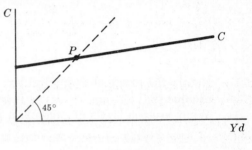

The marginal propensity to consume for the straight-line consumption function in Fig. 7-1 is constant since $\Delta C/\Delta Yd$, the slope of the line, is constant. However, the average propensity to consume, C/Yd, decreases as income increases. At point P, the APC is one; to the left of P, it is greater than one; to the right of P, the APC takes a value less than one and approaches the MPC as a limit for large values of disposable income.

Fig. 7-1

The relationship of consumption to disposable income is *proportional* when the average propensity to consume is the same for all levels of disposable income and *nonproportional* when it is not. The relationship of consumption to disposable income in Fig. 7-1 and Example 1 is nonproportional.

EXAMPLE 1. Suppose that the straight-line consumption function is $C = \$40 + 0.80\,Yd$. The APC and MPC for a range of disposable incomes Yd are given in Table 1. The consumption function is nonproportional since the APC falls as disposable income increases.

Table 1

Yd (\$)	C (\$)	APC	MPC
200	200	1.00	. . .
400	360	0.90	0.80
600	520	0.87	0.80
800	680	0.85	0.80
1000	840	0.84	0.80

7.2 NONINCOME DETERMINANTS OF CONSUMPTION DEMAND

In the linear consumption function $C = C_0 + bYd$, the parameter C_0 represents consumption at zero disposable income. Keynes speculated that nonincome determinants could influence aggregate consumption, although he believed them to be of minimal significance for a short-run model of economic activity. Thus, in the Keynesian analysis of aggregate consumer behavior, C_0 represents nonincome determinants that might affect consumption demand in the long run.

Keynesian analysis categorizes the nonincome determinants of consumption into subjective and objective factors. *Subjective factors* reflect psychological preferences. *Objective factors* include nonincome variables affecting households' ability to consume.

These subjective and objective factors are similar in concept to willingness and ability factors in microeconomic demand theory. Changes in these factors have similar effects upon the demand and aggregate consumption schedules. For instance, demand is a function of price but changes in one's willingness or ability to buy cause shifts of the demand schedule. Likewise, changes in subjective or objective factors shift the aggregate consumption function.

EXAMPLE 2. In Fig. 7-2, D_1 is the demand schedule for good X. C_1 is an aggregate consumption function.

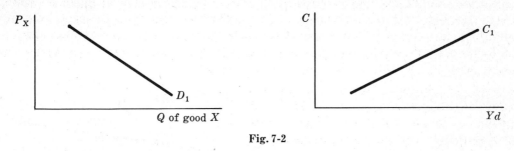

Fig. 7-2

D_1 shifts to the right if individuals are more willing or have increased capacity to buy good **X**. It shifts to the left if the good becomes less useful to them, or if their buying capacity falls.

C_1 shifts upward if households are more willing or able to spend their disposable income, and shifts downward if they prefer to save more or if they are less able to spend more at all income levels.

7.3 SUBJECTIVE FACTORS

Subjective or willingness variables are the underlying psychological factors affecting households' demand for goods. Buying attitudes are influenced by advertising, attractiveness of the product and by expectations about the price level, the future availability of goods or the future level of income. Problem 7.12 shows how changes in these subjective factors might cause upward or downward shifts in the aggregate consumption function.

7.4 OBJECTIVE FACTORS

The major objective factors affecting the aggregate consumption function are:

1. *Distribution of Income.* A change in income distribution affects the level of aggregate consumption if income recipients do not have the same average propensity to consume. As shown in Problems 7.9–7.11, a redistribution of income may cause a shift in the aggregate consumption function or a combined shift and change in the slope of the function.

2. *Consumer Installment Credit.* The cost and availability of consumer installment credit affects consumers' buying capacities. If credit is more readily available and/or its cost is lower, consumers are more likely to borrow and thereby in the aggregate save less at all levels of aggregate disposable income. Increased consumer borrowing, *ceteris paribus*, causes an upward shift of the aggregate consumption function.

3. *Stock of Assets.* Through annual saving flows, households add to their stock of assets (i.e., their wealth). Greater wealth, in turn, increases their ability to consume. It therefore follows that annual saving flows, *ceteris paribus*, increase households' stock of assets and shift the aggregate consumption function upward.

It is possible that price or interest rate changes negate the additive effect of annual saving flows to households' wealth. The real value of assets, measured in monetary terms, falls as the price level rises. Likewise, increases in the rate of interest decrease the money value of fixed income securities. Thus, annual saving flows will not shift the aggregate consumption function upward if price or interest rate increases cause a net reduction in households' stock of assets.

4. *The Rate of Interest.* Prior to *The General Theory*, the rate of interest was considered the primary determinant of saving and therefore of consumption. It was believed that saving was positively related to the rate of interest (i.e., households willingly increased their rate of saving for higher interest returns). Today most economists do not subscribe to this relationship. They do admit, however, that interest rate levels may affect consumption by altering the cost of borrowing and/or the current value of wealth. See 2 and 3 above.

7.5 THE DETERMINANTS OF CONSUMPTION DEMAND

Although nonincome variables might influence the level of aggregate consumption, Keynes believed that consumption is principally a function of disposable income. Economists have analyzed consumption data with the hope of establishing empirically the importance of income and nonincome variables. Their findings and evaluation of the Keynesian theory of consumption demand are presented in Chapter 8.

Review Questions

1. Keynes' fundamental psychological law states that (a) the change in income is greater than the change in consumption, (b) the change in consumption is greater than the change in income, (c) people stop consuming when they become affluent or (d) people stop saving when they become affluent.

2. The slope of the consumption function is defined as (a) nonincome factors, (b) the MPC, (c) the APC or (d) none of the above.

3. If $C = \$50 + 0.80\,Yd$, (a) the MPC is 0.50, (b) the MPC is 0.20, (c) the MPS is 0.80 or (d) the MPS is 0.20.

4. If a straight-line consumption function intercepts the vertical axis,
   (a) the MPC is constant and the APC rises as the level of disposable income increases,
   (b) the MPC and the APC rise as the level of disposable income increases,
   (c) the MPC is constant and the APC falls as the level of disposable income increases or
   (d) the MPC and the APC fall as the level of disposable income increases.

5. There is a proportional relationship between consumption and disposable income (a) if the APC is the same for all levels of disposable income, (b) if the consumption function is a straight line through the origin, (c) if the MPC equals the APC for all levels of disposable income or (d) all of the above.

6. A subjective determinant of consumption is a factor such as (a) a redistribution of income, (b) a change in the availability of credit, (c) a change in the wealth position of consumers or (d) a change in one's willingness to consume.

7. Keynes considered subjective and objective factors (a) important determinants of consumption, (b) unimportant determinants of consumption, (c) determinants of investment or (d) determinants of businessmen's willingness to supply.

8. Changes in subjective or objective factors (a) never affect the consumption function, (b) always cause downward shifts of the consumption function, (c) always cause upward shifts of the consumption function or (d) may cause upward or downward shifts of the consumption function.

9. Households' wealth increases (a) as a result of a current flow of saving, (b) if there is a decrease in the price level, (c) if there is a decrease in the rate of interest or (d) all of the above.

10.   Changes in the distribution of disposable income
  (a) cause upward shifts in the consumption function,
  (b) cause downward shifts in the consumption function,
  (c) have no effect upon the consumption function if income recipients have the same APC   or
  (d) cause the consumption function to shift if income recipients have the same APC.

Answers to Review Questions

1. (a) Review Section 7.1.
2. (b) Review Section 7.1.
3. (d) Review Section 7.1.
4. (c) Review Section 7.1.
5. (d) Review Section 7.1.

6. (d) Review Section 7.3.
7. (b) Review Section 7.2.
8. (d) Review Section 7.2.
9. (d) Review Section 7.4.
10. (c) Review Section 7.4.

Solved Problems

7.1.   What are the MPC and the APC for each household if (a) household A plans to consume $370 when disposable income is $400, $450 when it is $500 and $530 when it is $600, and (b) household B plans to consume $400 when disposable income is $500, $480 when it is $600 and $560 when it is $700?

  (a) The MPC for all changes in the level of disposable income is 0.80. The APC is 0.92 when disposable income is $400, 0.90 when it is $500 and 0.88 when it is $600.

  (b) The MPC for all changes in the level of disposal income is 0.80. The APC is also 0.80 for all levels of disposable income.

  (See Example 1.)

7.2.   Is the relationship between consumption and disposable income in Problem 7.1 proportional or nonproportional?

  The relationship between consumption and disposable income is proportional if the APC is constant and nonproportional if it varies with the level of disposable income. Household B's consumption function is proportional while A's is nonproportional.

7.3.   If the MPC is less than the APC, is the relationship between consumption and disposable income proportional or nonproportional?

  The relationship is nonproportional since the APC falls in adding $\Delta C/\Delta Yd$ to C/Yd.

7.4.   From Fig. 7-3, prove that consumption function (a) C_1 is proportional and (b) C_2 is nonproportional.

  A consumption function is proportional if the APC is constant and nonproportional if it changes with the level of disposable income. The APC will not change if the MPC is equal to the APC. The MPC of a straight-line consumption function is constant.

  (a) If $\Delta Yd = OYd_1$, the MPC equals OC_1/OYd_1. The APC for income level OYd_1 is OC_1/OYd_1. Since MPC = APC, the APC will not change as the level of disposable income increases, and C_1 is proportional.

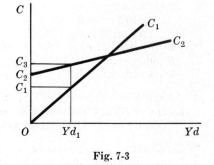

Fig. 7-3

(b) If $\Delta Yd = OYd_1$, the MPC equals $(OC_3 - OC_2)/OYd_1$ which is less than the APC of OC_3/OYd_1 for income level OYd_1. Since the MPC is less than the APC, the APC will fall as the level of disposable income increases, and C_2 is thus nonproportional.

(See Section 7.1.)

7.5. Assume a growing economy in which full employment output shifts to the right with time. Would a proportional or nonproportional consumption function necessitate the larger growth of investment spending over time?

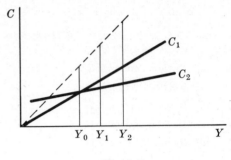

Figure 7-4 shows that the nonproportional consumption function C_2 necessitates larger increases in investment spending as full employment income shifts from Y_0 to Y_1 to Y_2 through time. This is due to the falling APC of the nonproportional consumption function C_2.

Fig. 7-4

7.6. What happens to the marginal propensity to consume if there are parallel and non-parallel shifts in a straight-line consumption function?

The MPC remains the same for parallel shifts of a straight-line consumption function and increases or decreases for nonparallel shifts.

7.7. An economy is composed of only three households (A, B and C). Their consumption equations are $C_A = \$10 + 0.80\,Yd$, $C_B = \$40 + 0.80\,Yd$ and $C_C = \$50 + 0.80\,Yd$ respectively. Determine the aggregate consumption equation for this hypothetical economy.

When the MPC for all households is constant, the aggregate consumption function is the summation of the constant term for individual functions plus the MPC (Yd). Thus, $C = \$10 + \$40 + \$50 + 0.80\,Yd = \$100 + 0.80\,Yd$.

7.8. Two households are added to the hypothetical economy in Problem 7.7. Their consumption equations are $C_D = \$5 + 0.80\,Yd$ and $C_E = \$7 + 0.80\,Yd$. (a) What is the new aggregate consumption equation? (b) If depicted graphically, explain what happens to the aggregate consumption function?

(a) The aggregate consumption equation becomes $C = \$112 + 0.80\,Yd$.

(b) As a result of an increase in the number of households, there is increased aggregate consumption for each level of aggregate disposable income. Thus, the aggregate consumption function has shifted upward.

7.9. Suppose that household C in Problem 7.7 voluntarily transfers income to household A and that preferences for consuming are not altered by this transfer. What effect does the transfer have upon the aggregate consumption function?

There is no change in the aggregate consumption function when a transfer has no effect upon households' preferences for consuming.

7.10. Continuing the situation in Problem 7.9, assume that preferences are affected by C's voluntary transfers. Since C plans to continue such transfers indefinitely, its consumption plans change from $50 + 0.80\,Yd$ to $48 + 0.80\,Yd$. Expecting continuous transfers, A changes its planned consumption from $10 + 0.80\,Yd$ to $15 + 0.80\,Yd$. What effect does this redistribution of income have upon the aggregate consumption function?

> The aggregate consumption function is now $115 + 0.80\,Yd$ instead of $112 + 0.80\,Yd$. Thus, the aggregate consumption function has shifted upward.

7.11. What type of redistribution of income has occurred if the aggregate consumption function changes from $112 + 0.80\,Yd$ to $115 + 0.85\,Yd$?

> There has been both an upward shift of the aggregate consumption function and a change in the marginal propensity to consume. The transfer recipients have a greater marginal propensity to consume and a greater preference for consuming than do those who are making the transfers. (See Example 2.)

7.12. How is the aggregate consumption function affected if

(a) an impending war is expected to result in a shortage of goods and an adoption of a rationing system,

(b) increased costs for steel, oil, etc. are expected to result in higher prices for consumer goods   or

(c) The President of the United States assures the public that economic policy is bringing the recession to an end?

> (a) Households will try to "hoard" goods before an actual shortage develops. The aggregate consumption function will shift upward.

> (b) The expected increase in prices encourages households to accelerate spending plans. The aggregate consumption function will shift upward.

> (c) If consumers believe that economic recovery is near, they will be more willing to consume. The aggregate consumption function will shift upward.

7.13. Suppose that the government institutes a higher rate of taxation on interest income. What effect might this action have upon the aggregate consumption function?

> The return from wealth (accumulated savings) is being more heavily taxed. This would probably result in increased consumption (increases in the MPC and the APC) as people decide to save less.

7.14. The central bank's monetary policy decreases credit availability to all sectors of the economy. How would this action affect the aggregate consumption function?

> If there is less consumer installment credit available, consumer demand might fall. That is, the aggregate consumption function might shift downward.

7.15. Inflation has reduced the purchasing power of debt outstanding. What effect might this event have upon the aggregate consumption function?

> The wealth of households has decreased. Their willingness to consume may fall, thereby shifting the aggregate consumption function downward.

7.16. Repayment provisions for consumer installment credit are extended from twenty-four to thirty-six months. How does this event affect the aggregate consumption function?

> With lower monthly installments, households may be more willing to purchase on an installment basis. If the volume of consumer credit increases, the aggregate consumption function shifts upwards.

Chapter 8

Postwar Theories of Consumption Demand

8.1 CONSUMPTION DATA

Data on consumption are available from a cross-sectional series which presents the consumption of households at different income levels and from a time series where aggregate consumption and aggregate disposable income are presented as quarterly, yearly or longer period flows.

Cross-sectional data show that high-income households have a smaller average propensity to consume than low-income ones. Thus, in plotting cross-sectional data, we derive a household consumption function with a positive vertical intercept.

The consumption function derived from a time series differs according to the periods chosen for analysis: (1) for *quarterly flows* of consumer spending, the aggregate consumption function is a straight line with a positive vertical intercept and (2) for *yearly or longer flows*, the consumption function is a straight line through the origin. Thus, although annual spending flows are the sum of quarterly spending flows, we derive distinct statistical consumption functions according to our specification of periods.

EXAMPLE 1. Figure 8-1 presents two distinct consumption functions. C_S represents the consumption function derived from cross-sectional and quarterly time series flows. C_L represents the aggregate consumption function derived from longer period time series flows.

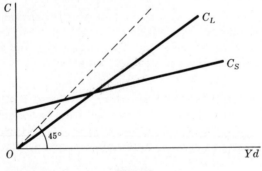

Fig. 8-1

C_S is nonproportional since the average propensity to consume falls as aggregate disposable income increases. Along C_L, the relationship between aggregate consumption and aggregate disposable income is proportional.

The next three sections focus on the ability of absolute, relative and permanent income theories to reconcile the short-run and long-run relationships between aggregate consumption and aggregate disposable income.

8.2 THE ABSOLUTE INCOME THEORY

Keynes originally theorized that aggregate consumption was directly but nonproportionately related to the current level of aggregate disposable income in both the short and long runs.

Since postwar data contradicted this theory for the long run, economists sought to restructure it by incorporating subjective and objective variables into the function. Non-income variables, it was suggested, shifted the consumption function upward with time. Thus, a short-run consumption function such as C_1 in Fig. 8-2 shifts upward, making C_L a locus of points observed from a number of short-run consumption functions. That is, C_L arises because aggregate consumption is equal to the amounts represented by points A, B, C and D on consumption schedules C_1, C_2, C_3 and C_4 at different levels of disposable income. This reconciliation of the short- and long-run consumption functions has been judged unsatisfactory, however, since the long-run proportionality of consumption and disposable income is not theoretically explained but is a chance phenomenon.

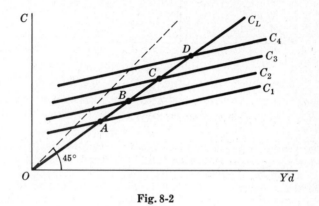

Fig. 8-2

8.3 THE RELATIVE INCOME THEORY

The relative income theory, developed by James Duesenberry, is judged superior to the absolute income theory in terms of reconciling the nonproportional and proportional relationship of aggregate consumption and aggregate disposable income. In presenting the theory, we initially hypothesize about individual behavior and then, using the assumptions in Section 1.4, we can generalize about aggregate consumption.

As viewed by Duesenberry, consumption and saving decisions are greatly influenced by the social environment in which one lives. Thus, an individual with a given income consumes more if he lives in an affluent neighborhood than if he lives in a poorer one. In addition, his consuming behavior within a neighborhood is relative to the consuming patterns of his neighbors (i.e., he spends in order to maintain a certain economic status within the neighborhood). If the distribution of income is relatively constant, it is highly probable that an individual's average propensity to consume is constant since his consumption is related to his relative income within a community and is not related to his absolute level of income. Therefore, in the aggregate, we would expect a proportional relationship between aggregate consumption and aggregate disposable income.

Duesenberry also theorized that households like to maintain a certain standard of living. Thus he thought it reasonable to present a household's consumption function as $C = f(Y_c, Y_{pp})$, where Y_c represents current income and Y_{pp} previous peak income. If current income always exceeds previous peak income, consumption is related to one's relative income within a given community. If current income should fall below previous peak income, consumption is related to the living standard established by the previous peak income. Thus, according to Duesenberry's theory, households would change their propensity to consume when income fell in order to maintain a given standard of living. In the short run, nonproportionality between aggregate consumption and aggregate disposable income would exist if current income fell below previous peak income.

EXAMPLE 2. Duesenberry's explanation of the proportional/nonproportional relationship of consumption and disposable income is illustrated by Fig. 8-3 and the following two situations.

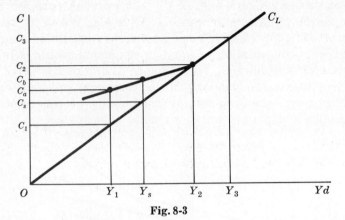

Fig. 8-3

Situation I: Constant Growth in the Absolute Level of Income. Households' consumption is interdependent and is therefore based upon relative income. Aggregate consumption equals C_1, C_2 and C_3 for absolute income levels Y_1, Y_2 and Y_3 respectively.

Situation II: Fluctuations in the Absolute Level of Income. Households try to maintain their previous standard of living when the level of income falls. We shall assume that the level of income falls from Y_2 to Y_1. Consumption declines from C_2 to C_a rather than C_1 since income level Y_2 is still influencing consumption. As the income level recovers to Y_s, consumption remains above C_s since consumption is still influenced by previous peak income Y_2. Once Y_2 is exceeded, consumption proceeds along consumption function C_L.

The relative income theory suggests the following relationships for the average propensity to consume and the marginal propensity to consume:

1. There is constant growth in the level of income. The APC is constant. The MPC equals the APC.

2. Current income is falling and is below a previous income level. The APC is rising. The MPC is less than the APC.

3. Income is rising but is below a previous income level. The APC is falling. The MPC is increasing. The MPC is less than the APC.

4. Income is rising and is above a previous income level. The APC is constant. The MPC equals the APC.

8.4 THE PERMANENT INCOME THEORY

Milton Friedman's permanent income theory resolves the proportional/nonproportional relationship between consumption and disposable income by theorizing that consumption is not based upon the current level of disposable income.

According to Friedman, current (measured) disposable income Ym is composed of permanent income Yp and transitory income Yt. Permanent income is that which households expect to receive over an extended number of years, while transitory income consists of any unexpected addition to or subtraction from permanent income. Thus, $Ym = Yp + Yt$.

The theory holds that permanent income determines consumption. In addition, it assumes that households, regardless of their level of permanent income, consume approximately the same proportion of their permanent income. Thus, if we relate consumption to permanent income, we get a fixed proportional relationship regardless of the distribution of permanent income. Only if we erroneously relate consumption to current measured income can we obtain a nonproportional relationship, since current measured income may contain positive or negative transitory income.

EXAMPLE 3.   The long-run relationship between consumption and income is 0.90.

Situation I: The current $420 level of income includes a positive $20 transitory component.   Consumption is currently $360.

If consumption is related to current income (C/Ym), the APC is 0.86.

If consumption is related to permanent income (C/Yp), the APC is 0.90.

Situation II: The current $420 level of income includes a negative $20 transitory component.   Consumption is currently $396.

If consumption is related to current income (C/Ym), the APC is 0.94.

If consumption is related to permanent income (C/Yp), the APC is 0.90.

If income changes are considered permanent, the marginal propensity to consume permanent income equals the average propensity to consume.   If the change in income is considered transitory, the marginal propensity to consume is zero.

Review Questions

1. The proportional relationship between consumption and income is supported by (*a*) cross-sectional data on family income, (*b*) quarterly time series data on aggregate consumption, (*c*) annual time series data on aggregate consumption or (*d*) all of the above.

2. According to the absolute income theory, (*a*) the average propensity to consume falls as disposable income increases, (*b*) the average propensity to consume is constant, (*c*) past and current incomes affect current consumption or (*d*) consumption is proportional to disposable income in the long run.

3. According to the relative income theory, (*a*) the APC is constant, (*b*) the APC is always rising, (*c*) the APC is always falling or (*d*) the APC may change if there are fluctuations in the level of income.

4. Duesenberry based the proportionality of aggregate consumption and aggregate disposable income in the long run upon the theory that
    (*a*) households based their consumption expenditures upon their absolute level of income,
    (*b*) households based their decision to consume upon their past peak income,
    (*c*) households based their decision to consume upon their relative level of income   or
    (*d*) households based their decision to consume upon their absolute level of income.

5. If current income falls below previous peak income, the relative income theory holds that
    (*a*) households will increase their rate of saving,
    (*b*) households will decrease their marginal propensity to consume,
    (*c*) the marginal propensity to consume will exceed the average propensity to consume   or
    (*d*) the marginal propensity to consume will equal the average propensity to consume.

6. According to the relative income theory, (*a*) the APC exceeds the MPC if past peak income exceeds current income, (*b*) the APC equals the APS in the long run, (*c*) the APC falls if past peak income exceeds current income or (*d*) all of the above.

7. The theories which support a proportionate relationship between consumption and income are (*a*) the permanent and absolute income theories, (*b*) the permanent and relative income theories, (*c*) the relative and absolute income theories or (*d*) none of the above.

8. According to the permanent income theory, all increases in (*a*) permanent income are saved, (*b*) permanent income are consumed, (*c*) transitory income are saved or (*d*) transitory income are consumed.

9. If current income includes a negative transitory component, relating consumption with current income will produce
    (*a*) an average propensity to consume that is lower than the long-run average propensity to consume,
    (*b*) an average propensity to consume that is higher than the long-run average propensity to consume,
    (*c*) an average propensity to consume that equals the long-run average propensity to consume   or
    (*d*) none of the above.

10.   Which of the following statements is *true*?

(*a*) The level of consumption will not change if transitory income increases.

(*b*) The level of consumption will not change if transitory income decreases.

(*c*) The level of consumption will increase if permanent income increases.

(*d*) All of the above.

Answers to Review Questions

1. (*c*) Review Section 8.1.

2. (*a*) Review Section 8.2.

3. (*d*) Review Section 8.3.

4. (*c*) Review Section 8.3.

5. (*b*) Review Section 8.3.

6. (*a*) Review Section 8.3.

7. (*b*) Review Sections 8.2-8.4.

8. (*c*) Review Section 8.4

9. (*b*) Review Section 8.4.

10. (*d*) Review Section 8.4.

Solved Problems

8.1.   From Fig. 8-4, establish whether the average propensity to consume current income at points L, M and N exceeds the long-run average propensity to consume.

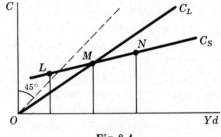

Fig. 8-4

The APC for long-run consumption function C_L is constant. The APC for C_S falls as income increases. Since M is a point on both C_S and C_L, the APC at point L exceeds the long-run APC while it is less than the long-run APC at point N.

8.2.   The long-run relationship between consumption and disposable income is 0.90. The relationship between consumption and disposable income for the past six quarters is shown in Table 1. (*a*) What is the consumption/income relationship for the six quarters and (*b*) what expectation might one hold about the future marginal propensity to consume?

Table 1

Quarter	Consumption ($)	Disposable Income ($)
1	360	400
2	368	410
3	375	420
4	382	430
5	390	440
6	398	450

(*a*) The marginal propensity to consume for the past six quarters has been less than 0.90 (since $\Sigma C/\Sigma Yd = 0.891$), resulting in a fall in the APC.

(*b*) If the long-run APC is to remain at 0.90, there must be an increase in the MPC in the near future.

8.3.   Is the absolute income theory supported by the data in Table 2?

Table 2

Quarter	Consumption ($)	Disposable Income ($)
1	360	400
2	378	420
3	396	440
4	414	460
5	432	480
6	450	500

　　According to the absolute income theory, the APC falls as disposable income increases. Since the APC is constant at 0.90, the data do not support the absolute income theory.

8.4.   Assume that consumption is a function of current disposable income and wealth. In Fig. 8-5, consumption is currently C_1. If disposable income falls to Y_2, what is the level of consumption?

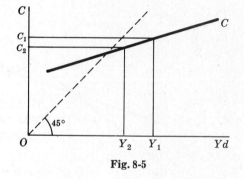
Fig. 8-5

　　Assuming no change in wealth, consumption will fall to C_2. If wealth falls with disposable income, there is a downward shift of the consumption function and consumption is less than C_2. If wealth increases as income falls, there is an upward shift of the consumption function and consumption is greater than C_2.

8.5.   Given $C = 0.80\,Yd + 0.10\,W$ and Yd currently at $400 while real wealth is $400, (*a*) what happens to the average propensity to consume if disposable income increases to $600 with no change in real wealth? (*b*) What happens to the average propensity to consume if the increase in disposable income is $600 and the increase in real wealth is to $480?

(*a*)   If Yd is $400 and W is $400, consumption is $360 and the APC is 0.90. If Yd is $600 and W is $400, consumption is $520 and the APC is 0.87. The average propensity to consume falls.

(*b*)   The average propensity to consume is 0.90 when disposable income is $400 and real wealth is $400. When Yd increases to $600 and W increases to $480, consumption is $528 and the APC is 0.88. The average propensity to consume falls.

8.6.   Given $C = 0.75\,Yd + 0.20\,W$ and Yd currently at $500, (*a*) what volume of wealth is needed to produce a consumption/income ratio of 0.90? (*b*) What volume of wealth is needed to retain the APC at 0.90 if disposable income doubles? (*c*) Is it realistic to assume that real wealth would increase by the amount established in (*b*)?

(*a*)   For ($375 + 0.20\,W)/$500 = 0.90, wealth must equal $375.

(*b*)   Wealth must equal $750.

(*c*)   To maintain a constant APC, wealth must increase at the same rate as the level of disposable income. To accomplish this, the rate of saving must be high to secure sufficient additions to wealth. This is unrealistic for a high consumption economy.

8.7.   Why is Duesenberry's theory of consumption considered an improvement upon the absolute income theory?

Keynes' short-run focus suggested that current consumption is principally a function of current disposable income. Other factors that affect consumption spending were considered unimportant, even in the long run. The absolute income theory proved unsatisfactory since it could not explain, other than by chance, the long-run proportionality of consumption and disposable income. Duesenberry's theory improved upon the absolute income theory by providing a theory of long-run behavior that might not hold in the short run if specific economic phenomenons occurred. According to Duesenberry, households consume a constant proportion of their disposable income. This proportionality is disturbed in the short run if current absolute income falls below a previous income level. Thus, short- and long-run consumption behaviors differ because of fluctuations in the level of income.

8.8.   Would consumption spending be more stable if the consumption function is proportional or nonproportional?

In Fig. 8-6, C_S is nonproportional while C_L is proportional. The MPC for $C_S[(C_2 - C_1)/(Y_2 - Y_1)]$ is less than the MPC of $C_L[(C_3 - C_1)/(Y_2 - Y_1)]$. Since changes in consumption are smaller for C_S, consumption spending is more stable when the consumption function is nonproportional.

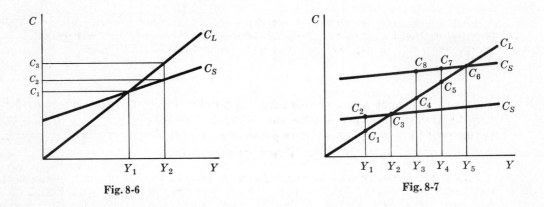

Fig. 8-6   Fig. 8-7

8.9.   Using the relative income theory as your point of reference, establish the change in consumption if, as given in Fig. 8-7 above, the income level changes from (a) Y_2 to Y_1, (b) Y_1 to Y_3, (c) Y_3 to Y_5 and (d) Y_5 to Y_4.

(a) Consumption falls from C_3 to C_2.

(b) Consumption increases from C_2 to C_4.

(c) Consumption increases from C_4 to C_6.

(d) Consumption falls from C_6 to C_7.

8.10.   Using the situations in Problem 8.9, establish whether the average propensity to consume and the marginal propensity to consume for each are constant, increasing or decreasing.

(a) The MPC equals the APC at income levels Y_2 and Y_1. If consumption falls to C_2 rather than C_1, the MPC has decreased. The APC has increased.

(b) Consumption has increased from C_2 to C_4 and therefore the MPC has increased. The APC has decreased.

(c) The MPC equals the APC along C_L, the long-run consumption function. The APC and MPC are constant.

(d) This situation is similar to that in (a). The MPC has decreased and the APC has increased.

8.11. The long-run relationship between consumption and disposable income is 0.90. Using the permanent income theory as your point of reference, establish the level of consumption for the following levels of measured disposable income: (1) $Ym = \$600$ and $Yt = 0$, (2) $Ym = \$650$ and $Yt = \$30$, (3) $Ym = \$700$ and $Yt = -\$20$ and (4) $Ym = \$800$ and $Yt = \$50$.

We saw in Section 8.4 that $Ym = Yp + Yt$, and that $C = f(Yp)$. It follows then, that in this case, $C = 0.90\,Yp$ and that the levels of consumption are (1) \$540, (2) \$558, (3) \$648 and (4) \$675.

8.12. Does the data in Table 3 support the permanent income theory?

Table 3

Consumption (\$)	360	390	420	450	480
Current income (\$)	400	440	480	520	560

There is no basis for support or contradiction. The permanent income theory holds that consumption is related to permanent disposable income. The data are for current measured disposable income which may or may not equal permanent disposable income.

8.13. By relating consumption to measured disposable income, one obtains the following APCs: (1) 0.91, (2) 0.89, (3) 0.88 and (4) 0.92. The long-run APC is 0.90. Using the permanent income theory as your point of reference, establish whether measured disposable income has a positive or negative transitory component.

According to the permanent income theory, measured income is composed of permanent and transitory incomes $(Ym = Yp + Yt)$, and $C/(Yp + Yt) = 0.90$ when $Yt = 0$. Thus, $C/(Yp + Yt) > 0.90$ when Yt is negative while $C/(Yp + Yt) < 0.90$ when Yt is positive. Measured income has a transitory component which is negative in (1), positive in (2), positive in (3) and negative in (4).

Chapter 9

The Marginal Efficiency of Capital

A technique for comparing the relative profitability of investment projects is the discounting of future returns. In this chapter we investigate the technique of discounting so that we can find what Keynes called the marginal efficiency of capital.

9.1 THE FUTURE VALUE OF A CURRENT SUM

In lending, we part with current dollars because we expect to receive a larger number of future dollars. That is, we lend because we expect to earn interest. For example, we might lend \$100 at a 0.06 annual rate of interest because we expect this loaned amount to total \$106 one year from now. The formula for the future value of a current sum is $S = P(1+i)$, where S is the future value of the current sum P and i is the annual rate of interest. Thus, \$106 = \$100(1.06).

When funds are invested for periods longer than one year, there is a compounding of interest (i.e., interest is paid on interest).

EXAMPLE 1. Suppose that \$100 is invested for two years at a 0.06 annual rate of interest.

Sum at the end of year one	Sum at the end of year two
$S_1 = P(1+i)$	$S_2 = S_1(1+i)$
$= \$100(1.06)$	$= \$106(1.06)$
$= \$106$	$= \$112.36$

The interest return is more than \$12 because the \$6 interest earned in year one earns interest of \$0.36 in year two.

The formula for a sum after two years is $S = P(1+i)^2$. After n years, it is $S = P(1+i)^n$, where P is the principal at the start of the first year. If interest is paid semiannually or quarterly, the formula is written $S = P(1+i/m)^n$, where i is the annual rate of interest, m is the number of times interest is paid in one year, and n is the number of periods that interest is received. Thus if interest is paid semiannually and the annual rate is 0.06, \$100 at the end of two years equals $\$100(1.03)^4$. It follows from the above formulation that S increases in value as the rate of interest increases and/or interest is paid more frequently within one year. If i equals zero, S equals P and no future dollar benefits accrue to the lender of funds.

9.2 THE PRESENT VALUE OF A FUTURE SUM

The formula $S = P(1+i/m)^n$ is used to calculate the future value S of a current sum P. By rearranging terms,

$$P = \frac{S}{(1+i/m)^n} \quad \text{or} \quad P = S\left[\frac{1}{(1+i/m)^n}\right]$$

We now have a formula for the current or present value P of a future sum S. The interest rate is renamed the rate of discount, the rate at which a future sum is reduced to a current value. This change in terminology is noted by replacing i with r $\{P = S[1/(1 + r/m)^n]\}$.

The present value of a future sum can be computed with the use of Table I, which gives values for $1/(1 + r/m)^n$ of the present value formula. The quantity $1/(1 + r/m)^n$ is, in effect, the present value of a future dollar. The present value of a future dollar is found (1) by going down the first column until the row corresponding to the correct number of interest periods n is reached and (2) by going across that row until the applicable r/m column is reached. At the intersection of the applicable n row and the applicable r/m column, we obtain the present value of a future dollar. Multiplying this value by S, we establish the present value P of a future sum S.

Table I

Present Value of $1 Received at the End of Period														
n (Periods)	r/m													
	0.01	0.02	0.04	0.06	0.08	0.10	0.12	0.14	0.15	0.16	0.18	0.20	0.22	0.24	0.25
1	0.990	0.980	0.962	0.943	0.926	0.909	0.893	0.877	0.870	0.862	0.847	0.833	0.820	0.806	0.800
2	0.980	0.961	0.925	0.890	0.857	0.826	0.797	0.769	0.756	0.743	0.718	0.694	0.672	0.650	0.640
3	0.971	0.942	0.889	0.840	0.794	0.751	0.712	0.675	0.658	0.641	0.609	0.579	0.551	0.524	0.512
4	0.961	0.924	0.855	0.792	0.735	0.683	0.636	0.592	0.572	0.552	0.516	0.482	0.451	0.423	0.410
5	0.951	0.906	0.822	0.747	0.681	0.621	0.567	0.519	0.497	0.476	0.437	0.402	0.370	0.341	0.328
6	0.942	0.888	0.790	0.705	0.630	0.564	0.507	0.456	0.432	0.410	0.370	0.335	0.303	0.275	0.262
7	0.933	0.871	0.760	0.665	0.583	0.513	0.452	0.400	0.376	0.354	0.314	0.279	0.249	0.222	0.210
8	0.923	0.853	0.731	0.627	0.540	0.467	0.404	0.351	0.327	0.305	0.266	0.233	0.204	0.179	0.168
9	0.914	0.837	0.703	0.592	0.500	0.424	0.361	0.308	0.284	0.263	0.225	0.194	0.167	0.144	0.134
10	0.905	0.820	0.676	0.558	0.463	0.386	0.322	0.270	0.247	0.227	0.191	0.162	0.137	0.116	0.107
11	0.896	0.804	0.650	0.527	0.429	0.350	0.287	0.237	0.215	0.195	0.162	0.135	0.112	0.094	0.086
12	0.887	0.788	0.625	0.497	0.397	0.319	0.257	0.208	0.187	0.168	0.137	0.112	0.092	0.076	0.069
13	0.879	0.773	0.601	0.469	0.368	0.290	0.229	0.182	0.163	0.145	0.116	0.093	0.075	0.061	0.055
14	0.870	0.758	0.577	0.442	0.340	0.263	0.205	0.160	0.141	0.125	0.099	0.078	0.062	0.049	0.044
15	0.861	0.743	0.555	0.417	0.315	0.239	0.183	0.140	0.123	0.108	0.084	0.065	0.051	0.040	0.035
16	0.853	0.728	0.534	0.394	0.292	0.218	0.163	0.123	0.107	0.093	0.071	0.054	0.042	0.032	0.028
17	0.844	0.714	0.513	0.371	0.270	0.198	0.146	0.108	0.093	0.080	0.060	0.045	0.034	0.026	0.023
18	0.836	0.700	0.494	0.350	0.250	0.180	0.130	0.095	0.081	0.069	0.051	0.038	0.028	0.021	0.018
19	0.828	0.686	0.475	0.331	0.232	0.164	0.116	0.083	0.070	0.060	0.043	0.031	0.023	0.017	0.014
20	0.820	0.673	0.456	0.312	0.215	0.149	0.104	0.073	0.061	0.051	0.037	0.026	0.019	0.014	0.012

EXAMPLE 2. The use of Table I in determining the present value of a future sum is illustrated in the following two situations.

Situation I: The present value of $100 received at the end of five years is $74.70 if the annual rate of discount is 0.06.

From Table I we find that the present value of $1 five years from now with a 0.06 annual rate of discount is 0.747. That is, $\$1/(1.06)^5 = 0.747$. The present value of a sum is given by

$$P = S\left[\frac{1}{(1 + r)^n}\right]$$

Thus, $P = \$100(0.747) = \$74.70$

Situation II: The present value of $100 received at the end of five years is $55.80 if the rate of discount is 0.12 compounded semiannually.

The present value of $1 five years from now at a 0.12 rate of discount compounded semiannually is 0.558. That is, $\$1/(1.06)^{10} = 0.558$. The present value of a sum is given by

$$P = S\left[\frac{1}{(1 + r/m)^n}\right]$$

Thus, $P = \$100(0.558) = \$55.80$

If the current and future sums are known, Table I is used to find the rate of discount that equates the current sum with the present value of the future sum.

EXAMPLE 3. The annual rate of discount that relates a loan of $676 with the promise to repay $1000 at the end of ten years is 0.04.

$$P = \frac{S}{(1+r)^{10}}$$

$$\$676 = \frac{\$1000}{(1+r)^{10}}$$

Rearranging,
$$\frac{\$676}{\$1000} = \frac{1}{(1+r)^{10}}$$

we have the present value of $1 ten years from now. From Table I, 0.676 for $n = 10$ gives us the discount rate of 0.04.

9.3 THE PRESENT VALUE OF FUTURE SUMS

When sums are not returned at one future date but at the end of a number of future periods, the present value of the flow is found by totaling the present value of each sum.

EXAMPLE 4. $100 is received at the end of year 1, $200 at the end of year 2 and $300 at the end of year 3. The present value of this flow is $502.20 if the annual rate of discount is 0.08.

The present value of a flow is found by summing the present value of each annual sum (i.e., by summing $P_1 + P_2 + P_3$). From Table I, we find:

$$P_1 = S_1\left(\frac{1}{1+r}\right) = \$100(0.926) = \$\ 92.60$$

$$P_2 = S_2\left[\frac{1}{(1+r)^2}\right] = \$200(0.857) = \quad 171.40$$

$$P_3 = S_3\left[\frac{1}{(1+r)^3}\right] = \$300(0.794) = \quad \underline{238.20}$$

The present value of the three year flow $= \$502.20$

The formula for the present value of a flow of future dollars is

$$P = \frac{S_1}{1+r} + \frac{S_2}{(1+r)^2} + \cdots + \frac{S_n}{(1+r)^n}$$

where P represents the present value of this flow, S_1 represents the sum received at the end of year 1, S_2 the sum received at the end of year 2, etc., and r represents the rate of discount. When $S_1 = S_2 = \cdots = S_n = S$, the formula reduces to

$$P = \frac{S}{r}\left[1 - \frac{1}{(1+r)^n}\right]$$

Here, the quantity
$$\frac{1}{r}\left[1 - \frac{1}{(1+r)^n}\right]$$

is the present value of a dollar received at the end of each period for n periods. Table II gives values for the present value of a dollar received at the end of each period for n periods and is used in the same way as Table I.

EXAMPLE 5. By using Table II, we find that the present value of $100 received at the end of each year for five years is $379.10 if the annual rate of discount is 0.10.

From Table II we find that the present value of $1 received at the end of each year for five years is 3.791 for a 0.10 annual rate of discount. That is,

$$\frac{1}{0.10}\left[1 - \frac{1}{(1.10)^5}\right] = 3.791$$

The present value of a flow is given by

$$P = S\left\{\frac{1}{r}\left[1 - \frac{1}{(1+r)^n}\right]\right\}$$

Thus, $P = \$100(3.791) = \$379.10$

Table II

n (Periods)	\multicolumn{15}{c}{Present Value of \$1 Received Annually at the End of Each Period for n Periods}

Present Value of $1 Received Annually at the End of Each Period for n Periods

n (Periods)	0.01	0.02	0.04	0.06	0.08	0.10	0.12	0.14	0.15	0.16	0.18	0.20	0.22	0.24	0.25
1	0.990	0.980	0.962	0.943	0.926	0.909	0.893	0.877	0.870	0.862	0.847	0.833	0.820	0.806	0.800
2	1.970	1.942	1.886	1.833	1.783	1.736	1.690	1.647	1.626	1.605	1.566	1.528	1.492	1.457	1.440
3	2.941	2.884	2.775	2.673	2.577	2.487	2.402	2.322	2.283	2.246	2.174	2.106	2.042	1.981	1.952
4	3.902	3.808	3.630	3.465	3.312	3.170	3.037	2.914	2.855	2.798	2.690	2.589	2.494	2.404	2.362
5	4.853	4.713	4.452	4.212	3.993	3.791	3.605	3.433	3.352	3.274	3.127	2.991	2.864	2.745	2.689
6	5.795	5.601	5.242	4.917	4.623	4.355	4.111	3.889	3.784	3.685	3.498	3.326	3.167	3.020	2.951
7	6.728	6.472	6.002	5.582	5.206	4.868	4.564	4.288	4.160	4.039	3.812	3.605	3.416	3.242	3.161
8	7.652	7.325	6.733	6.210	5.747	5.335	4.968	4.639	4.487	4.344	4.078	3.837	3.619	3.421	3.329
9	8.566	8.162	7.435	6.802	6.247	5.759	5.328	4.946	4.772	4.607	4.303	4.031	3.786	3.566	3.463
10	9.471	8.983	8.111	7.360	6.710	6.145	5.650	5.216	5.019	4.833	4.494	4.192	3.923	3.682	3.571
11	10.368	9.787	8.760	7.887	7.139	6.495	5.988	5.453	5.234	5.029	4.656	4.327	4.035	3.776	3.656
12	11.255	10.575	9.385	8.384	7.536	6.814	6.194	5.660	5.421	5.197	4.793	4.439	4.127	3.851	3.725
13	12.134	11.343	9.986	8.853	7.904	7.103	6.424	5.842	5.583	5.342	4.910	4.533	4.203	3.912	3.780
14	13.004	12.106	10.563	9.295	8.244	7.367	6.628	6.002	5.724	5.468	5.008	4.611	4.265	3.962	3.824
15	13.865	12.849	11.118	9.712	8.559	7.606	6.811	6.142	5.847	5.575	5.092	4.675	4.315	4.001	3.859
16	14.718	13.578	11.652	10.106	8.851	7.824	6.974	6.265	5.954	5.669	5.162	4.730	4.357	4.003	3.887
17	15.562	14.292	12.166	10.477	9.122	8.022	7.120	6.373	6.047	5.749	5.222	4.775	4.391	4.059	3.910
18	16.398	14.992	12.659	10.828	9.372	8.201	7.250	6.467	6.128	5.818	5.273	4.812	4.419	4.080	3.928
19	17.226	15.678	13.134	11.158	9.604	8.365	7.366	6.550	6.198	5.877	5.316	4.844	4.442	4.097	3.942
20	18.046	16.351	13.590	11.470	9.818	8.514	7.469	6.623	6.259	5.929	5.353	4.870	4.460	4.110	3.954

Present Value Table II is also used to find the rate of discount that equates a current cash outlay with the present value of a future flow of cash.

EXAMPLE 6.   The rate of discount that equates a current cash outlay of \$1041.20 with the present value of \$200 received at the end of each year for seven years is 0.08.

$$P = \frac{S}{r}\left[1 - \frac{1}{(1+r)^7}\right]$$

$$\$1041.20 = \frac{\$200}{r}\left[1 - \frac{1}{(1+r)^7}\right]$$

$$5.206 = \frac{1}{r}\left[1 - \frac{1}{(1+r)^7}\right] \qquad \begin{array}{l}\text{the present value of \$1} \\ \text{received at the end of} \\ \text{each year for seven years}\end{array}$$

and from Table II, $r = 0.08$.

9.4   THE MARGINAL EFFICIENCY OF CAPITAL

In purchasing a machine, a buyer spends a current cash sum anticipating future cash returns. Keynes named the rate of discount that equates the cost of a new machine with the present value of the cash flow from this capital addition *the marginal efficiency of capital* (MEC).

EXAMPLE 7.   A new machine costs \$10,000 to purchase and install. It is expected that this machine will have no scrap value and a ten year life. It is expected that 1500 units of output are produced annually, selling for \$2 per unit. The expenses of operating the machine (materials, labor, floor space, etc.)

total $700 annually. There is a corporate income tax of 50% on dollar receipts after expenses. Annual net dollar receipts are calculated as follows:

Annual Gross Dollar Receipts from Sales (1500 units @ $2)		$3000
Expenses:		
Operating Expenses	$ 700	
Depreciation Allowance*	1000	1700
Dollar Receipts after Expenses		$1300
Less: Corporate Income Taxes		650
Net Dollar Receipts after Taxes		$ 650
Plus: Depreciation Allowance*		1000
Annual Net Dollar Receipts		$1650

* Annual depreciation allowance is here taken as the cost of the machine divided by the number of productive years for the machine. Since depreciation is a bookkeeping expense (a noncash expense), it must be added to net dollar receipts after taxes to obtain the machine's annual net dollar receipts.

The marginal efficiency of capital is computed by using the present value formula from Section 9.3.

$$P = \frac{S_1}{1 + r} + \frac{S_2}{(1 + r)^2} + \cdots + \frac{S_n}{(1 + r)^n}$$

$$\$10,000 = \frac{\$1650}{1 + r} + \frac{\$1650}{(1 + r)^2} + \cdots + \frac{\$1650}{(1 + r)^{10}}$$

Since the annual cash flows are equal, the formula for the present value of a dollar received annually can be used. Thus,

$$\$10,000 = \frac{\$1650}{r}\left[1 - \frac{1}{(1 + r)^{10}}\right]$$

$$6.06 = \frac{1}{r}\left[1 - \frac{1}{(1 + r)^{10}}\right]$$

and from Table II, r is approximately 0.10.

9.5 CHANGES IN THE MARGINAL EFFICIENCY OF CAPITAL

The marginal efficiency of capital for an investment proposal depends upon (1) the current cost of the asset, (2) the quantity of funds returned over the life of the asset and (3) the distribution of these returns. The marginal efficiency of capital increases if the cost of the asset falls, the quantity of funds returned increases or the return of funds is concentrated in earlier periods. The marginal efficiency of capital falls if asset costs increase, less future funds are returned or the flow of funds is concentrated in later periods.

EXAMPLE 8. Costs, size of flows and distribution of flows can be affected by (1) a government action, (2) market forces or (3) expectations.

Given: r approximates 0.10 (Example 7) if a current cash outlay equals $10,000 and $1650 is returned at the end of each year for ten years.

Situation I: The price of new machines increases 10% as a result of increased demand in the capital goods industry. The $10,000 machine now costs $11,000. Thus,

$$\$11,000 = \frac{\$1700}{r}\left[1 - \frac{1}{(1 + r)^{10}}\right]$$

$$6.47 = \frac{1}{r}\left[1 - \frac{1}{(1 + r)^{10}}\right]$$

$$r \cong 0.09$$

The increased price for new capital lowers the marginal efficiency of capital.

Situation II: The government institutes a 10% investment tax credit whereby (1) the firm is able to reduce its federal taxes by 10% of the purchase price on a capital addition and (2) the firm is allowed to depreciate capital additions at original cost. A $10,000 machine now has a $9000 net cost to the firm with no change in the receipt of funds. Thus,

$$\$9000 \ = \ \frac{\$1650}{r}\left[1 - \frac{1}{(1+r)^{10}}\right]$$

$$5.45 \ = \ \frac{1}{r}\left[1 - \frac{1}{(1+r)^{10}}\right]$$

$$r \ \cong \ 0.13$$

Passage of an investment tax credit increases the marginal efficiency of capital.

Situation III: The government permits firms to depreciate machinery in one-half the time previously allowed. For tax purposes, a machine with a ten-year productive life is depreciated in five years. The cash flow for the proposed investment is now $2150 for years 1 through 5 and $1150 for years 6 through 10. Thus,

$$\$10,000 \ = \ \frac{\$2150}{1+r} + \cdots + \frac{\$2150}{(1+r)^5} + \frac{\$1150}{(1+r)^6} + \cdots + \frac{\$1150}{(1+r)^{10}}$$

$$r \ \cong \ 0.12$$

A more rapid depreciation of machinery increases the marginal efficiency of capital.

Situation IV: It is expected that a higher demand for the product will increase the selling price of each item from $2.00 to $2.20. Annual cash flows increase from $1650 to $1800. Thus,

$$\$10,000 \ = \ \frac{\$1800}{r}\left[1 - \frac{1}{(1+r)^{10}}\right]$$

$$5.56 \ = \ \frac{1}{r}\left[1 - \frac{1}{(1+r)^{10}}\right]$$

$$r \ \cong \ 0.12$$

An increase in demand that results in a higher priced item increases the marginal efficiency of capital.

Situation V: Cost pressures are expected to develop in the labor sector, causing operating expenses to increase from $700 to $1000. Annual cash flows fall from $1650 to $1500 a year. Thus,

$$\$10,000 \ = \ \frac{\$1500}{r}\left[1 - \frac{1}{(1+r)^{10}}\right]$$

$$6.67 \ = \ \frac{1}{r}\left[1 - \frac{1}{(1+r)^{10}}\right]$$

$$r \ \cong \ 0.08$$

An increase in production costs that reduces the flow of funds lowers the marginal efficiency of capital.

Review Questions

1. The present value of $1000 five years from now at an 0.08 rate of discount is $681. Thus,
    (a) $681 today is preferred to $1000 five years from now,
    (b) $600 today is preferred to $1000 five years from now   or
    (c) $750 today is preferred to $1000 five years from now.

2. $100 invested at 0.06 will amount to the largest sum when interest is compounded (a) annually, (b) semiannually, (c) quarterly or (d) continuously.

3. Which of the following has the highest rate of discount?
    (a) A current sum of $399.90 with returns of $50 semiannually for five years.
    (b) A current sum of $399.90 with returns of $100 annually for five years.
    (c) A current sum of $421.20 with returns of $25 quarterly for five years.
    (d) A current sum of $421.20 with returns of $100 annually for five years.

4. The marginal efficiency of capital is

    (a) the rate of discount that equates the current cost of real capital with the present value of the flow of cash generated by real investment,

    (b) the rate of discount that equates the current cost of a financial investment with the present value of the flow of cash generated by a financial investment,

    (c) the rate of interest that equates the current cost of real capital with the present value of the flow of cash generated by real investment   or

    (d) the rate of interest that equates the current cost of a financial investment with the present value of the flow of cash generated by a financial investment.

5. Which of the following $10,000 flows generates the lowest marginal efficiency of capital?

    (a) $1000 received at the end of each year for ten years.

    (b) $500 received at the end of each six-month period for ten years.

    (c) $250 received at the end of each three-month period for ten years.

    (d) $200 received at the end of each two-month period for ten years.

6. Which of the following $10,000 flows generates the highest MEC?

    (a) $1000 received at the end of each year for ten years.

    (b) $1250 received at the end of each year for eight years.

    (c) $2000 received at the end of each year for five years.

    (d) $2500 received at the end of each year for four years.

7. The MEC for a proposed capital addition will fall (a) if there is a reduction in the purchase price of new machines, (b) if there is an increase in the purchase price of new machines, (c) if future flows are distributed in earlier rather than later periods   or (d) if the corporate income tax rate is reduced.

8. The MEC for a proposed capital addition will increase (a) if the government reduces the corporate income tax rate, (b) if the government allows firms to depreciate new capital more rapidly, (c) if technological change in the capital goods industry lowers the supply price of new capital   or (d) all of the above.

9. Which of the following expectations will *not* increase the MEC for a proposed capital addition?

    (a) Firms expect an increase in the selling price of the good because of increased demand.

    (b) Firms expect a larger inflow of funds as a result of inflation.

    (c) Firms expect production costs to increase.

    (d) Firms expect a reduction in corporate income taxes.

10. The MEC for a proposed capital addition will decrease (a) if the government introduces an investment tax credit, (b) if the supply price of new machines rises as a result of increased demand in the capital goods industry, (c) if the government reduces the corporate income tax rate   or (d) all of the above.

Answers to Review Questions

1. (c) Review Section 9.2.

2. (d) Review Section 9.1.

3. (a) Review Section 9.3.

4. (a) Review Section 9.4.

5. (a) Review Section 9.4.

6. (d) Review Section 9.4.

7. (b) Review Section 9.5.

8. (d) Review Section 9.5.

9. (c) Review Section 9.5.

10. (b) Review Section 9.5.

Solved Problems

9.1. $100 will amount to what sum one year from now if the rate of interest is 0.08 and (a) interest is paid annually, (b) interest is compounded semiannually or (c) interest is compounded quarterly?

Since the value of a sum is $S = P(1 + i/m)^n$,

(a) $$S = \$100(1.08) = \$108$$

(b) $$S = \$100(1.04)^2 = \$108.16$$

(c) $$S = \$100(1.02)^4 = \$108.24$$

9.2. What is the present value of $108 one year from now if the rate of discount is 0.08?

$$P = \frac{S}{1+r} = \frac{\$108}{1.08} = \$100$$

9.3. What is the present value of $100 one year from now if the annual rate of discount is (a) 0.06, (b) 0.08 and (c) 0.10? (d) What happens to the present value of $100 one year from now as the rate of discount increases?

(a) $94.30.

(b) $92.60.

(c) $90.90.

(d) The present value of $100 falls as the rate of discount increases.

9.4. Assuming a rate of discount of 0.08, identify the preferred alternative in each of the following situations: (1) $750 today or $1000 five years from now, (2) $681 today or $1000 five years from now and (3) $600 today or $1000 five years from now.

Since

$$P = \frac{S}{(1+r)^5} = \frac{\$1000}{(1.08)^5} = \$1000(0.681) = \$681$$

$681 today amounts to $1000 five years from now if the rate of interest is 0.08. Therefore, in (1) preference is for $750 today since it would total more than $1000 five years from now, in (2) there is no preference since $681 today equals $1000 five years from now and in (3) preference is for $1000 five years from now since $600 today would total less than $1000 five years from now.

9.5. What is the present value of $100 received at the end of each year for two years if the rate of discount is 0.08?

Using Table I, in the first year,

$$P = \frac{S}{1+r} = \frac{\$100}{1.08} = \$100(0.926) = \$\ 92.60$$

In the second year,

$$P = \frac{S}{(1+r)^2} = \frac{\$100}{(1.08)^2} = \$100(0.857) = \underline{\quad 85.70}$$
$$\$178.30$$

Using Table II,

$$P = \frac{S}{r}\left[1 - \frac{1}{(1+r)^2}\right] = \frac{100}{0.08}\left[1 - \frac{1}{(1.08)^2}\right] = \$100(1.783) = \$178.30$$

9.6. What is the sum of $178.30 at the end of two years if the rate of interest is 0.08? Does the flow of Problem 9.5 ($100 at the end of year 1 plus $100 at the end of year 2) amount to the same sum at the end of two years?

> A loan of $178.30 at an annual 0.08 rate of interest equals $208 after two years. The flow in Problem 9.5 also equals $208 at the end of two years. The $100 received at the end of year 1 equals $108 at the end of year 2. This sum added to the $100 at the end of year 2 totals $208.

9.7. The present value of a flow is found by use of Table I or Table II. Can these tables be used interchangeably to find the present value of a flow?

> Table II is used only if the sums in the flow are equal. Table I can be used for any present value calculation.

9.8. Assuming a 0.10 rate of discount, calculate the present values of (a) $1000 at the end of year 1, $3000 at the end of year 2 and $5000 at the end of year 3, (b) $3000 at the end of each year for 3 years and (c) $5000 at the end of year 1, $3000 at the end of year 2 and $1000 at the end of year 3.

(a)
$$P = \frac{S_1}{1+r} + \frac{S_2}{(1+r)^2} + \frac{S_3}{(1+r)^3}$$

$$= \frac{\$1000}{1.10} + \frac{\$3000}{(1.10)^2} + \frac{\$5000}{(1.10)^3}$$

$$= \$1000(0.909) + \$3000(0.826) + \$5000(0.751)$$

$$= \$909 + \$2478 + \$3755$$

$$= \$7142$$

(b)
$$P = \frac{S}{r}\left[1 - \frac{1}{(1+r)^3}\right]$$

$$= \frac{\$3000}{r}\left[1 - \frac{1}{(1+r)^3}\right]$$

$$= \$3000(2.487)$$

$$= \$7461$$

(c)
$$P = \frac{S_1}{1+r} + \frac{S_2}{(1+r)^2} + \frac{S_3}{(1+r)^3}$$

$$= \frac{\$5000}{1.10} + \frac{\$3000}{(1.10)^2} + \frac{\$1000}{(1.10)^3}$$

$$= \$5000(0.909) + \$3000(0.826) + \$1000(0.751)$$

$$= \$4545 + \$2478 + \$751$$

$$= \$7774$$

9.9. Why do the present values in Problem 9.8 differ although each flow totals $9000 and has the same rate of discount?

> A sum has a larger present value the sooner it is received. For example, $100 one year from now has a greater present value than $100 received two years from now. Thus, the flow in Problem 9.8(c) has the highest present value since $5000 of a $9000 flow is received at the end of the first year.

9.10. Each of the following flows equals $10,000. Rank their present values in descending order, assuming that the same rate of discount is applied to each flow:

    (1) $2500 at the end of each year for four years,

    (2) $3000 at the end of each year for the first three years and $1000 at the end of the fourth year,

    (3) $2000 at the end of each year for five years   and

    (4) $750 at the end of each quarter for the first three years and $250 at the end of each quarter for the fourth year.

Ranking: (4) (2) (1) (3). An annual sum of $3000 is received in both (2) and (4) but (4) has the higher present value since sums are received quarterly rather than annually. The flow in (2) has a higher present value than in (1) since annual sums are received earlier in (2). The present value of (1) exceeds the present value of (3) since the flow in (1) is received in fewer years.

9.11. What is the relationship between discounting flows and calculating the rate of return from an investment proposal?

In acquiring a new machine, a businessman purchases a stream of future cash sums. By discounting the flow of future cash, he has a technique for comparing the relative profitability of investment projects. Keynes termed the rate of discount that equates the present cost of a project with the present value of the expected income stream the marginal efficiency of capital.

9.12. Find the marginal efficiency of capital (MEC) for a machine that costs $3433 to purchase and install and that generates a cash sum of $1000 at the end of each year for five years.

From the equation

$$P = \frac{S}{r}\left[1 - \frac{1}{(1+r)^5}\right]$$

we have

$$\$3433 = \frac{\$1000}{r}\left[1 - \frac{1}{(1+r)^5}\right]$$

$$3.433 = \frac{1}{r}\left[1 - \frac{1}{(1+r)^5}\right]$$

$$r = 0.14$$

9.13. Find the marginal efficiency of capital for a machine costing $4000 to purchase and install. The machine will produce 1600 units of output annually. It is expected that output will sell for $1 per unit. The machine has an expected life of four years and no scrap value. Other annual production expenses total $300. There is no corporate income tax.

Annual Gross Dollar Receipts from Sales (1600 units @ $1)		$1600
Expenses:		
Other Production Costs	$ 300	
Depreciation	1000	1300
Dollar Receipts after Expenses		$ 300
Less: Corporate Income Taxes		...
Net Dollar Receipts after Taxes		$ 300
Plus: Depreciation Allowances		1000
Annual Net Dollar Receipts		$1300

$$P = \frac{S}{r}\left[1 - \frac{1}{(1+r)^4}\right]$$

$$\$4000 = \frac{\$1300}{r}\left[1 - \frac{1}{(1+r)^4}\right]$$

$$3.08 = \frac{1}{r}\left[1 - \frac{1}{(1+r)^4}\right]$$

$$r \cong 0.12$$

9.14. (*a*) Recalculate the marginal efficiency of capital in Problem 9.13 assuming a corporate income tax rate of 50%. (*b*) How does a change in corporate income taxes affect the rate of return from investment proposals?

(*a*)

Dollar Receipts after Expenses	$ 300
Less: Corporate Income Taxes	150
Net Dollar Receipts after Taxes	$ 150
Plus: Depreciation Allowances	1000
Annual Net Dollar Receipts	$1150

$$P = \frac{S}{r}\left[1 - \frac{1}{(1+r)^4}\right]$$

$$\$4000 = \frac{\$1150}{r}\left[1 - \frac{1}{(1+r)^4}\right]$$

$$3.48 = \frac{1}{r}\left[1 - \frac{1}{(1+r)^4}\right]$$

$$r \cong 0.06$$

(*b*) The MEC is inversely related to the rate of corporate income taxes, *ceteris paribus*. Thus, the government can increase the rate of return on investment proposals by lowering corporate income tax rates and decrease the rate of return by raising corporate income tax rates.

9.15. Find the MEC for a machine that costs $16,000 to purchase and install. The production of 3000 units of output annually will be sold for $2 per unit. The machine has an expected life of eight years and no scrap value. Other production costs total $900. There is a 50% tax on receipts after expenses.

Annual Gross Dollar Receipts from Sales (3000 units @ $2)		$6000
Expenses:		
Other Production Costs	$ 900	
Depreciation	2000	2900
Dollar Receipts after Expenses		$3100
Less: Corporate Income Taxes		1550
Net Dollar Receipts after Taxes		$1550
Plus: Depreciation Allowances		2000
Annual Net Dollar Receipts		$3550

$$P = \frac{S}{r}\left[1 - \frac{1}{(1+r)^8}\right]$$

$$\$16,000 = \frac{\$3550}{r}\left[1 - \frac{1}{(1+r)^8}\right]$$

$$4.51 = \frac{1}{r}\left[1 - \frac{1}{(1+r)^8}\right]$$

$$r \cong 0.15$$

9.16. What happens to the MEC of the machine in Problem 9.15 if purchase and installation costs increase to $18,000?

Annual Gross Dollar Receipts from Sales (3000 units @ $2)		$6000
Expenses:		
Other Production Costs	$ 900	
Depreciation	2250	3150
Dollar Receipts after Expenses		$2850
Less: Corporate Income Taxes		1425
Net Dollar Receipts after Taxes		$1425
Plus: Depreciation Allowances		2250
Annual Net Dollar Receipts		$3675

$$P = \frac{S}{r}\left[1 - \frac{1}{(1+r)^8}\right]$$

$$\$18,000 = \frac{\$3675}{r}\left[1 - \frac{1}{(1+r)^8}\right]$$

$$4.90 = \frac{1}{r}\left[1 - \frac{1}{(1+r)^8}\right]$$

$$r \cong 0.12$$

9.17. What happens to the MEC of the machine in Problem 9.15 if increased demand allows the firm to sell the product for $2.50 an item instead of $2.00?

Annual Gross Dollar Receipts from Sales (3000 units @ $2.50)	$7500
Expenses	2900
Dollar Receipts after Expenses	$4600
Less: Corporate Income Taxes	2300
Net Dollar Receipts after Taxes	$2300
Plus: Depreciation Allowances	2000
Annual Net Dollar Receipts	$4300

$$P = \frac{S}{r}\left[1 - \frac{1}{(1+r)^8}\right]$$

$$\$16,000 = \frac{\$4300}{r}\left[1 - \frac{1}{(1+r)^8}\right]$$

$$3.72 = \frac{1}{r}\left[1 - \frac{1}{(1+r)^8}\right]$$

$$r \cong 0.21$$

9.18. What happens to the MEC when (a) labor's demands for higher wages increase the cost of production, (b) the cost of new capital rises as the capital goods industry is unable to meet the increased demand for new capital or (c) government allows firms to depreciate machinery at a faster rate.

(a) The MEC falls as the flow of expected income falls.

(b) The MEC falls as the cost of new capital increases.

(c) The MEC increases since faster depreciation allows firms to recover funds sooner.

Chapter 10

Theories of Investment

As classified in the national income accounts, investment expenditure includes spending on new plant and equipment, net inventory investment and new residential construction. This chapter presents theories explaining the level of these three classes of investment expenditure.

10.1 THE MARGINAL EFFICIENCY OF CAPITAL SCHEDULE

As developed in Chapter 9, a proposal to invest in new equipment can be evaluated by finding the rate of discount that equates a current cash outlay with the present value of future cash receipts. Since a firm will have more than one investment proposal to evaluate, it is possible to construct a marginal efficiency of capital schedule where the dollar volumes of proposed investments are listed in descending order of expected rate of return.

EXAMPLE 1. A firm's expected return from six investment proposals is as follows:

- (*A*) An investment of $10,000 with a 0.14 return
- (*B*) An investment of $5,000 with a 0.18 return
- (*C*) An investment of $15,000 with a 0.12 return
- (*D*) An investment of $8,000 with a 0.10 return
- (*E*) An investment of $4,000 with a 0.16 return
- (*F*) An investment of $6,000 with a 0.20 return

The proposals in descending order of expected return are *F, B, E, A, C, D*.

Table 1

The Firm's MEC Schedule		
Investments Returning at Least	Proposals	Dollar Volume of Investment
0.20	*F*	6,000
0.18	*F, B*	11,000
0.16	*F, B, E*	15,000
0.14	*F, B, E, A*	25,000
0.12	*F, B, E, A, C*	40,000
0.10	*F, B, E, A, C, D*	48,000

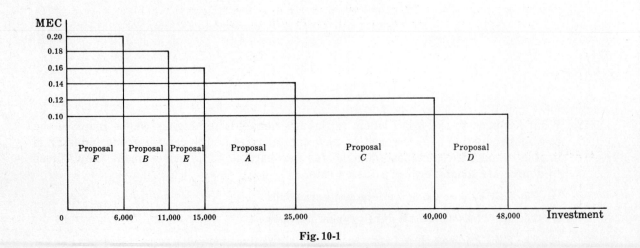

Fig. 10-1

A marginal efficiency of capital schedule for the entire economy can be constructed by summing the marginal efficiency of capital schedules for all firms. Since each firm's project is a very small fraction of the total, the aggregate marginal efficiency of capital schedule appears in Fig. 10-2 as a continuous function. By construction, the MEC schedule is negatively sloped, since investment proposals are listed in descending order of expected rate of return.

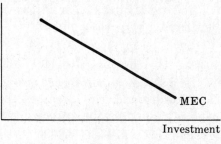

Fig. 10-2

The MEC schedule shifts if there are additional proposals that offer similar or higher expected rates of return or if, as noted in Section 9.5, the expected rates of return on current proposals change as a result of government actions, market forces or expectations.

10.2 THE MARGINAL EFFICIENCY OF INVESTMENT

Implicit in the marginal efficiency of capital schedule (Section 10.1) is the assumption that the capital-producing industry is able to supply an unlimited quantity of new equipment at a constant average cost. Thus, in Fig. 10-3, the average supply cost of new equipment is P_0 regardless of the demand for new capital.

It is likely, however, that the average supply cost of new capital will rise as the utilization of production facilities increases. If it does, then the

Fig. 10-3

marginal efficiency of capital of all investment proposals decreases and the aggregate marginal efficiency of capital schedule is steeper than if the supply cost of new capital were constant. The effect of a rising supply cost of new capital schedule upon the expected rates of return on investment proposals is noted in macroeconomic theory by renaming the steeper schedule the *marginal efficiency of investment*.

EXAMPLE 2.   The supply of new capital schedule is given as S_1 and S_2 in Fig. 10-4(a).

Situation I: In Fig. 10-4(b), MEC_1 is derived from supply schedule S_1, where the supply of new capital is available at a constant supply cost of P_1. Capital additions I_1 and I_2 have expected rates of return of at least r_4 and r_3, respectively.

Situation II: In Fig. 10-4(b), MEI_2 is derived from supply schedule S_2 where new capital I_1 and I_2 are available at supply costs P_2 and P_3. Since the marginal efficiency of capital on investment proposals falls as the supply cost of new capital increases, I_1 and I_2 have lower expected rates of return (r_2 and r_1, respectively) than when the supply cost of new capital is constant at P_1.

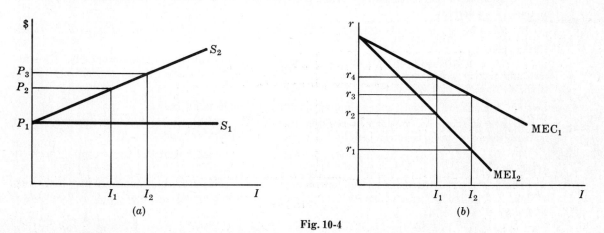

Fig. 10-4

To simplify the analysis, however, we assume that the capital-producing industries supply new capital at a constant cost.

10.3 A SCHEDULE OF INVESTMENT DEMAND

In macroeconomic theory, we assume that firms add to their stock of capital as long as each capital addition increases their level of profits. That is, firms add to their stock of capital as long as the expected rate of return r from an investment proposal exceeds the cost i of borrowing or using the funds required to purchase the new equipment. Such behavior is depicted in Fig. 10-5(a). If the rate of interest is i_0, firms are willing to add I_0 proposals. If the rate of interest is lower, say at i_1, additional investment proposals are profitable and firms are willing to add I_1 to their stock of capital. The investment demand schedule is therefore presented in Fig. 10-5(b) as $I = I(i)$ since the level of investment is a decreasing function of the rate of interest.

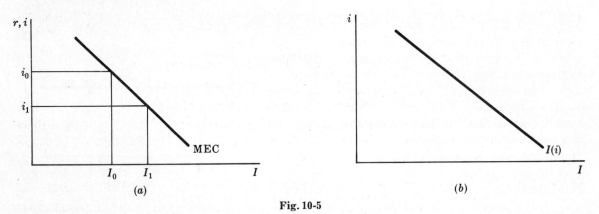

Fig. 10-5

10.4 THE COST OF FUNDS

We shall assume that firms base their investment decisions upon the *current rate of interest i* even though numerous objections to this assumption have been raised in financial theory. Example 3 identifies situations where the firm's relevant cost of funds is *not* the current rate of interest.

EXAMPLE 3.   The current rate of interest is 0.08.

Situation I: The rate of interest is expected to average less than 0.06 for the major portion of the life of new equipment.

   The firm's cost of funds is lower than 0.08 since, through the call provision, the firm can refinance at a lower rate of interest sometime in the future. Thus, the firm should not base its investment decision on the current rate of interest but upon the *average rate of interest* paid over the life of the new equipment.

Situation II: The rate of interest on the firm's debt increases if it continues borrowing large sums in the market place.

   Investors question the firm's ability to invest increasing quantities of funds profitably. This uncertainty factor results in a larger interest cost. Thus, the firm's cost of funds is positively related to the *volume of funds borrowed*.

Situation III: Lenders will supply only a limited quantity of funds to an individual firm.

   Even if the firm has investment projects that have a return greater than the current rate of interest, net investment is determined by the *current availability of funds*.

Situation IV: In raising funds in the market, the firm has maintained a ratio of $3 of equity (stock) to $1 of debt (bonds).

   The firm's cost of funds is a weighted average of its various sources of funds. Thus, if the cost of debt is 0.08 and the cost of equity funds is 0.12, the firm's *average cost of funds* is $0.25(0.08) + 0.75(0.12) = 0.11$.

Situation V: The firm generates funds internally through depreciation write-offs or by the retention of earnings.

The cost of internally generated funds is the rate of interest on funds invested in the financial markets. Since the firm normally invests internally generated funds on a short-term basis, the cost of such funds is the current short-term rate of interest.

10.5 THE ACCELERATOR THEORY OF INVESTMENT

The accelerator theory of investment explains net investment in terms of growth in aggregate spending. We shall assume that firms, in the aggregate, maintain a given relationship between their stock of capital and the aggregate level of output. For example, the relationship of the stock of capital K to the aggregate level of output Y is given as $K = wY$ where w, the capital/output ratio, is the ratio of the desired stock of capital to the aggregate level of output. Thus, net investment ΔK equals $w\Delta Y$.

EXAMPLE 4. When the capital/output ratio is 2, net investment equals $2\Delta Y$. Given the aggregate output schedule in Table 2, net investment is $20 in period B, $40 in period C, $20 in period D and $0 in period E.

Table 2

Period	A	B	C	D	E
Aggregate Output ($)	600	610	630	640	640

Changes in the aggregate level of output may affect replacement investment as well as capital additions. If aggregate spending declines, firms may elect to postpone replacement investment during that period.

EXAMPLE 5. The capital/output ratio is 2. A $2000 stock of capital was accumulated uniformly over ten periods and has a useful life of ten periods. As shown in Table 3, beginning in period 11, replacement investment is $200 per period for the next ten periods. Aggregate output is $1000 in period 11, $1100 in period 12, $1300 in period 13, $1400 in period 14, $1400 in period 15 and $1300 in period 16.

Table 3

Period	Y ($)	ΔY ($)	K ($)	Net I ($)	Replacement I ($)
11	1000	0	2000	0	200
12	1100	100	2200	200	200
13	1300	200	2600	400	200
14	1400	100	2800	200	200
15	1400	0	2800	0	200
16	1300	−100	2600	0	0

The value of net investment ranges from $0 to $400 between periods 11 and 16 as a result of changes in the level of aggregate output. Replacement investment is $200 in each period but falls to $0 in period 16 as a result of the $100 decline in aggregate output in that period.

Numerous objections can be raised to the accelerator theory of investment.

1. There may be lags in capital additions either because capital takes time to build or because there are backlogs in the capital-producing industries.

2. Replacement and net investment are based upon long-term expectations and not current variations in output.

3. It is possible that developments in technology may increase or decrease the amount of capital needed for a specific level of output.

4. Although there are minimal changes in aggregate output, investment will increase if some firms accumulate excess capacity as demand falls while other firms add to their stock of capital as demand increases.

With the exception of objection 3, these criticisms of the accelerator theory point to its limited usefulness as a model of short-run changes in plant and equipment investment.

10.6 INVENTORY INVESTMENT

The accelerator theory is suitable as a model of short-run changes in inventory investment in some situations.

The practicalities of production and distribution require that firms carry inventories of finished and unfinished goods. It is therefore reasonable to assume that inventory investment is a positive linear function of the volume of aggregate sales. That is, $I_{inv} = nR$, where I_{inv} represents aggregate inventory investment, R is the volume of aggregate sales and n is the inventory/sales ratio.

The accelerator can be used as a theory of aggregate inventory investment only if there is some stability in the structure of sales.

EXAMPLE 6. An economy has only three suppliers of goods, each with a monthly sales volume of $3000. Supplier A has an inventory/sales ratio of 0.3, B has an inventory/sales ratio of 0.5 and C has an inventory/sales ratio of 1.0. Given an equal distribution of sales among these three suppliers, the aggregate inventory/sales ratio is 0.6.

Situation I: A $300 increase in sales is shared equally by all suppliers.

$$\Delta I_{inv} = n\,\Delta R \qquad (n = \text{aggregate inventory/sales})$$
$$\Delta I_{inv} = 0.6(\$300)$$
$$\Delta I_{inv} = \$180$$

Situation II: A $300 increase in sales is realized only by supplier A.

$$\Delta I_{inv} = n\,\Delta R \qquad (n = \text{inventory/sales ratio of supplier } A)$$
$$\Delta I_{inv} = 0.3(\$300)$$
$$\Delta I_{inv} = \$90$$

Situation III: A $300 increase in sales is realized only by supplier C.

$$\Delta I_{inv} = n\,\Delta R \qquad (n = \text{inventory/sales ratio of supplier } C)$$
$$\Delta I_{inv} = 1.0(\$300)$$
$$\Delta I_{inv} = \$300$$

These situations show that the increase in inventory investment depends upon the distribution of incremental aggregate sales. Obviously, it is not possible to formulate a theory explaining changes in inventory investment if there is variability in the distribution of incremental demand.

10.7 INVESTMENT IN RESIDENTIAL HOUSING

In purchasing a house, an individual borrows a current sum, promising payment of interest and repayment of principal over a specified number of periods.

EXAMPLE 7. The present value formula

$$P = \frac{S}{1+i} + \frac{S}{(1+i)^2} + \cdots + \frac{S}{(1+i)^n}$$

is used to find the constant annual cash outlay needed to retire a mortgage plan. P represents the amount borrowed, i is the stated rate of interest and S is the constant annual cash outlay required for the payment of interest and the repayment of principal over n years.

Situation I: $30,000 is borrowed for 25 years at an annual interest cost of 0.06.

$$\$30,000 = \frac{S}{1.06} + \frac{S}{(1.06)^2} + \cdots + \frac{S}{(1.06)^{25}}$$

$$S = \$2346.87$$

Situation II: $30,000 is borrowed for 25 years at an annual interest cost of 0.08.

$$\$30,000 = \frac{S}{1.08} + \frac{S}{(1.08)^2} + \cdots + \frac{S}{(1.08)^{25}}$$

$$S = \$2810.30$$

Example 7 shows that the annual sum needed for interest payments and the repayment of principal increases as the rate of interest rises. If these higher annual payments exceed households' current budgetary allowances for housing, rising interest rates will prohibit some household units from purchasing new housing. This will cause the demand for new housing to be negatively related to the rate of interest.

In most instances, residential builders borrow a major portion of the funds needed to purchase land and materials for the construction of new housing. The rate of interest, therefore, affects the builder's return from new construction. For example, the value of the future sum received from the sale of a completed house falls as the interest cost of a current borrowed sum increases. The value of this future sum is further reduced if the builder must wait additional periods to sell a completed house because higher interest rates have caused a drop in the demand for new housing.

Generally, then, both the supply of and demand for new housing are affected by changes in the rate of interest.

Review Questions

1. Net investment is represented by the (*a*) replacement of a machine, (*b*) addition of a new machine, (*c*) purchase of AT&T bonds or (*d*) purchase of a new car.

2. The aggregate marginal efficiency of capital schedule is a schedule of (*a*) investment demand, (*b*) the rate of return on investment proposals, (*c*) the dollar volume of investments undertaken by the firm or (*d*) the dollar volume of investment proposals listed in descending order of expected rate of return.

3. A shift in the aggregate MEC schedule will *not* occur if (*a*) the government lowers the corporate income tax rate, (*b*) there is a growth in population, (*c*) the supply cost of new capital increases   or (*d*) there is a reduction in the rate of interest.

4. An increase in the volume of investment will *not* occur if interest rates
   (*a*) remain constant while corporate income taxes are increased,
   (*b*) are lowered by increasing the quantity of money,
   (*c*) remain constant while the government institutes an investment tax credit   or
   (*d*) are constant, but businessmen expect demand to increase as a result of a decrease in personal income tax rates.

5. There is a marginal efficiency of investment schedule if
   (*a*) the average cost of new capital is constant,
   (*b*) the average cost of new capital is positively related to the quantity of new capital produced,
   (*c*) the government institutes an investment tax credit on capital additions   or
   (*d*) the government rations the production of new capital through a selective tax policy.

6. If the firm is able to generate funds internally, then its cost of funds is (*a*) zero, (*b*) the long-term rate of interest, (*c*) a weighted average of the various sources of long-term funds or (*d*) the short-term rate of interest.

7. The accelerator theory of investment relates the
   (*a*) current rate of investment to the long-term rate of interest,
   (*b*) current rate of investment to the firm's availability of funds,
   (*c*) current level of investment to the current level of output   or
   (*d*) current level of investment to the change in the level of output.

8. If the aggregate capital/output ratio is 2, then a $100 increase in aggregate income will result in capital additions of (a) $50, (b) $80, (c) $100 or (d) $200.

9. Which of the following is a criticism of the accelerator theory?

    (a) Investment decisions are based upon long-term and not short-term changes in output.

    (b) Technological change can affect the capital/output ratio.

    (c) Capital changes may not synchronize with changes in output.

    (d) All of the above.

10. According to the accelerator theory of inventory investment, desired changes in the level of inventory are explained by the (a) amount of goods the firm has failed to sell, (b) amount of goods the firm expects to sell, (c) current level of sales or (d) change in sales volume.

Answers to Review Questions

1. (b) Review Introduction.

2. (d) Review Section 10.1.

3. (d) Review Section 10.1.

4. (a) Review Section 10.1.

5. (b) Review Section 10.2.

6. (d) Review Section 10.4.

7. (d) Review Section 10.5.

8. (d) Review Section 10.5.

9. (d) Review Section 10.5.

10. (d) Review Section 10.6.

Solved Problems

10.1. Differentiate among financial investment, net investment and replacement investment.

Financial investment is the acquisition of securities that are claims against real capital. Replacement investment is the replacement of capital goods that have been used up in the production of goods and services. Net investment is the addition of new capital to the current stock of capital.

10.2. Which of the following represent investment in macroeconomics: (1) building a new public school, (2) building a sewage treatment center, (3) an increase in inventory, (4) the purchase of a new car, (5) new residential construction, (6) additions to plant capacity or (7) investment in new machinery?

In economics, investment refers to those goods which are not directly or currently consumed or those that are held as inventory. Technically, then, all of the above expenditures could represent investment. It is the custom in macroeconomics, however, to adopt the classifications of the national income accounts and include as investment only (3) inventory, (5) residential construction, (6) additions to plant capacity and (7) investment in new machinery. In macroeconomics, investment theory is primarily concerned with explaining investment in new plant and equipment.

10.3. Suppose that a firm has the investment proposals given in Table 4. Derive, in tabular form, a marginal efficiency of capital schedule.

Table 4

Investment	A	B	C	D	E	F
Cost ($)	25,000	50,000	10,000	35,000	5,000	30,000
Expected Return	0.15	0.10	0.08	0.12	0.05	0.07

The marginal efficiency of capital schedule is given in Table 5.

Table 5

MEC	Proposals	Volume of Investment ($)
0.15	A	25,000
0.12	A, D	60,000
0.10	A, D, B	110,000
0.08	A, D, B, C	120,000
0.07	A, D, B, C, F	150,000
0.05	A, D, B, C, F, E	155,000

(See Example 1.)

10.4. Which investment proposals in Problem 10.3 are acceptable if the cost of funds is 0.09?

Investment proposals are acceptable as long as each expected rate of return exceeds the cost of funds. With a 0.09 cost of funds, proposals A, D and B are acceptable for a total commitment of $110,000.

10.5. What behavioral assumption is implicit in the answer to Problem 10.4?

Profit maximization is assumed. That is, businessmen are willing to add to their stock of capital as long as the expected rate of return r from a capital addition exceeds the cost of funds i for purchasing the capital.

10.6. From Fig. 10-6, find net investment when the rate of interest is (a) i_1, (b) i_2 and (c) i_3.

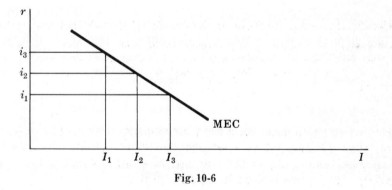

Fig. 10-6

(a) Investment is I_3 when the rate of interest is i_1.

(b) Investment is I_2 when the rate of interest is i_2.

(c) Investment is I_1 when the rate of interest is i_3.

10.7. How is the aggregate MEC schedule affected if (a) there is a growth in population, (b) there is increasing uncertainty about the future level of demand or (c) the government allows a 10% tax credit on capital replacements and additions?

(a) With an increase in demand, there is need for additional capacity. The MEC schedule shifts to the right.

(b) Future proceeds are expected to fall, thereby lowering the expected rate of return from all projects. The MEC schedule shifts to the left.

(c) The cost of capital replacements and additions is lowered, increasing the expected rate of return on all investment proposals. The MEC schedule shifts to the right.

10.8. If the current rate of interest is i_0, with reference to Fig. 10-7, find net investment when (a) the MEC schedule is MEC_0, (b) uncertainty about demand causes the MEC schedule to shift to MEC_1 and (c) technological change in the capital goods industry results in a reduction in capital costs and the MEC schedule shifts to MEC_2.

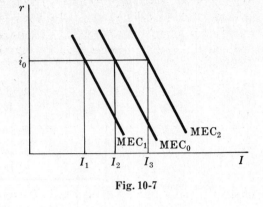

Fig. 10-7

(a) Net investment is I_2.

(b) Net investment is I_1.

(c) Net investment is I_3.

10.9. Does the rate of interest determine the volume of investment?

The rate of interest determines the volume of investment provided that businessmen desire to maximize profits, there are no changes in factors affecting the marginal efficiency of capital for investment proposals and funds are available in unlimited supply at the stated rate of interest for the desired volume of investment. (See Section 10.3.)

10.10. As shown in Fig. 10-8 below, a firm's investment demand schedule is MEC_0. What is its level of investment under the following conditions?

(a) The firm is able to generate internally a sufficient volume of funds to finance its investment proposals. The short-term rate of interest is i_1.

(b) The firm must secure funds in the financial markets. Its weighted cost of funds is i_2.

(c) The firm must secure funds in the financial markets. Its weighted cost of funds is i_2 but fund availability is I_1.

(d) The firm's supply of funds is depicted by curve P_1.

(a) Investment is I_4 determined by the short-term rate of interest i_1.

(b) Investment is I_3 determined by the weighted cost of funds i_2.

(c) Investment is I_1 determined by I_1 availability of funds.

(d) Investment is I_2 determined by the rising supply of funds schedule P_1.

(See Section 10.4.)

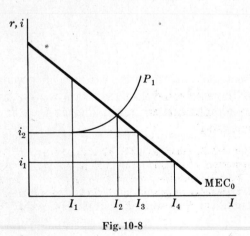

Fig. 10-8

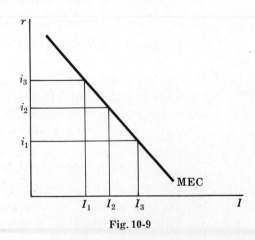

Fig. 10-9

10.11. In Fig. 10-9 (page 84), i_1, i_2 and i_3 represent a short-term rate of interest, a long-term rate of interest and a weighted cost of funds respectively. Find the volume of investment when (a) investment is financed by internally generated funds or (b) investment is financed by external funds which are obtained in proportion to the current capital structure.

(a) The short-term rate of interest i_1 is the relevant rate for investments financed by internal funds. The volume of investment is I_3.

(b) The firm's weighted cost of capital is i_3 since the cost of equity exceeds the cost of long-term debt. The volume of investment is I_1.

10.12. Differentiate between the MEC and MEI schedules.

A MEC schedule is constructed holding constant the supply cost of new capital and the expected rate of return on future cash flows. The MEI schedule also holds the expected rate of return of future cash flows constant but assumes that the supply cost of new capital is positively related to the production of new capital. Since the expected rate of return from investment proposals falls as the supply cost of new capital rises, the MEI schedule has a steeper slope and is to the left of the MEC schedule.

10.13. What is the appropriate investment schedule if the supply cost of new capital is (a) S_1, (b) S_2 or (c) S_3 as shown in Fig. 10-10?

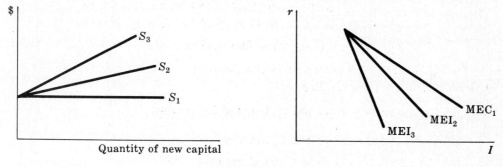

Fig. 10-10

(a) Holding other factors constant, the slope of the investment schedule increases along with increases in the slope of the supply cost of new capital schedule (see Section 10.2). Thus, the appropriate investment schedule is MEC_1 when the supply schedule for new capital is S_1.

(b) It is MEI_2 when the supply schedule is S_2.

(c) It is MEI_3 when the supply schedule is S_3.

10.14. What happens to the interest elasticity of investment demand (the responsiveness of investment volume to changes in the rate of interest) when the supply cost of new capital is upward sloping rather than horizontal?

In Fig. 10-11 (page 86), we shall assume that MEC_1 represents the situation when the supply cost of new capital is horizontal and MEI_2 the situation when it is upward sloping. Assuming that the rate of interest falls from i_0 to i_1, we find that investment volume increases to I_1 for MEI_2 and I_2 for MEC_1. Thus, investment is more responsive (more interest elastic) to interest rate changes when the supply cost of new capital is constant than when it is positively related to the quantity of new capital produced.

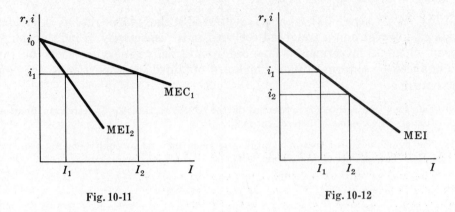

Fig. 10-11   Fig. 10-12

10.15. In Fig. 10-12 above, the capital goods industry's maximum production of new capital is I_1. If the rate of interest falls from i_1 to i_2, what is the current volume of investment?

> The current volume of investment cannot exceed I_1, the maximum output of new capital produced by the capital goods industry. Since the demand for new capital I_2 exceeds supply I_1, the supply price of new capital will rise. This will shift the MEI schedule to the left, eliminating the excess demand for new capital.

10.16. Can the monetary authority regulate investment volume through the cost of funds?

> The monetary authority can regulate the volume of investment through the cost of funds if (1) businessmen desire to maximize profits, (2) there is a stable investment demand schedule, (3) funds are available in unlimited supply at the stated cost of funds for the desired volume of investment and (4) the capital goods industry is able to supply the quantity of capital demanded at the current cost of capital.

10.17. Suppose that the aggregate capital/output ratio is 3, output is initially $100 and increases as follows: period 1, $120; period 2, $140; period 3, $155; period 4, $165 and period 5, $170. Find the level of investment for each period.

> Since $\Delta K = w\,\Delta Y$, the level of investment for each period is as given in Table 6.

Table 6

Period	Change in Output ($)	Investment ($)
1	20	60
2	20	60
3	15	45
4	10	30
5	5	15

10.18. If a firm wishes to keep a desired capital/output ratio, what happens to the volume of investment if output is increasing at a decreasing rate?

> The volume of investment is falling. If incremental output is decreasing (Problem 10.17), then the need for additional capacity is falling.

10.19. The desired inventory/sales ratio is 0.20. Find the change in the desired level of inventory if sales are currently $2000 and expand in period 1 to $2200, in period 2 to $2250, in period 3 to $2400, in period 4 to $2250 and in period 5 to $2350.

Period 1: $\Delta I_{\text{inv}} = 0.20(\$200) = +\$40$

Period 2: $\Delta I_{\text{inv}} = 0.20(\$50) = +\$10$

Period 3: $\Delta I_{\text{inv}} = 0.20(\$150) = +\$30$

Period 4: $\Delta I_{\text{inv}} = 0.20(-\$150) = -\$30$

Period 5: $\Delta I_{\text{inv}} = 0.20(\$100) = +\$20$

10.20. Why is new housing investment believed to be inversely related to the rate of interest?

The rate of interest is believed to affect both the supply of and demand for new housing. Builders finance a major portion of the cost of constructing a new house so that the supply cost of new housing is directly related to the rate of interest. If the demand for new housing is inversely related to price, then the quantity of new housing demanded should fall as interest rates rise. When purchasing a house, most individuals borrow a major portion of the purchase price with a promise to amortize this sum plus interest over a specified number of future periods. As the interest cost on borrowed funds increases, amortization payments increase, thereby decreasing the ability and willingness of prospective buyers to purchase new houses.

Chapter 11

Equilibrium in the Commodity Markets

We now incorporate the marginal efficiency of capital theory of investment into the model of income determination. In doing so, we find that the equilibrium level of income varies inversely with the rate of interest.

11.1 THE *IS* SCHEDULE FOR A TWO-SECTOR MODEL

In the two-sector model developed in Chapter 2, equilibrium income occurred where planned saving equaled planned investment or, equivalently, where the value of output equals planned spending. Thus, given $C = C_0 + bY$ and $I = I_0$, equilibrium income occurs where

$$Y = \frac{C_0 + I_0}{1 - b}$$

In the preceding model, investment spending is exogenous (i.e., determined by forces outside the model). If $I = I_0 - gi$, as theorized in Section 10.3, equilibrium income occurs where

$$Y = \frac{C_0 + I_0 - gi}{1 - b}$$

With investment negatively related to the rate of interest, equilibrium income varies inversely with the rate of interest. The schedule of equilibrium income consistent with different rates of interest is generally called the *IS schedule*.

EXAMPLE 1. The following situations illustrate the derivation of an *IS* schedule.

Given: $I = \$55 - 200i$ and $S = -\$40 + 0.20\,Y$.

Situation I: When the rate of interest is 0.09, investment equals $37. Equilibrium income is $385, occurring where planned saving equals planned investment.

$$S = I$$
$$-\$40 + 0.20\,Y = \$37$$
$$Y = \$385$$

Situation II: When the rate of interest is 0.07, investment equals $41 and equilibrium income is $405.

$$S = I$$
$$-\$40 + 0.20\,Y = \$41$$
$$Y = \$405$$

Situation III: When the rate of interest is 0.05, investment equals $45 and equilibrium income is $425.

$$S = I$$
$$-\$40 + 0.20\,Y = \$45$$
$$Y = \$425$$

Situation IV: When the rate of interest is 0.03, investment equals $49 and equilibrium income is $445.

$$S = I$$
$$-\$40 + 0.20\,Y = \$49$$
$$Y = \$445$$

As the rate of interest falls from 0.09 to 0.07, the volume of investment increases from $37 to $41, raising the income level through the multiplier from $385 to $405. Thus, a 0.09 rate of interest is consistent with a $385 equilibrium level of income while a 0.07 rate of interest is consistent with a $405 equilibrium level of income. The equilibrium level of income consistent with these different rates of interest is presented in Fig. 11-1.

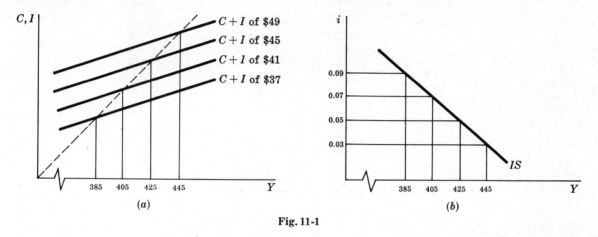

Fig. 11-1

Given a specified investment demand function, we are able to derive an equation for the IS schedule and can then establish the equilibrium levels of income that are consistent with different rates of interest.

EXAMPLE 2.   Given $I = \$55 - 200i$ and $S = -\$40 + 0.20\,Y$,   equilibrium income occurs where

$$S = I$$
$$-\$40 + 0.20\,Y = \$55 - 200i$$
$$\$95 - 0.20\,Y = 200i$$
$$0.20\,Y = \$95 - 200i$$
$$Y = \$475 - 1000i \quad \text{the } IS \text{ equation}$$

11.2   SHIFTS OF THE *IS* SCHEDULE

Autonomous changes in spending cause parallel shifts of the IS schedule. Since the IS schedule is a schedule of equilibrium income, the magnitude of the shift is governed by the autonomous change in spending and the value of the expenditure multiplier (see Section 3.3).

EXAMPLE 3.   In Fig. 11-2(a), an autonomous increase in investment demand shifts the investment demand schedule rightward by ΔI. For interest rate i_0, the schedule of equilibrium income [Fig. 11-2(b)] shifts by ΔY since changes in investment cause equilibrium income to change by $k_e\,\Delta I$.

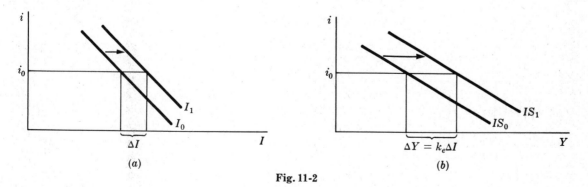

Fig. 11-2

In Fig. 11-3(a), there is an autonomous increase in consumption demand and therefore a decrease in autonomous saving. For interest rate i_0, the schedule of equilibrium income [Fig. 11-3(b)] shifts rightward by ΔY, which equals $k_e \Delta C$.

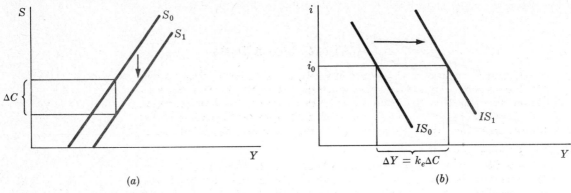

(a) (b)

Fig. 11-3

11.3 THE *IS* SCHEDULE FOR A THREE-SECTOR MODEL

Addition of the government sector, where $G = G_0$ and $Tx = Tx_0$, to the two-sector model (where $C = C_0 + bYd$ and $I = I_0 - gi$) results in an equilibrium level of income of

$$Y = \frac{C_0 + I_0 - gi + G_0 - bTx_0}{1 - b}$$

Since investment continues to depend upon the rate of interest, we retain the model where there is a schedule of equilibrium income. The *IS* schedule for the three-sector model shifts from changes in autonomous spending and taxes, with the magnitude of the shift depending upon the size of the autonomous change and the applicable multiplier (see Section 4.5).

EXAMPLE 4. Shifts in the *IS* schedule for the three-sector model are illustrated in the situations below.

Situation I: Given IS_0, the schedule of equilibrium income, and ΔG, an autonomous increase in government spending, the *IS* schedule in Fig. 11-4 shifts rightward by $k_e \Delta G$.

Situation II: Given IS_0, the schedule of equilibrium income, and ΔTx, an autonomous increase in taxes, the *IS* schedule in Fig. 11-5 shifts leftward by $k_{tx} \Delta Tx$.

Situation III: Given IS_0, the schedule of equilibrium income, and ΔG, an equal increase in government spending and taxes, the *IS* schedule in Fig. 11-6 shifts rightward by $k_b \Delta G$.

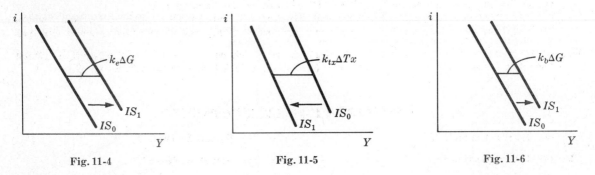

Fig. 11-4   Fig. 11-5   Fig. 11-6

EXAMPLE 5. With specified behavioral equations for the household, business and government sectors, we are able to derive an *IS* equation for a three-sector model.

Given $C = \$40 + 0.80\,Yd$, $I = \$55 - 200i$, $G = \$20$ and $Tx = \$20$, equilibrium income occurs where

$$Y = C + I + G$$
$$Y = \$40 + 0.80(Y - \$20) + \$55 - 200i + \$20$$
$$0.20\,Y = \$99 - 200i$$
$$Y = \$495 - 1000i \quad \text{the } IS \text{ equation}$$

Review Questions

1. Investment is a function of the rate of interest. A decrease in the rate of interest
   (a) increases the level of investment which then decreases the level of income,
   (b) increases the level of investment which then increases the level of income,
   (c) decreases the level of investment which then decreases the level of income   or
   (d) decreases the level of investment which then increases the level of income.

2. The IS curve shows
   (a) a positive relationship between the rate of interest and the level of income,
   (b) a negative relationship between the rate of interest and the level of income,
   (c) a positive relationship between the rate of interest and the level of investment   or
   (d) a negative relationship between the rate of interest and the level of investment.

3. The equation for planned investment is $\$70 - 400i$ while the equation for planned saving is $-\$30 + 0.20\,Y$. Given a 0.05 rate of interest, equilibrium income is   (a) \$350, (b) \$400, (c) \$450   or   (d) \$500.

4. The IS equation is $Y = \$500 - 2000i$. Which of the following sets of interest and income does *not* represent a point on the IS schedule?   (a) $i = 0.02$ and $Y = \$450$,   (b) $i = 0.05$ and $Y = \$400$,   (c) $i = 0.07$ and $Y = \$360$ or   (d) $i = 0.10$ and $Y = \$300$.

5. An autonomous increase in investment (a) has no effect on the IS schedule, (b) has no effect on the IS schedule but causes a multiple change in the level of income, (c) causes the IS schedule to shift to the right   or   (d) causes the IS schedule to shift to the left.

6. Given a MPC of 0.80 and a \$10 increase in investment, the IS schedule shifts (a) to the right by \$50, (b) to the right by \$10, (c) to the left by \$50   or   (d) to the left by \$10.

7. Which of the following statements is *incorrect*?
   (a) The IS schedule shifts to the left if there is an increase in taxes.
   (b) The IS schedule shifts to the right if there is an increase in taxes and government spending.
   (c) The IS schedule shifts to the right if the rate of interest falls.
   (d) The IS schedule shifts to the right if there is an increase in investment.

8. Given $C = \$40 + 0.80\,Yd$, $Tx = \$20$, $G = \$20$ and $I = \$70 - 400i$, a \$10 increase in taxes will shift the IS schedule (a) to the right by \$10, (b) to the left by \$10, (c) to the right by \$40   or   (d) to the left by \$40.

9. Which of the following statements is *correct* given $C = \$40 + 0.80\,Yd$, $Tx = \$20$, $G = \$20$ and $I = \$70 - 400i$?
   (a) A \$10 increase in government spending will shift the IS schedule to the right by \$10.
   (b) A \$10 increase in taxes will shift the IS schedule to the right by \$10.
   (c) A \$10 increase in taxes and government spending will shift the IS schedule to the right by \$10.
   (d) A \$10 increase in taxes and government spending will shift the IS schedule to the left by \$10.

10. An equal increase in taxes and government spending (a) has no effect upon the IS schedule, (b) shifts the IS schedule to the right by $k_b \Delta G$ or   (c) shifts the IS schedule to the left by $k_b \Delta G$.

Answers to Review Questions

1.	(b) Review Example 1.		6.	(a) Review Example 3.
2.	(b) Review Section 11.1.		7.	(c) Review Section 11.3.
3.	(b) Review Example 2.		8.	(d) Review Example 5.
4.	(a) Review Example 2.		9.	(c) Review Example 4.
5.	(c) Review Section 11.2.		10.	(b) Review Section 11.3.

Solved Problems

11.1. Assume that the equation for investment is $\$100 - 500i$. Find the level of investment when the interest rate is (a) 0.04, (b) 0.05, (c) 0.06 or (d) 0.07.

(a) When $i = 0.04$, $I = \$100 - 500(0.04) = \$80$.

(b) When $i = 0.05$, $I = \$100 - 500(0.05) = \$75$.

(c) When $i = 0.06$, $I = \$100 - 500(0.06) = \$70$.

(d) When $i = 0.07$, $I = \$100 - 500(0.07) = \$65$.

11.2. Using the investment equation in Problem 11.1, if the saving equation is $S = -\$40 + 0.25\,Y$, find the level of income when the interest rate is (a) 0.04, (b) 0.05, (c) 0.06 or (d) 0.07.

(a) When i is 0.04, I is \$80.   Equilibrium income equals \$480.

$$I = S$$
$$\$80 = -\$40 + 0.25\,Y$$
$$\$480 = Y$$

(b) When i is 0.05, I is \$75.   Equilibrium income equals \$460.

(c) When i is 0.06, I is \$70.   Equilibrium income equals \$440.

(d) When i is 0.07, I is \$65.   Equilibrium income equals \$420.

11.3. Using the information in Problems 11.1 and 11.2, find an equation that represents equilibrium between saving and investment.

The equation is

$$S = I$$
$$-\$40 + 0.25\,Y = \$100 - 500i$$
$$0.25\,Y = \$140 - 500i$$
$$Y = \$560 - 2000i$$

11.4. Why is there a schedule of equilibrium income?

Given a two-sector model of the economy and a stable consumption function, equilibrium income varies directly with the level of investment. If investment in turn varies inversely with the rate of interest, so too does the equilibrium level of income. Thus, for each rate of interest, there is an equilibrium level of income. For a family of interest rates, there is a schedule of equilibrium income.

11.5. If $C = \$40 + 0.80\,Y$ and $I = \$70 - 200i$, find (a) the IS equation and (b) the equilibrium levels of income when the rate of interest is 0.10 and 0.05.

(a) Equilibrium exists where

$$Y = C + I$$
$$Y = \$40 + 0.80\,Y + \$70 - 200i$$
$$0.20\,Y = \$110 - 200i$$
$$Y = \$550 - 1000i$$

(b) When i is 0.10, the equilibrium level of income is \$450.

When i is 0.05, the equilibrium level of income is \$500.

11.6. Which of the following equations represent (a) IS_1 and (b) IS_2 in Fig. 11-7?

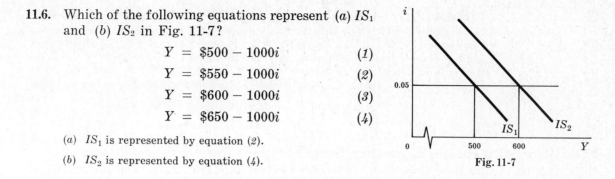

$$Y = \$500 - 1000i \qquad (1)$$

$$Y = \$550 - 1000i \qquad (2)$$

$$Y = \$600 - 1000i \qquad (3)$$

$$Y = \$650 - 1000i \qquad (4)$$

(a) IS_1 is represented by equation (2).

(b) IS_2 is represented by equation (4).

Fig. 11-7

11.7. The IS equations in Problem 11.6 differ only in the value of the constant. (a) Find the equilibrium level of income for each of these equations if the rate of interest is 0.05. (b) Assuming that there is a $50 difference in the constant of the IS equations as well as in the equilibrium level of income at a 0.05 rate of interest, what is the magnitude of the exogenous change in spending and/or taxes?

(a) When i is 0.05, Y is $450 for IS equation (1), $500 for IS equation (2), $550 for IS equation (3) and $600 for IS equation (4).

(b) Parallel shifts in the IS schedule reflect exogenous changes in spending (ΔI, ΔC or ΔG) where $\Delta Y = k_e \Delta G$ or taxes where $\Delta Y = k_{tx} \Delta Tx$. If the $50 shift was caused by increased government spending, then there must have been a $10 autonomous increase in government spending since $\Delta Y = k_e \Delta G = \$50 = 5\Delta G$. If caused by a reduction in taxes, the tax decrease equals $12.50 since $\$50 = -4\,\Delta Tx$.

11.8. In Fig. 11-8, the demand for investment is plotted in quadrant 1. Quadrant 2 depicts the equality of saving and investment. The saving function is plotted in quadrant 3. Derive the IS curve in quadrant 4 as a schedule of equilibrium income where planned saving equals planned investment.

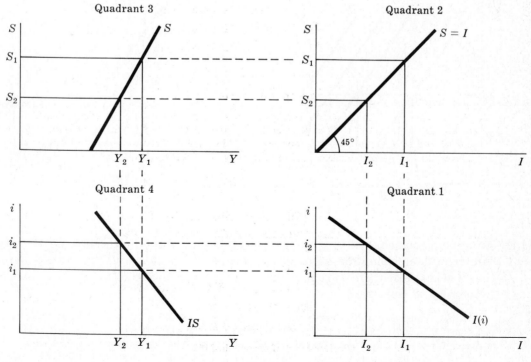

Fig. 11-8

With the interest rate at i_1, investment equals I_1. To have equilibrium, saving must equal S_1, which it does at an income level of Y_1. In quadrant 4, we see that an interest rate of i_1 is consistent with an income level of Y_1. If the interest rate is i_2, investment equals I_2. For the equality of planned saving and planned investment, saving volume must equal S_2 at income level Y_2. Thus an interest rate of i_2 is consistent with an income level of Y_2 in quadrant 4. By continuous choosing of the rate of interest, we derive a curve that represents equilibrium income for various rates of interest.

11.9. Autonomous changes in spending cause multiple changes in the equilibrium level of income. Given the IS equation $Y = \$550 - 1000i$, a MPC $= 0.80$, and a 0.05 rate of interest, (*a*) what happens to the equilibrium level of income if $5 in government spending is added to the model? (*b*) What happens to the IS schedule as a result of adding government spending to the model?

(*a*) At a 0.05 rate of interest, the equilibrium level of income increases from $500 to $525.

(*b*) The IS schedule is shifted to the right by $25, i.e., by $k_e \, \Delta G$. (See Example 4.)

11.10. In Fig. 11-9 below, if IS_0 represents the equation $Y = \$500 - 800i$ and the MPS is 0.20, what increase in government spending would cause the IS schedule to shift to (*a*) IS_1, (*b*) IS_2 and (*c*) IS_3?

The expenditure multiplier k_e equals $1/\text{MPS} = 5$.

(*a*) IS_1 represents a $10 increase in government spending.

(*b*) IS_2 represents a $15 increase in government spending.

(*c*) IS_3 represents a $20 increase in government spending.

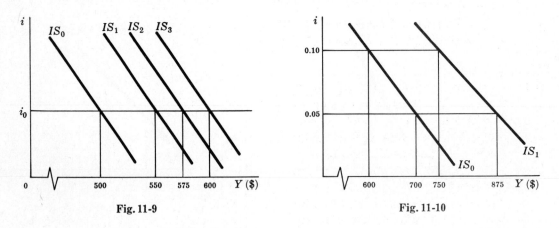

Fig. 11-9   Fig. 11-10

11.11. An autonomous change in spending causes the IS schedule to shift by the expenditure multiplier times the autonomous change in spending. What would happen to the IS schedule if there were a change in a behavioral coefficient such as the marginal propensity to consume?

In Fig. 11-10 above, IS_0 represents equilibrium income for a two-sector model with behavioral equations $C = \$50 + 0.75 Y$ and $I = \$150 - 500i$. If the MPC increases to 0.80, the IS schedule shifts rightward to IS_1. The rightward shift of the IS schedule is $150 at a 0.10 rate of interest and $175 at a 0.05 rate of interest. Thus, a change in a behavioral coefficient causes a nonparallel shift of the IS schedule.

11.12. What happens to the *IS* schedule if there is an increase in (*a*) imports, (*b*) taxes, (*c*) investment or (*d*) exports.

> (*a*) An increase in imports represents an increase in saving leakages. The *IS* schedule shifts to the left.
>
> (*b*) An increase in taxes represents an increase in saving leakages. The *IS* schedule shifts to the left.
>
> (*c*) An increase in investment represents an autonomous increase in spending. The *IS* schedule shifts to the right.
>
> (*d*) An increase in exports represents an autonomous increase in spending. The *IS* schedule shifts to the right.

11.13. Given $k_e = 4$ and $k_{tx} = 3$, explain the direction and magnitude of the shift in the *IS* schedule when there is a (*a*) \$50 decrease in government spending, (*b*) \$10 increase in consumption, (*c*) \$25 increase in both taxes and government spending or (*d*) \$10 decrease in both taxes and government spending.

> (*a*) The *IS* schedule shifts to the left by \$200.
>
> (*b*) The *IS* schedule shifts to the right by \$40.
>
> (*c*) The *IS* schedule shifts to the right by \$25.
>
> (*d*) The *IS* schedule shifts to the left by \$10.

11.14. Suppose that $C = \$40 + 0.75(Y - tY)$, $t = 0.20$, $Tx = 0$, $G = \$90$ and $I = \$150 - 500i$. Explain the direction and magnitude of the shift in the *IS* schedule when there is a (*a*) \$10 increase in G, (*b*) \$10 increase in Tx or (*c*) \$10 increase in G and Tx.

> The expenditure multiplier equals $1/(1 - b + bt) = 1/(1 - 0.75 + 0.15) = 2.5$ and the tax multiplier equals $-b/(1 - b + bt) = -0.75/(1 - 0.75 + 0.15) = -1.875$. Therefore,
>
> (*a*) the *IS* schedule shifts to the right by \$25.
>
> (*b*) The *IS* schedule shifts to the left by \$18.75.
>
> (*c*) The *IS* schedule shifts to the right by \$6.25.

11.15. The expenditure multiplier is 5, the tax multiplier is 4, the balanced budget multiplier is 1 and the current *IS* curve is IS_0 in Fig. 11-11. Determine the new *IS* curve if there is (*a*) a \$20 reduction in taxes, (*b*) a \$20 reduction in taxes and government expenditures, (*c*) a \$20 increase in government expenditures and (*d*) a \$20 decrease in autonomous investment.

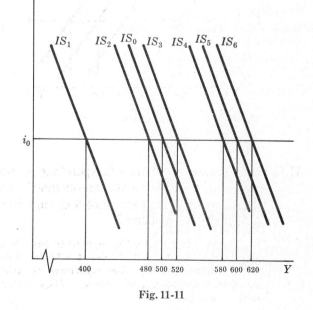

Fig. 11-11

> (*a*) There is a rightward shift of the *IS* curve. The new *IS* curve is IS_4.
>
> (*b*) There is a leftward shift of the *IS* curve. The new *IS* curve is IS_2.
>
> (*c*) There is a rightward shift of the *IS* curve. The new *IS* curve is IS_5.
>
> (*d*) There is a leftward shift of the *IS* curve. The new *IS* curve is IS_1.

Chapter 12

Money and the Level of Income

12.1 A SIMPLE MONETARY MODEL OF THE LEVEL OF MONEY INCOME

In most economies, money is the basis for exchanging goods and services. Thus, it can be said that the ability to spend is limited by the amount of money that potential spenders have at their disposal. From this point of view, the stock of money M is the means of acquiring output.

The contemporary approach to the equation of exchange, $MV = Y$, views money as the means of spending. Velocity V, in this income equation of exchange, measures the average number of times that the money stock is used to purchase the output of final goods and services. In the Cambridge version of the equation of exchange, $1/V$ represents the proportion of the level of money income held in the form of money. By using the Cambridge version of the equation of exchange, we are able to formulate a theory of the demand for money.

EXAMPLE 1. The equation of exchange $MV = Y$ can be rewritten as $M = (1/V)Y$. Letting $k = 1/V$, we have $M = kY$, where k represents the proportion of money income that people desire to hold as money. Thus, $M = kY$ represents, in equation form, the demand for money.

Given the demand for money and an exogenous money supply, we can establish the level of money income where there is equilibrium between the demand for and supply of money. It follows that changes in the stock of money result in multiple changes in the level of money income.

EXAMPLE 2. Suppose that the money supply Ms equals \$100 and the demand for money Md equals $0.20\,Y$. Equilibrium in the demand for and supply of money exists at a \$500 level of money income.

Equilibrium condition:
$$Ms = Md$$
$$\$100 = 0.20\,Y$$
$$\$500 = Y$$

EXAMPLE 3. If the money supply increases from \$100 (Example 2) to \$110 and the demand for money is $0.20\,Y$, the level of money income consistent with equilibrium in the supply of and demand for money increases from \$500 to \$550.

Equilibrium condition:
$$Ms = Md$$
$$\$110 = 0.20\,Y$$
$$\$550 = Y$$

Dividing the dependent by the independent variable $\Delta Y/\Delta M$, we find a money multiplier $1/k$ of 5 associated with changes in the quantity of money.

$$\frac{\Delta Y}{\Delta M} = \frac{\$50}{\$10} = 5 = V = \frac{1}{k}$$

12.2 INTEGRATING THE MONETARY AND KEYNESIAN MODELS OF THE LEVEL OF MONEY INCOME

The monetary model developed in Section 12.1 and the Keynesian expenditure model developed in Chapters 2 through 6 may be integrated as follows:

$$Monetary\ model: \qquad Y = \frac{M_0}{k}$$

given:
$$Md = kY$$
$$Ms = M_0$$

$$Keynesian\ model: \quad Y = k_e(C_0 + I_0 + G_0 - bTx_0 + X_0 - Z_0)$$

given:
$$C = C_0 + b(Y - Tx) \qquad X = X_0$$
$$Tx = Tx_0 \qquad\qquad\qquad Z = Z_0$$
$$I = I_0 \qquad\qquad\qquad\quad k_e = 1/(1 - b)$$
$$G = G_0$$

Since both are models of the level of money income, it follows that

$$\frac{M_0}{k} = k_e(C_0 + I_0 + G_0 - bTx_0 + X_0 - Z_0)$$

The reconciling equation above shows that money supply changes, given a stable demand for money, must result in changes in consumption, investment, government or net export spending while changes in fiscal policy necessitate changes in either the stock of or demand for money.

EXAMPLE 4. *Given*: A \$400 level of money income, $Ms = \$100$, $k = 0.25$, $C = \$330$, $I = \$60$, $G = \$50$, $Tx = \$50$, $b = 0.80$, $k_e = 5$ and $k_{tx} = 4$.

Situation I: Suppose that there is a \$10 increase in the money supply with no change in k, G or Tx. Since $1/k$ equals 4, there is a \$40 increase in the level of money income. With no changes in the government sector, private spending $(C + I)$ increases \$40.

Situation II: Suppose that there is a \$10 increase in the money supply with no change in C, I, G or Tx. Since spending has not increased, there is no change in the level of money income. Thus, the increase in the demand for money is equal to the increase in the supply of money.

Situation III: Suppose that there is a \$10 increase in G and Ms with no change in k or Tx. Since k_e equals 4 and $1/k$ equals 4, there is a \$40 increase in the level of money income. The \$10 increase in government spending induces a \$30 increase in consumption spending.

Situation IV: Suppose that there is a \$10 increase in G and no change in k, Ms or Tx. There is no change in the level of money income since there is no change in k or Ms. There must be a decrease in I and/or C equal to the increase in G.

The interdependence of the monetary and expenditure models is further developed in Chapters 16 and 17.

12.3 THE CREATION OF PAPER CURRENCY

In economics, money is an asset that provides its owner with ultimate liquidity. That is, the owner of money is able to purchase goods and services with this asset without incurring additional transaction costs. We shall define money as consisting of currency and demand deposits, although other assets also provide their owner with a high degree of liquidity.

Currency is composed of both coins and paper currency. In the United States, we have token coins and fiat paper currency. *Token coins* arise when the issued coin is not worth its face value as a commodity. Thus, token coins do not include an amount of metal equal to the face value of the coin. *Credit or fiat paper currency* arises when there is no commodity backing the issue.

Examples 5 through 7 demonstrate various ways the government could change the quantity of fiat paper currency.

EXAMPLE 5.   Paper currency is printed by the government and given to households. Households receive an asset, paper currency. The government increases a liability, paper currency. The balancing entry for the household and government sectors is good will.

HOUSEHOLD SECTOR		GOVERNMENT SECTOR	
Assets	Liabilities	Assets	Liabilities
Paper currency +	Good will +	Good will +	Paper currency +

EXAMPLE 6.   The government creates paper currency and uses it to purchase goods and services from the business sector. The business sector changes the composition of its assets, giving up goods and services for paper currency. The government sector increases the quantity of goods and services it receives by issuing a liability, paper currency.

BUSINESS SECTOR		GOVERNMENT SECTOR	
Assets	Liabilities	Assets	Liabilities
Goods & services −		Goods & services +	Paper currency +
Paper currency +			

EXAMPLE 7.   The government issues paper currency in exchange for government securities owned by the household sector. The household sector changes the composition of its assets from an interest-bearing government liability to a non-interest-bearing government liability. There is a similar change in the liabilities of the government sector.

HOUSEHOLD SECTOR		GOVERNMENT SECTOR	
Assets	Liabilities	Assets	Liabilities
Government securities −			Government securities −
Paper currency +			Paper currency +

As a general rule, the government creates additional paper currency by purchasing government securities (Example 7). This method is classified as a *monetization of debt* since the government is exchanging interest-bearing for non-interest-bearing debt. Creation of paper currency by the outright purchase of goods and services (Example 6) was used only during the Civil War. Currency creation has never taken the form of Example 5 although some abstract economic theories assume this method.

Let us now consider the effect of currency creation upon the level of money income. (We shall assume that the household sector receives additional paper currency in exchange for government securities.) If households decide to hold the increased supply of paper currency, there is no effect upon the level of spending and therefore no change in the level of money income. In this case, the increased money supply is completely offset by an equal increase in the demand for money. However, if households spend the larger currency balances or lend them to the business sector, the level of money income rises as consumption plus investment spending increases. Of crucial importance, then, is the behavior of those who receive the additional paper currency. This is treated in Chapter 13.

12.4   THE CREATION AND CONTROL OF DEMAND DEPOSIT MONEY

Demand deposits are the largest component of the money supply. Demand deposits arise from either the depositing of currency or the process of lending.

EXAMPLE 8.   The household sector deposits $100 of paper currency in the commercial banking system, receiving a credit to its demand deposit account.

HOUSEHOLD SECTOR			COMMERCIAL BANKING SYSTEM		
Assets		Liabilities	Assets		Liabilities
Paper currency	−$100		Paper currency	+$100	Demand deposit +$100
Demand deposit	+$100				

Assuming that the household sector chooses to leave this $100 on deposit indefinitely, the commercial banking system can elect to create additional deposits by making loans to the business or household sectors.

COMMERCIAL BANKING SYSTEM			BUSINESS SECTOR		
Assets		Liabilities	Assets		Liabilities
Loans	+$50	Demand deposit +$50	Demand deposit +$50		IOU to bank +$50

The government, through its central bank, regulates deposit creation by the commercial banking system by controlling the commercial banks' reserve requirement and the volume of reserves owned by the commercial banking system.

EXAMPLE 9.   Reserve requirements limit deposit expansion by the commercial banking system. Reserves, in the United States, are defined as vault cash (coins plus paper currency) plus deposits at the central bank. A 20% reserve requirement means that the commercial bank must have 20¢ in reserve assets for each $1 of demand deposits.

If a commercial banking system has $100 in reserves, demand deposit liabilities cannot exceed $500. By lowering the requirement to, say, 10%, the central bank can double demand deposit volume since $100 of reserves will support a $1000 volume of demand deposits. The central bank could have increased demand deposit volume to $100 by retaining the 20% reserve requirement and increasing reserve volume to $200.

In the United States, the central bank relies upon changes in reserve volume to effect changes in the volume of demand deposit money. This is accomplished by the buying and selling of government securities. The effect of changes in reserve volume upon the money supply depends upon the commercial banking system's willingness to lend and create demand deposits and business' willingness to borrow from commercial banks. In Example 10, we assume that there is an unlimited demand for loans and that the commercial banking system creates the maximum quantity of demand deposits that the reserve requirement allows.

EXAMPLE 10.   The following transactions establish the increase in reserve volume and the resultant potential increase in demand deposit volume from a purchase of government securities by the central bank:

(A)   The central bank purchases $100 in securities from households and pays for these securities by issuing a check drawn upon itself.

(B)   The household sector deposits its check drawn upon the central bank in the commercial banking system, electing to hold a demand deposit with commercial banks.

(C)   The commercial banking system collects on the check issued by the central bank by having the central bank credit its deposit account. Commercial bank reserves increase by $100.

(D)   Assuming a 20% reserve requirement, the commercial banking system has excess reserves of $80 ($20 of the $100 increase in reserves must be used to support the demand deposit created in B). It is therefore in a position to create $400 of demand deposits by making loans of $400.

HOUSEHOLD SECTOR			
Assets			Liabilities
(A) { Government securities	−$100		
(A) { Check liability of the central bank	+$100		
(B) { Check liability of the central bank	−$100		
(B) { Demand deposit at commercial banks	+$100		

COMMERCIAL BANKING SYSTEM

	Assets		Liabilities		
(B)	Check liability of the central bank	+$100	Demand deposit of households	+$100	(B)
(C) {	Check liability of the central bank	−$100	Demand deposits	+$400	(D)
	Deposit at the central bank	+$100	Change in demand deposits	+$500	
(D)	Loans & investments	+$400			
	Change in assets	+$500			

CENTRAL BANK

	Assets		Liabilities		
(A)	Government securities	+$100	Check payable to households	+$100	(A)
			Check payable to households	−$100	(C)
			Deposit of commercial banks	+$100	

A $100 increase in reserves increases demand deposit money $500. It is possible, though, that deposit volume may increase less than $500. A commercial bank may elect to hold reserves in excess of its requirements. Thus, the $100 increase in reserves might change demand deposits by only $450 if a commercial bank elects to hold excess reserves of $10. This and other complicating factors are not considered here although they are of crucial importance to money supply determination.

Demand deposit creation, like increases in the paper currency component of the money supply, involves monetization of public and private debt. In transaction (D) of Example 10, demand deposit volume increased $400 as commercial banks exchanged their non-interest-bearing liability (deposit money) for an interest-bearing liability of a firm, household or government. Likewise, the central bank's purchase of a government security also involves debt monetization. Since the central bank is a part of the government sector, its exchange of an interest-bearing government security for a non-interest-bearing deposit at the central bank reduces the interest-bearing liabilities of the government sector.

The effect upon income of an increase in demand deposit or paper currency money depends upon what households or firms do with their additional money balances. If households keep their additional money balances, there is no increase in spending and therefore no change in the level of money income. Likewise, the demand deposits created through commercial bank lending have no effect upon spending if firms hold these additional balances idle.

Review Questions

1. In the $MV = Y$ version of the equation of exchange, (a) M measures the change in the stock of money, (b) M measures the demand for money, (c) V measures the average number of times that the money stock is used for purchasing goods and services or (d) V measures the number of times each component of the money supply is used to transact exchange.

2. The Cambridge version of the equation of exchange is (a) $MV = Y$, (b) $Mk = Y$, (c) $MY = k$ or (d) $M = kY$.

3. The equation of exchange can be formulated into a monetary theory of income if

   (a) the demand for money is a function of income and the money supply is an exogenous variable,

   (b) the demand for money and the supply of money are exogenous variables or

   (c) the demand for money is a function of the rate of interest and the money supply is an exogenous variable.

4. If the demand for money equals $0.33\,Y$ and there is a $10 increase in the money supply, the level of money income (a) does not change, (b) increases by $3.33, (c) increases by $10 or (d) increases by $30.

5. The current equilibrium level of money income is $500. The money supply equals $100 and the expenditure multiplier is 5. If the demand for money is a stable function of income and there is a $10 increase in autonomous investment,

   (a) the money supply must increase $50 for the money income level to increase $50,

   (b) the money supply must increase $10 for the money income level to increase $50,

   (c) the money supply must increase $10 for the money income level to increase $10   or

   (d) the money income level will increase $50 regardless of the change in the money supply.

6. The equilibrium level of money income is $500. The money supply equals $100 and the expenditure multiplier is 5. A $10 increase in government expenditures

   (a) has no effect upon the level of money income if there is no change in the stock of money and the demand for money is a stable function of the level of income,

   (b) increases the money income level $50 if there is no change in the stock of money and the demand for money is a stable function of income,

   (c) increases the money income level $10 if there is no change in the stock of money and the demand for money is a stable function of income   or

   (d) increases the level of money income $10 if there is a $10 increase in the stock of money and the demand for money is a stable function of income.

7. Which of the following statements is *incorrect*?

   (a) Money is an asset used in the exchange of goods and services.

   (b) Money is an asset that provides its owner with liquidity.

   (c) The United States money supply is composed largely of fiat or credit money.

   (d) The United States money supply has commodity backing.

8. Which of the following best represents the way in which the government increases the paper currency component of the money supply?

   (a) Households sell gold to the government in return for currency.

   (b) The government gives newly created currency to households.

   (c) The government pays for goods and services with newly issued currency.

   (d) The government exchanges paper currency for government securities.

9. The central bank can increase the demand deposit component of the money supply by

   (a) lowering reserve requirements or decreasing the volume of reserves,

   (b) lowering reserve requirements or increasing the volume of reserves,

   (c) increasing reserve requirements or decreasing the volume of reserves   or

   (d) increasing reserve requirements or increasing the volume of reserves.

10. Demand deposit volume is currently $2000. Reserves total $400 and the reserve requirement is 20%. Which of the following statements is *incorrect*?

   (a) There is no change in the volume of demand deposits if the reserve requirement is increased to 25% and the volume of reserves increases $500.

   (b) Potential demand deposit volume increases $160 if reserves increase $30.

   (c) Potential demand deposit volume increases $100 if reserves increase $20.

   (d) Potential demand deposit volume increases $125 if reserves increase $25.

11. If the demand for money equals $0.25 Y$, the money multiplier is (a) 0.25, (b) 2.50, (c) 4.00 or (d) 5.20.

12. Assume that households sell $100 of government securities to the central bank in return for $100 in paper currency. If households elect to deposit this paper currency in the commercial banking system and the reserve requirement is 25%, the money supply increases by (a) $100, (b) $200, (c) $400 or (d) $500.

Answers to Review Questions

1. (c) Review Section 12.1.

2. (d) See Example 1.

3. (a) See Example 2.

4. (d) See Example 3.

5. (b) Review Section 12.2.

6. (a) See Example 4.

7. (d) Review Section 12.3.

8. (d) Review Examples 5 through 7 and discussion of the monetization of debt.

9. (b) Review Section 12.4.

10. (b) See Example 10.

11. (c) See Example 3.

12. (c) Review Section 12.4.

Solved Problems

12.1. Compare the models $Y = C + I + G$ and $M = kY$.

The approach in the Keynesian model $(Y = C + I + G)$ is on the household, business and government sectors' spending. The Cambridge version of the equation of exchange, $M = kY$, views income through the equilibrium of the demand for and supply of money. While both models can be used as theories of income, their emphases differ. The equation of exchange model stresses the effect of autonomous changes in the stock of money upon the level of money income while the Keynesian model analyzes the effect of autonomous changes in spending upon income.

12.2. Find velocity when (a) $C = \$525$, $I = \$130$, $G = \$80$, $X = \$15$ and $Ms = \$150$; (b) $C = \$525$, $I = \$130$, $G = \$80$, $X = \$15$ and $Ms = \$100$ and (c) $C = \$500$, $I = \$110$, $G = \$75$, $X = \$15$ and $Ms = \$100$.

(a) $Y = C + I + G + X = \$750$, therefore $V = Y/M = 5$.

(b) Velocity is 7.5.

(c) Velocity is 7.

12.3. Derive (a) the value of k and (b) the quantity of money demanded for each situation in Problem 12.2.

(a) $k = 1/V$. Therefore the value of k is 1/5 in (a), 1/7.5 in (b) and 1/7 in (c).

(b) The demand for money equals kY. The quantity of money demanded is \$150 in (a), \$100 in (b) and \$100 in (c).

12.4. Assuming that $Ms = \$100$ and $Md = 0.20\,Y$, calculate (a) the value of the money multiplier, (b) the level of money income and (c) the level of money income if there is a \$10 increase in the supply of money.

(a) The value of the money multiplier equals $1/k$. Given $k = 0.20$, the money multiplier equals 5.

(b) The demand for and supply of money are in equilibrium when there is a \$500 level of money income.

(c)
$$Ms = Md$$
$$\$110 = 0.20\,Y$$
$$\$550 = Y$$

Thus, a \$10 increase in the supply of money results in a \$50 increase in the level of money income.

12.5. Why does a change in the money supply result in a multiple change in the level of money income?

If the money supply is increased, it must be held by someone. Given $Md = kY$ (a stable demand for money equation), the increased money supply is demanded if there is an increase in the level of money income. Since k, the proportion of income held as money, is less than one, the increase in income must exceed the increase in the supply of money. Thus, a change in the supply of money, given a constant value for k, results in a multiple change in the level of money income.

12.6. Does a change in the supply of money always result in a multiple change in the level of money income?

The change in the level of money income equals $\Delta Y = \Delta M/k$, given a stable demand for money function. If there is a change in the behavioral coefficient of the function, then the change in the level of income depends upon the magnitude and direction of change in the value of k. For instance, given $Ms = \$100$ and $Md = 0.20\,Y$, a \$25 increase in the supply of money has no effect upon the level of income if the value of k increases to 0.25. When the demand for money changes along with a change in the money supply, the change in the level of income equals

$$\Delta Y \;=\; \Delta MV + M\,\Delta V + \Delta M\,\Delta V$$

12.7. From Fig. 12-1, what is the value of k when the demand for money is represented by (a) Md_1, (b) Md_2 or (c) Md_3?

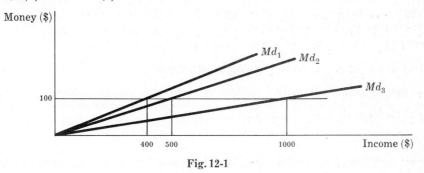

Fig. 12-1

$Md = kY$. Substituting the values for Md and Y from Fig. 12-1, we have

(a) Md_1:

$\qquad\qquad\qquad\qquad\qquad \$100 \;=\; k(\$400)$

$\qquad\qquad\qquad\qquad\qquad 0.25 \;=\; k$

(b) Md_2:

$\qquad\qquad\qquad\qquad\qquad \$100 \;=\; k(\$500)$

$\qquad\qquad\qquad\qquad\qquad 0.20 \;=\; k$

(c) Md_3:

$\qquad\qquad\qquad\qquad\qquad \$100 \;=\; k(\$1000)$

$\qquad\qquad\qquad\qquad\qquad 0.10 \;=\; k$

12.8. Will an increase in the supply of money result in an increase in prices?

Assuming no change in the value of k, an increase in the money supply results in increased spending and therefore an increase in the level of money income. Whether this increased income reflects increased output of goods and services or increased prices depends upon the economy's ability to expand output (see Chapter 20).

12.9. Suppose that $Ms = \$100$, $Md = 0.25\,Y$, $Y = \$400$ and the expenditure multiplier is 5. What is the increase in the level of money income if there is a \$15 increase in government spending and no change in the supply of and demand for money?

According to spending multiplier analysis, $\Delta Y = k_e\,\Delta G$. Thus, there is a \$75 increase in income from a \$15 increase in government spending. We have seen, however, that in a money economy there must be either an increased money supply or a decrease in k if the level of money income is to rise. Since both Ms and k are assumed constant, there can be no multiple increase in the level of money income from increased government spending. We find in Chapters 16 and 17 that the stimulative effect of increased government spending is offset by an equal decrease in investment spending when there is no change in Ms or k.

12.10. There are numerous assets such as saving accounts and U.S. saving bonds that provide their owners with liquidity. Are these assets money?

Money provides its owners with *ultimate* liquidity. That is, the possessor can use the asset in its current form to acquire goods and services directly without transaction costs. Assets such as saving accounts and U.S. saving bonds cannot be used in their current form to acquire goods and services. They must be converted into a demand deposit or currency before goods and services are purchased and traditionally have not been classified as money. Some economists, however, have favored inclusion of saving accounts in the definition of money since their conversion into a demand deposit or currency does not involve a transaction cost.

12.11. What is fiat money?

We have fiat money when the issuer does not promise to convert money into a specified commodity. For example, the U.S. government does not promise to convert a \$5 bill into gold or any other commodity. When a country has a fiat money supply, it is able to increase its quantity by the monetization of public and/or private debt.

12.12. How does the government monetize its debt?

The government monetizes its debt by exchanging newly printed paper currency for federal debt. Current owners of the debt willingly exchange government bonds for paper currency if they are offered a "good price" for these bonds.

12.13. Does monetization of the federal debt result in increased spending and therefore a higher level of money income?

The increased money supply results in a higher level of money income if the additional money balance is spent. If owners of the increased money balance decide to hold it as an idle balance, there is no additional spending and therefore no change in the level of money income. In the latter situation, the relative increase in the supply of money is met by an equal relative increase in the demand for money.

12.14. Assume that the money income level is currently \$800, given $Ms = \$200$ and $Md = 0.25\,Y$. What happens to the level of money income and the demand for money if the central bank issues \$50 in paper currency to households in exchange for \$50 of government securities and (*a*) households elect to spend all of the \$50 increase in paper currency? (*b*) If households elect to hold the entire \$50 increase in paper currency?

(*a*) Given no change in the demand for money, the level of money income equals

$$Y = \frac{M + \Delta M}{k}$$

$$Y = \frac{\$200 + \$50}{0.25}$$

$$Y = \$1000$$

(*b*) Assuming that the additional money supply is not spent, there is no change in the level of money income and k now equals

$$Y = \frac{M + \Delta M}{k}$$

$$\$800 = \frac{\$200 + \$50}{k}$$

$$0.3125 = k$$

There is an increase in the demand for money.

12.15. Why is the commercial banking system able to create money?

The use of checks is both a convenient and safe means of payment. Thus, the volume of transactions carried out through demand deposits greatly exceeds that of paper currency. Given a preference for demand deposits, a central bank purchase of government securities will result in more paper currency deposited with commercial banks than held by the business and household sectors. Assuming that the owners of demand deposits will not convert to paper currency, the commercial banking system is able to create demand deposits in the process of lending to the business and household sectors. The central bank limits commercial banks' capacity to create demand deposits by reserve requirements and by control over the quantity of reserves held by them.

12.16. (a) Show by means of T-accounts what happens (1) if the central bank purchases $150 of government securities from the household sector by paying for them with newly issued paper currency and (2) if households elect to deposit $120 of this paper currency in the commercial banking system. (Assume that the reserve requirement for the commercial banking system is 20%.) (b) Calculate the change in the quantity of money (demand deposits plus currency) held by households.

(a)

HOUSEHOLD SECTOR

Assets			Liabilities
(1) { Government securities	−$150		
Paper currency	+$150		
(2) { Paper currency	−$120		
Demand deposits	+$120		

COMMERCIAL BANKING SYSTEM

Assets		Liabilities	
(2) { Paper currency	+$120	Demand deposits	+$120
Loans	+$480	Demand deposits	+$480

(b) $\Delta Ms = \$600 + \$30 = \$630$. The change in the money supply equals the change in demand volume plus the change in currency held by the household sector.

12.17. Suppose that reserves total $1250 and the volume of demand deposits equals $5000 given a reserve requirement of 25%. Calculate the volume of demand deposits if (a) the reserve requirement is lowered to 20%, (b) the volume of reserves is decreased $250 and (c) the volume of reserves is decreased $250 and the reserve requirement is lowered to 20%.

(a) Deposit volume is found by the formula $D = R/r$, where R is the volume of reserves, r the reserve requirement and D the volume of demand deposits. Therefore, $D = \$1250/0.20 = \$6250$. The volume of demand deposits increases $1250.

(b) $D = \$1000/0.25 = \$4000$. The volume of demand deposits decreases $1000.

(c) $D = \$1000/0.20 = \$5000$. There is no change in the volume of demand deposits.

12.18. Is the change in the volume of demand deposits always equal to $\Delta D = \Delta R/r$?

The formula $\Delta D = \Delta R/r$ is used to estimate the maximum change in the volume of demand deposits from a change in the volume of reserves. This maximum is not realized if the commercial banking system elects not to expand loans and investments as additional reserves are received. If the commercial banking system holds reserves in excess of rD, it is said to be holding excess reserves and is therefore not fully expanded.

12.19. Will an increase in the volume of demand deposits always result in an increase in the level of money income?

Demand deposit volume increases as the commercial banking system receives additional reserves and uses these additional reserves to make loans to and/or purchase securities from the household and business sectors. When an increase in demand deposits is associated with increased loans, we expect increased spending and therefore an increase in the level of money income. There is less certainty when commercial banks create demand deposits in acquiring reserves and purchasing securities from households and others. If the depositor of reserves or the seller of securities holds the newly created deposit balances, deposit creation has no impact upon spending and the level of money income. If these additional money balances are spent, the level of money income rises.

12.20. Suppose that $Md = 0.20\,Y$, $r = 0.25$, $\Delta D = \Delta R/r$, the central bank purchases \$20 of government securities from the household sector and the household sector deposits the proceeds in the commercial banking system. Derive the change in the money supply and the level of money income if (a) households spend their additional demand deposit balances and the commercial banking system expands deposit volume by making loans to the business sector or (b) households elect to hold their additional demand deposit balances, the commercial banking system expands deposit volume by purchases of securities and the sellers of securities to the commercial banks elect to hold these additional deposit balances.

In each situation $\Delta D = \Delta R/r = \$20/0.25 = \$80$.

(a) Assuming that the business sector has borrowed from the commercial banking system to buy goods and services, \$80 of the \$80 increase in the money supply results in increased spending. The change in the level of money income equals $\Delta Y = \Delta M/k = \$80/0.20 = \$400$.

(b) All of the additional demand deposit balances are held. There is no additional spending and therefore no change in the level of money income.

Chapter 13

The Keynesian Theory of the Demand for Money

13.1 MOTIVES FOR HOLDING MONEY

Keynes recognized three distinct motives for holding money: (1) a *transaction motive* where idle money is needed for the future exchange of goods and services, (2) a *precautionary motive* where money balances are held because of uncertainty about the future course of events and (3) a *speculative motive* where money is held if financial investments are expected to have a negative return over a stipulated period.

13.2 THE TRANSACTION DEMAND FOR MONEY

Households, firms and the government hold idle money balances if there is imperfect synchronization between money receipts and expenditures. The longer the lag between the receipt and expenditure of money income, the greater the money balances held.

EXAMPLE 1. Suppose that a household's annual disposable income is $7300. We shall assume that this household spends its *entire* income *uniformly* over the year so that consumption spending totals $20 a day.

Situation I: The household is paid daily. The household never holds more than $20 for transaction purposes.

Situation II: The household is paid $140 weekly. Since this household is spending $20 a day, transaction balances must be held for expenditures throughout the week. We shall assume that this household is paid Saturday mornings before stores are opened. Money balances at the end of each day are shown in Table 1.

Table 1

Money Balance ($) Held at the End of Each Day

Saturday	Sunday	Monday	Tuesday	Wednesday	Thursday	Friday
120	100	80	60	40	20	0

Situation III: The household is paid $280 every other week. Assuming that it is paid Saturday morning before stores open, its money balance at the end of each day is as given in Table 2.

Table 2

Money Balance ($) Held at the End of Each Day

Week	Saturday	Sunday	Monday	Tuesday	Wednesday	Thursday	Friday
1	260	240	220	200	180	160	140
2	120	100	80	60	40	20	0

When expenditures are uniform, the average money balance held for a pay period equals $\Sigma H/\gamma$, where H is the average money balance held each day and gamma γ is the number of days in a pay period.

EXAMPLE 2. When the average daily balances held from Saturday to Friday are $130, $110, $90, $70, $50, $30 and $10 respectively, the average money balance held for a *seven day pay period*, given a $140 income for the period, is

$$\frac{\Sigma H}{\gamma} = \frac{\$490}{7} = \$70$$

When the average daily balances held from Saturday of the first week to Friday of the second week equal $270, $250, $230, ..., $50, $30 and $10 respectively, the average money balance held for a *fourteen day pay period*, given a $280 income for the period, equals

$$\frac{\Sigma H}{\gamma} = \frac{\$1960}{14} = \$140$$

Given uniform spending and constant per diem income, the average money balance held per pay period doubles as the number of days in a pay period doubles.

Given uniform expenditures, a household's average holding of money balances for transactions is found by the formula

$$Mt = \frac{1}{2}\left(\frac{Y}{365}\right)\gamma$$

where Mt is the average holding of money balances for transactions, Y is the annual level of disposable income and γ is the number of days in a pay period.

EXAMPLE 3.   If a household's annual income is $7300 and its expenditures are uniform, its average holding of money balances for transactions when paid every 14 days is

$$Mt = \frac{1}{2}\left(\frac{Y}{365}\right)\gamma$$

$$= \frac{1}{2}\left(\frac{\$7300}{365}\right)14 = \$140 \qquad \text{the average holding of money balances for transactions}$$

When paid every 28 days,

$$Mt = \frac{1}{2}\left(\frac{Y}{365}\right)\gamma$$

$$= \frac{1}{2}\left(\frac{\$7300}{365}\right)28 = \$280 \qquad \text{the average holding of money balances for transactions}$$

EXAMPLE 4.   The relationship between Mt, Y and γ can also be presented graphically, as in Fig. 13-1. The number of days in a pay period γ is measured along the horizontal axis while Mt, the average holding of money for transactions, is measured along the vertical axis. OY_1 represents a $7300 level of disposable income while OY_2 represents a $14,600 level of disposable income.

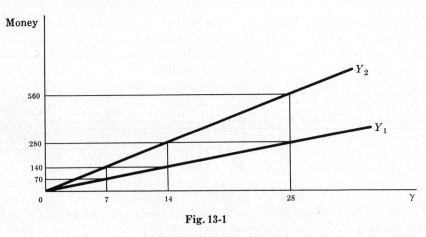

Fig. 13-1

Given uniform expenditures, we can see that the household's average holding of money balances increases as the number of days in a pay period increases. For example, a household's average holding of money is $70 if it has an annual disposable income of $7300 and is paid weekly. If this household is paid biweekly (every 14 days), its average holding of money is $140.

The average holding of money for transactions is also related to the level of disposable income. Given weekly receipt of income, a household's average holding of money for transactions increases from $70 to $140 if its annual level of disposable income increases from $7300 ($OY_1$) to $14,600 ($OY_2$).

In the short run, the number of days in a pay period is generally constant so that a household's average holding of money for transactions is solely a function of its level of disposable income. Thus, in Fig. 13-2(a), with $0\gamma_1$ representing the weekly receipt of income, the average holding of money for transactions increases from $70 to $105 to $140 as the income level increases from $7300 to $10,950 to $14,600.

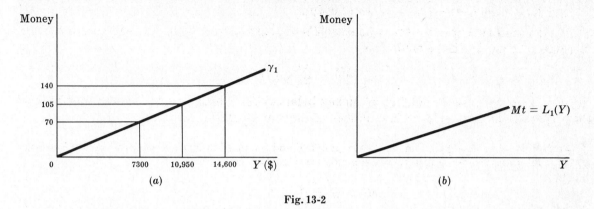

Fig. 13-2

Assuming that the holding of money for transactions by businesses and government, as well as households, is determined by similar forces, it follows that the aggregate transaction demand for money in the short run is a function of the level of aggregate income. Thus, $Mt = L_1(Y)$ in Fig. 13-1(b) is the aggregate transaction demand for money.

13.3 THE PRECAUTIONARY DEMAND FOR MONEY

Precautionary money balances are held because of *uncertainty* about the receipt and expenditure of future income. For instance, a household which consumes its entire income each month would be in a difficult position if receipt of income were temporarily delayed. Similarly, a household would be unable to take advantage of a "good buy" if idle money balances were unavailable.

The determinants of the precautionary demand for money are similar to those for the transaction demand. There is less need for precautionary balances if income is received more frequently.   As the level of income increases, precautionary balances also rise since consumption levels are increasing. However, unlike the transaction demand, the precautionary demand for money might increase as economic activity contracts. Households and firms might demand larger precautionary balances as they become uncertain about receiving funds. Similarly, precautionary balances might fall as economic activity recovers. Unless otherwise specified, we shall assume a stable precautionary demand for money schedule. Furthermore, we shall assume that receipt of income is constant in the short run so that income is the sole determinant of the precautionary demand for money. Thus, we can present both the transaction and precautionary demands for money as $Mt = L_1(Y)$.

13.4 THE SPECULATIVE DEMAND FOR MONEY

Classical economists recognized the transaction and precautionary motives as rational reasons for holding money. They considered it irrational, however, to hold money balances in excess of these needs since interest can be earned on idle money. Keynes introduced the speculative motive as an additional rational reason for holding money. He reasoned that, depending on the relationship between the current and future rates of interest, money might be a better store of value than bonds.

EXAMPLE 5.   Assume a bond contract that promises to pay interest of $60 each year for five years and the repayment of $1000 principal five years from now.   The current price of a bond is found by discounting the future cash returns from the bond at the current rate of interest.

Situation I: The current rate of interest is 0.06.   Since

$$P = \frac{S_1}{1+r} + \frac{S_2}{(1+r)^2} + \cdots + \frac{S_n}{(1+r)^n}$$

$$P = \frac{\$60}{1.06} + \frac{\$60}{(1.06)^2} + \frac{\$60}{(1.06)^3} + \frac{\$60}{(1.06)^4} + \frac{\$1060}{(1.06)^5}$$

From Table II (page 67), the present value of $60 a year for four years at 0.06 is

$$\$60(3.465) \;=\; \$207.90$$

From Table I (page 65), the present value of $1060 received five years from now at 0.06 is

$$\$1060(0.747) \;=\; \underline{791.82}$$

Current price of the bond is $999.72

Situation II: The current rate of interest is 0.08.   Thus,

$$P = \frac{\$60}{1.08} + \frac{\$60}{(1.08)^2} + \frac{\$60}{(1.08)^3} + \frac{\$60}{(1.08)^4} + \frac{\$1060}{(1.08)^5}$$

From Table II (page 67), the present value of $60 a year for four years at 0.08 is

$$\$60(3.312) \;=\; \$198.72$$

From Table I (page 65), the present value of $1060 received five years from now at 0.08 is

$$\$1060(0.681) \;=\; \underline{721.86}$$

Current price of the bond is $920.58

These two situations show that the price of a bond is inversely related to the current market rate of interest.

In holding bonds with a distant maturity, there is the possibility of a capital loss if interest rates rise and the bond is sold before maturity.   Thus, the effective yield from holding a bond includes not only the receipt of interest payments but the capital gain or loss on the bond at the time of sale as well.

EXAMPLE 6.   Assume that a six-year bond was purchased one year ago for $1000.   This bond promised to pay interest of $60 a year plus repayment of $1000 principal at maturity.   One year later, the rate of interest has risen to 0.08.   From Situation II in Example 5, we find that this bond, with only five more years to maturity, now sells for $920.58.

If the bond is sold now, the investor will receive a $60 interest payment after one year and lose $79.42 upon sale of the bond. Thus, the effective return from this bond is −$19.42 for an effective yield of −0.01942.

If an investor expects a capital loss upon sale of the bond to exceed interest payments, he will prefer to hold money since there is a negative yield from holding bonds.   If the expected capital loss equals the interest payments, he will be indifferent about holding money or bonds.   And if interest payments exceed the expected capital loss, he will hold bonds.   Money, then, is held as a hedge against negative returns from bonds.   The holding of money or bonds depends upon the relationship between the *current* rate of interest and the *expected* rate of interest for the period in which conversion will take place.   Individuals differ regarding the period for which funds will be invested.   They also differ with respect to expectations about the future rate of interest.   Thus, the demand for speculative money balances depends upon the current rate of interest and the diversity of opinion about the future rate of interest.

In Fig. 13-3(a), we construct a demand schedule for bonds. Up to interest rate i_1, there is no demand for bonds. Why? There is a general consensus that the future long-term rate of interest will be considerably higher than the current rate i_1 so that if bonds are purchased at or below i_1 negative returns will be earned. Between i_1 and i_2, opinions differ regarding the existence of negative returns. Thus, an increasing number of investors are willing to hold bonds as the current rate of interest rises above i_1. Above i_2, all investors prefer to hold bonds since there is a general belief that positive returns will be earned.

A demand schedule for money is presented in Fig. 13-3(b) using the information in Fig. 13-3(a). At a current rate of interest above i_2, investors believe that there is a positive return from holding bonds. Therefore, there is no demand for money. Between i_1 and i_2, opinions differ. However, as the current rate of interest approaches i_1, an increasing number of investors believe that negative returns will be earned from holding bonds and therefore larger speculative money balances are demanded. At interest rate i_1, all investors believe that there are negative returns from holding bonds and all prefer to hold money. As presented, the speculative demand for money L_2 is negatively related to the rate of interest.

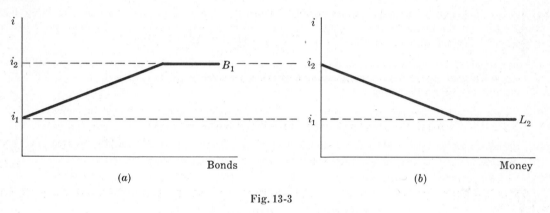

Fig. 13-3

Review Questions

1. Keynes held that money is used (a) to exchange goods and services, (b) to meet unexpected contingencies, (c) to avoid a negative effective yield from long-term bonds or (d) all of the above.

2. The average holding of money for transactions

   (a) increases if the lag between the receipt and expenditure of income is shortened,

   (b) increases if the lag between the receipt and expenditure of income is lengthened,

   (c) decreases if the lag between the receipt and expenditure of income is lengthened or

   (d) increases if income payments are received more frequently.

3. If expenditures are uniform, the average holding of money for transactions is (a) $100 if $200 is received weekly, (b) $100 if $400 is received biweekly, (c) $100 if $800 is received monthly or (d) none of the above.

4. A household's average holding of money for transactions (a) increases as the number of days in a pay period increases, (b) decreases as the number of days in a pay period increases, (c) decreases as the level of disposable income increases or (d) increases as the level of disposable income decreases.

5. Which of the following statements is *incorrect*?

   (a) A household's average holding of money for transactions increases as the level of disposable income increases.

   (b) A household's average holding of money for transactions decreases if instead of uniform spending, expenditures are concentrated in the first part of the pay period.

   (c) A household's average holding of money for transactions is unrelated to its pattern of expenditure.

   (d) A household's average holding of money for transactions increases as the number of days in a pay period increases.

6. Which of the following statements is *incorrect*?

   (a) The precautionary demand for money is unrelated to the level of income.

   (b) There is a precautionary demand for money because of uncertainty about the receipt of future income.

   (c) The quantity of money held for precautionary needs falls as households are paid more frequently.

   (d) There is a precautionary demand for money to meet unexpected expenditures.

7. According to Keynes, there is a speculative demand for money because (a) people like to speculate in the stock market, (b) there is considerable risk in holding money, (c) bonds may yield less than money or (d) people may not wish to buy securities.

8. Investors prefer holding money rather than bonds if they expect (a) a capital loss from holding a bond, (b) the rate of interest to fall, (c) the rate of interest to rise or (d) the capital loss from a bond to exceed its interest return.

9. A horizontal speculative demand for money at interest rate i_0 indicates that there is (a) no speculative demand for money, (b) a small but limited demand for money, (c) an unlimited demand for money or (d) an unlimited demand for bonds.

10. Which situation best reflects an investor's preference to hold money rather than bonds?

   (a) An interest return of $50 and a capital gain of $50 in holding a bond for one year.

   (b) An interest return of $50 and a capital loss of $50 in holding a bond for one year.

   (c) An interest return of $50 and a capital loss of $40 in holding a bond for one year.

   (d) An interest return of $50 and a capital loss of $60 in holding a bond for one year.

Answers to Review Questions

1. (d) Review Section 13.1.   5. (c) Review Section 13.2.   8. (d) See Example 6.

2. (b) Review Section 13.2.   6. (a) Review Section 13.3.   9. (c) See Fig. 13-3.

3. (a) See Example 3 and Problem 13.4.   7. (c) Review Section 13.4.   10. (d) See Example 6.

4. (a) See Example 3.

Solved Problems

13.1. What is the average money balance held over a pay period for situations (a), (b) and (c) in Table 3 if weekly income is $140?

Table 3

Average Daily Money Balances Held			
	(a)	(b)	(c)
Monday	$130	$140	$100
Tuesday	110	130	80
Wednesday	90	120	60
Thursday	70	110	30
Friday	50	40	10
Saturday	30	20	0
Sunday	10	0	0
Sum	$490	$560	$280

The average holding of money over a pay period is the sum of the average daily holdings divided by the number of days in the pay period. In situation (a), the average holding of money is $70 ($490/7). This represents uniform expenditure of weekly income. In situation (b), spending is concentrated in the latter part of the week and the average holding of money is $80. (Note that no expenditure is made on Monday and the entire weekly income is held throughout this day.) In situation (c), spending is concentrated in the earlier part of the week. The average holding of money is $40.

13.2. Why is there a transaction demand for money?

As shown in Problem 13.1, idle money balances are held to budget expenditures over a given period. The magnitude of the average money balance held depends upon the timing of expenditures, the size of the income level and the length of the pay period.

13.3. (a) What is a household's average holding of money for transactions if it receives $210 weekly and spends this entire sum uniformly over the period? (b) What happens to the average holding of money if spending is not uniform?

(a) When spending is uniform over the period, the average holding of money equals one-half the sum received for the period. Thus, the average holding of money for the week is $210/2 = $105 when the entire sum is allocated evenly over the period.

(b) If a majority of expenditures occurs early in the week, the average holding of money is less than $105. If a majority of expenditures occurs later in the week, the average holding of money exceeds $105.

13.4. When spending is uniform, $Mt = \frac{1}{2}(Y/365)\gamma$ can be used for finding the average holding of money for transactions. How does this formula relate to the simpler one used in Problem 13.3?

$(Y/365)\gamma$ measures the receipt of income for a pay period composed of γ days. Thus if a household has an annual level of disposable income of $10,950, it is receiving $10,950/365, or $30 a day or 30\gamma$ ($210) a week.

13.5. For the five situations in Table 4, calculate (a) the daily level of income, (b) the pay period level of income and (c) the average holding of money for transactions if spending is uniform.

Table 4

Situation	Y ($)	γ (days)
A	10,950	7
B	10,950	14
C	10,950	28
D	16,425	7
E	21,900	7

(a) The daily level of income equals $Y/365$. The daily level of income is $30 in A, B and C, $45 in D and $60 in E.

(b) The level of income for a pay period equals $(Y/365)\gamma$. The pay period income for A is $210, B is $420, C is $840, D is $315 and E is $420.

(c) The average holding of money for transactions equals $\frac{1}{2}(Y/365)\gamma$. The average holding of money for A is $105, B is $210, C is $420, D is $157.50 and E is $210.

13.6. Explain how Mt, Y and γ are related in Problem 13.5.

In situations A, B and C, Y is held constant and the relative change in Mt is equal to the relative change in γ (i.e., Mt increases from $105 to $210 to $420 as γ increases from 7 to 14 to 28 days). In situations A, D and E, γ is held constant. The relative increase in Mt is now equal to the relative increase in Y. Given uniform expenditures, then, the relative change in the average holding of money is equal to the relative change in the number of days in a pay period and/or the level of income.

13.7. What happens to a household's average holding of money for transactions if (*a*) it is paid weekly rather than biweekly, (*b*) its disposable income increases 10% or (*c*) it begins using credit cards?

(*a*) Mt is cut in half.

(*b*) Mt increases 10%.

(*c*) The disbursement of money is no longer uniform. There is less need to hold idle money for transactions and the average quantity of money held for transactions falls.

13.8. Mt, Y and γ are plotted in Fig. 13-4 below. If expenditures are uniform, find the annual level of disposable income for (*a*) Y_1 and (*b*) Y_2.

(*a*)
$$Y = \frac{2Mt(365)}{\gamma}$$

$$Y_1 = \$10,950$$

(*b*)
$$Y_2 = \$21,900$$

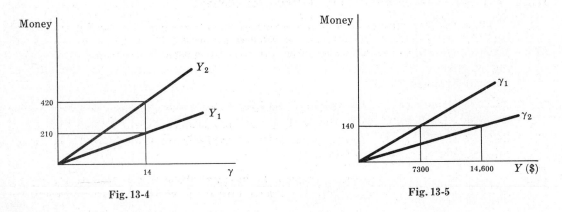

Fig. 13-4   Fig. 13-5

13.9. Mt, Y and γ are plotted in Fig. 13-5 above. If expenditures are uniform, find the number of days in the pay period for (*a*) γ_1 and (*b*) γ_2.

(*a*)
$$\gamma = 2Mt\left(\frac{365}{Y}\right)$$

$$\gamma_1 = 14 \text{ days}$$

(*b*)
$$\gamma_2 = 7 \text{ days}$$

13.10. What assumptions are made in presenting the aggregate transaction demand for money as L_1 in Fig. 13-6 (page 115)?

It is assumed here that expenditure patterns and the number of days in a pay period are both constant.

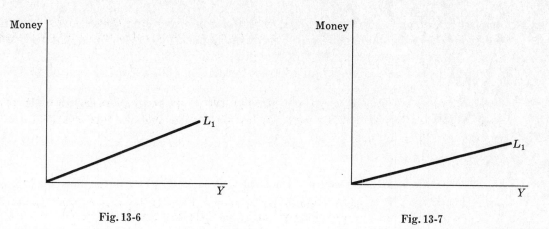

Fig. 13-6   Fig. 13-7

13.11. With reference to Fig. 13-7 above, what happens to the aggregate transaction demand for money if (1) income is paid more frequently and (2) the interval between receipt and disbursement of income narrows?

In both situations there is a reduction in the average money balance held. The L_1 function pivots toward the income axis since there is a smaller demand for money at each level of income.

13.12. Why is there a precautionary demand for money?

Precautionary money balances are needed if income receipts and expenditure patterns are uncertain. For instance, "extra" money balances are needed if income is not received on time. There is also a need for additional money balances for unplanned spending.

13.13. Explain what happens to the level of precautionary money balances when (a) income payments are made more frequently, (b) businessmen become uncertain about the level of spending or (c) economic activity expands, making households more optimistic about the receipt of income.

If a future event is less certain, there is an increased likelihood that receipts and expenditures will not coincide and therefore there is a greater need for precautionary money balances.

(a) As income payments are made more frequently, there is less likelihood that the payment of income will be delayed for a given number of days. Thus, the precautionary demand for money falls.

(b) Increased uncertainty about spending raises the probability that sales and therefore the receipt of income will be delayed. Businesses will prefer to hold larger precautionary money balances.

(c) Greater certainty about receiving income reduces the need for precautionary money balances.

13.14. Why is there a speculative demand for money?

Bonds promise to pay the investor an interest return and repayment of capital at a stipulated future date. If a bondholder elects to sell a bond prior to its maturity date and interest rates are higher than when he purchased the bond, there is a capital loss since the bond is sold for less than its purchase price. Investors prefer to hold money rather than bonds when they expect the capital loss to exceed the interest return. The speculative demand for money develops during periods of rising interest rates when money may prove to be a better store of value than long-term bonds. (See Section 13.4.)

13.15. Assume that funds are going to be invested for a one-year period only. Would an investor prefer to hold money or long-term bonds if he had the following expectations: (a) an interest return of $60, a capital gain of $30, (b) an interest return of $60, a capital loss of $30 and (c) an interest return of $60, a capital loss of $70?

(a) The investor would hold bonds. An investor receives no return from money while receiving $90 from the bond investment.

(b) The investor would hold bonds. An investor receives no return from money while receiving $30 from the bond investment.

(c) The investor would hold money. The bond returns −$40, which is less than the zero return from money.

13.16. Is it possible that some investors will prefer to hold money while others will prefer to hold bonds?

Investors' preferences for bonds or money depend upon their expectations about the effective yield from holding bonds. For instance, investor A might believe that the future rate of interest will be the same as the current rate of interest and thereby prefer holding bonds because of the positive effective yield in doing so. Investor B, however, might believe that the future rate of interest will be substantially above the current rate of interest. He will prefer holding money if he expects a negative effective yield from holding bonds.

13.17. Explain the speculative demand for money schedule in Fig. 13-8 below.

If the current rate of interest declines from i_3 to i_2, a larger number of investors prefer to hold money given their expectation of the future rate of interest. If the current rate of interest is i_1, there is a consensus among investors that, at this rate, bonds provide a negative effective yield.

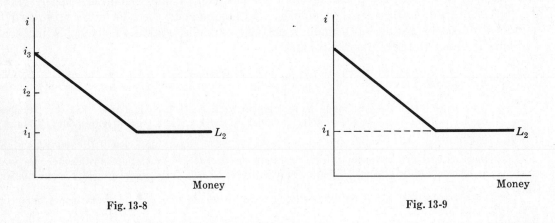

Fig. 13-8   Fig. 13-9

13.18. Assume that in Fig. 13-9 above i_1 is the current rate of interest and that the central bank buys government bonds from households in exchange for paper currency. What is the effect of this increase in the supply of money?

Holders of the public debt welcome these central bank purchases because they prefer to hold money. Given such preferences, the increased money balances are held and there is no change in spending.

13.19. If interest rate i_1 (Fig. 13-9) persists for an extended period of time, will speculative demand schedule L_2 be stable?

   If a rate of interest persists for an extended period of time, it is likely to affect investors' expectations about the future rate of interest and thereby cause shifts in the speculative demand for money schedule.

13.20. What effect will central bank actions of minimizing fluctuations in the rate of interest have upon the speculative demand for money?

   If there are minimal fluctuations in the rate of interest as a result of central bank actions, bonds will probably have an effective yield greater than zero. Thus, there would most likely be no speculative demand for money.

Chapter 14

Equilibrium in the Money Markets

14.1 THE COMBINED DEMAND FOR MONEY

The transaction, precautionary, and speculative demands for money can be combined into a single demand function as follows:

Transaction-precautionary demand: $\qquad Mt = L_1(Y)$

Speculative demand: $\qquad Ma = L_2(i)$

Combined demand for money: $\qquad Md = Mt + Ma$

Thus, $\qquad Md = L(Y, i)$

EXAMPLE 1. *Given*: linear functions Mt and Ma in Figs. 14-1(a) and (b). The combined demand for money Md equals $Ma + Mt$. The quantity of money demanded for transaction-precautionary needs is m_1 at income level Y_1. If income is assumed constant at Y_1, the combined demand for money schedule equals $Ma + m_1$ in Fig. 14-1(c).

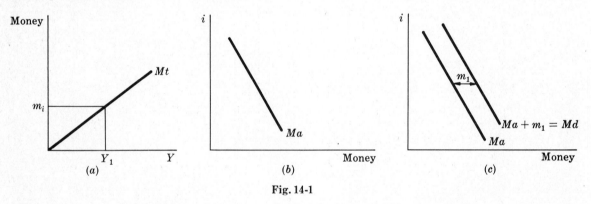

Fig. 14-1

EXAMPLE 2. The quantity of money demanded is m_1 at income level Y_1, m_2 at income level Y_2 and m_3 at income level Y_3. The combined demand for money schedule in Fig. 14-2(c) is $Ma + m_1$ for income level Y_1, $Ma + m_2$ for income level Y_2 and $Ma + m_3$ for income level Y_3. Thus, there is a demand for money schedule for each level of income.

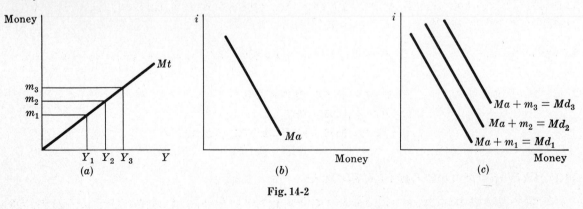

Fig. 14-2

14.2 THE *LM* SCHEDULE

Equilibrium in the monetary sector occurs where the supply of money Ms equals the demand for money Md. In Fig. 14-3, Md_1 is the demand for money when the level of income is Y_1. At higher income level Y_2, Md_2 is the applicable schedule. Thus, equilibrium between the supply of and demand for money occurs at either an i_1 or i_2 rate of interest, depending upon the level of income.

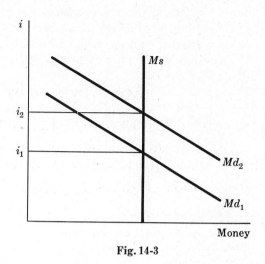

Fig. 14-3

Given a supply of money, combinations of the rate of interest and the level of income exist where there is equilibrium between the supply of and demand for money. Those combinations of i and Y consistent with equilibrium in the money markets comprise the *LM* schedule.

EXAMPLE 3. Suppose that the money supply is constant at Ms_0 in Fig. 14-4(a). As the demand for money increases because of higher income levels, equilibrium between the supply of and demand for money occurs at i_1 when income is Y_1, i_2 when income is Y_2, and i_3 when income is Y_3. The combinations of i and Y consistent with equilibrium in the money markets is labeled LM in Fig. 14-4(b).

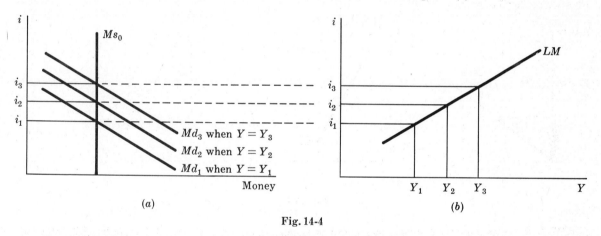

Fig. 14-4

Given specified equations for the transaction-precautionary and speculative demands for money and a fixed quantity of money, we are able to derive an equation for the *LM* schedule. From this equation, we can find the rates of interest that are consistent with different levels of income.

EXAMPLE 4. Given $Ms = \$200$, $Mt = 0.25\,Y$ and $Ma = \$50 - 200i$, monetary equilibrium occurs where

$$Ms = Md$$
$$\$200 = 0.25\,Y + \$50 - 200i$$
$$0.25\,Y = \$150 + 200i$$
$$Y = \$600 + 800i \quad \text{the } LM \text{ equation}$$

14.3 SHIFTS IN THE *LM* SCHEDULE

A schedule of monetary equilibrium exists given a supply of money and the combined money demand functions. If either supply or demand changes, there is a shift in the *LM* schedule. In general, the *LM* schedule shifts (1) to the right if there is an increase in the quantity of money or a decrease in the demand for money and (2) to the left if the money supply decreases or there is an increase in the demand for money. The shift in the *LM* schedule from a change in the supply of money is equal to the money multiplier $1/k$ times the change in the supply of money ΔM.

EXAMPLE 5. An increase in the quantity of money in Fig. 14-5 causes a rightward shift in the *LM* schedule. As a result of the increased quantity of money, equilibrium between the supply of and demand for money at income level Y_0 occurs at rate of interest i_1 rather than i_0.

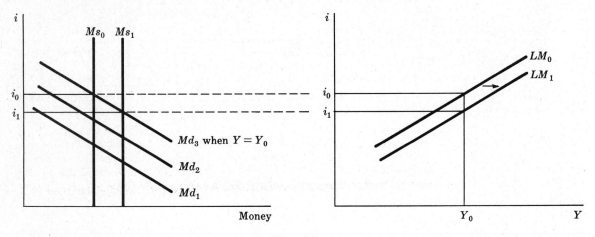

Fig. 14-5

EXAMPLE 6. Assume that the *LM* equation is $Y = \$600 + 800i$, given $Ms = \$200$, $Ma = \$50 - 200i$ and $Mt = 0.25\,Y$.

Situation I: Suppose that the money supply increases from \$200 to \$220. The *LM* equation is

$$Y = \$600 + 800i + \Delta M(1/k)$$

which is equal to

$$Y = \$680 + 800i$$

Situation II: Suppose that the money supply increases from \$220 to \$240. The *LM* equation is

$$Y = \$680 + 800i + \Delta M(1/k)$$

which is equal to

$$Y = \$760 + 800i$$

Note that the constant of the *LM* equation increases \$80 for each \$20 increase in the money supply. The \$80 rightward shift of the *LM* schedule equals $\Delta M(1/k)$.

14.4 THE SHAPE OF THE *LM* SCHEDULE

As theorized in Section 13.4, the speculative demand for money exists within a band of interest rates. Given expectations about the future rate of interest, investors prefer to hold bonds rather than money if the current rate of interest is equal to or greater than i_2 in Fig. 14-6(*a*). Thus, there is no speculative demand for money if the current rate of interest is equal to or greater than i_2. If the current rate of interest is i_1, investors prefer to hold money rather than bonds and the speculative demand for money becomes horizontal. Thus, the *LM* schedule in Fig. 14-6(*b*) is positively sloped if the current rate of interest is between i_1 and i_2, horizontal at interest rate i_1 and vertical when the current rate of interest is equal to or greater than i_2.

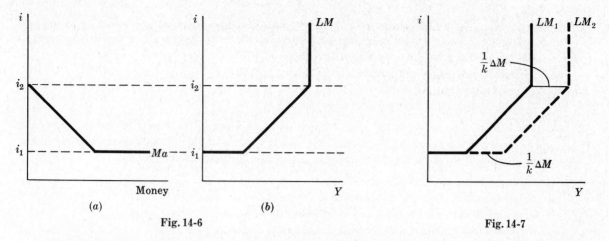

Fig. 14-6

Fig. 14-7

Changes in the supply of money do not change the horizontal and vertical boundaries of the *LM* schedule. Money supply increases (Fig. 14-7) elongate the horizontal portion and shift the vertical region of the *LM* schedule by $\Delta M(1/k)$. *There must be a change in the speculative demand for money to change the horizontal and vertical boundaries.*

Review Questions

1. The demand for money is a family of schedules

   (a) because the influence of the rate of interest upon the demand for money is constantly changing,
   (b) because the influence of the level of income upon the demand for money is constantly changing,
   (c) when the demand for money is presented on a three-dimensional graph   or
   (d) when the demand for money is presented on a two-dimensional graph.

2. The demand for money is

   (a) positively related to the level of income and negatively related to the rate of interest,
   (b) negatively related to the level of income and the rate of interest,
   (c) positively related to the rate of interest and the level of income   or
   (d) negatively related to the level of income and positively related to the rate of interest.

3. Suppose that the money supply is constant and the demand for money is a function of income and the rate of interest. If the level of income increases, there is

   (a) an increase in the quantity of money demanded and an increase in the rate of interest,
   (b) an increase in the quantity of money demanded and a decrease in the rate of interest,
   (c) a decrease in the quantity of money demanded and a decrease in the rate of interest   or
   (d) a decrease in the quantity of money demanded and an increase in the rate of interest.

4. The *LM* schedule is a schedule of monetary equilibrium where (a) the supply of money equals the demand for goods, (b) the supply of money equals the demand for money, (c) the demand for money equals the demand for goods or (d) the transaction-precautionary demand for money equals the speculative demand for money.

5. Given $Ms = \$200$, $Ma = \$50 - 400i$ and $Mt = 0.20\,Y$, the *LM* equation is (a) $Y = \$1000 + 2000i$, (b) $Y = \$750 + 2000i$, (c) $Y = \$750 - 2000i$ or   (d) $Y = \$1000 - 2000i$.

6. When the *LM* equation is $Y = \$750 + 2000i$, there is equilibrium between the supply of and the demand for money if

   (a) the rate of interest is 0.10 and the level of income is $750,
   (b) the rate of interest is 0.10 and the level of income is $800,
   (c) the rate of interest is 0.10 and the level of income is $950   or
   (d) the rate of interest is 0.10 and the level of income is $900.

7. If the *LM* equation is $Y = \$600 + 800i$, which of the following combinations of the rate of interest and the level of income *do not* represent equilibrium between the supply of and demand for money?
    (*a*) The rate of interest is 0.10 and the level of income is $680.
    (*b*) The rate of interest is 0.08 and the level of income is $660.
    (*c*) The rate of interest is 0.06 and the level of income is $648.
    (*d*) The rate of interest is 0.05 and the level of income is $640.

8. The *LM* schedule shifts (*a*) to the right if there is an increase in the supply of money, (*b*) to the right if there is an increase in the demand for money, (*c*) to the left if there is an increase in the supply of money or (*d*) to the left if there is a decrease in the demand for money.

9. When $Mt = 0.25\,Y$, the *LM* schedule shifts
    (*a*) rightward $20 if there is a $20 increase in the supply of money,
    (*b*) leftward $20 if there is a $20 increase in the supply of money,
    (*c*) rightward $20 if there is a $5 increase in the supply of money   or
    (*d*) leftward $20 if there is a $5 increase in the supply of money.

10. Which of the following statements is *correct*?
    (*a*) The *LM* schedule is vertical if there is no speculative demand for money.
    (*b*) The *LM* schedule is horizontal if there is no speculative demand for money.
    (*c*) Money supply changes have no effect upon the *LM* schedule if the *LM* schedule is positively sloped.
    (*d*) Money supply changes have no effect upon the *LM* schedule if the *LM* schedule is vertical.

Answers to Review Questions

1. (*d*) See Example 1.
2. (*a*) Review Section 14.1.
3. (*a*) Review Section 14.2.
4. (*b*) See Example 3.
5. (*b*) Review Section 14.2.

6. (*c*) Review Section 14.2.
7. (*b*) Review Section 14.2.
8. (*a*) Review Section 14.3.
9. (*c*) See Example 4.
10. (*a*) Review Section 14.4.

Solved Problems

14.1. From the schedules for the transaction-precautionary and speculative demand for money given in Table 1, find the quantity of money demanded when the rate of interest is 0.08 and the level of income equals $600.

Table 1

Transaction-Precautionary Schedule		Speculative Schedule	
Y ($)	M ($)	i	M ($)
500	100	0.10	35
550	110	0.08	50
600	120	0.06	75
650	130	0.04	115

The quantity of money demanded is

$$Md = Mt + Ma$$
$$Md = \$120 + \$50$$
$$Md = \$170$$

14.2. Using the demand for money schedules in Table 1, find the quantity of money demanded when (a) the rate of interest is 0.06 and the income level equals \$500, (b) the rate of interest is 0.06 and the income level equals \$550, (c) the rate of interest is 0.04 and the income level equals \$500 and (d) the rate of interest is 0.04 and the income level equals \$600.

Since $Md = Mt + Ma$,

(a) $Md = \$100 + \$75 = \$175$,

(b) $Md = \$110 + \$75 = \$185$,

(c) $Md = \$100 + \$115 = \$215$ and

(d) $Md = \$120 + \$115 = \$235$.

14.3. The transaction demand for money is presented by $Mt = 0.20\,Y$. The speculative demand for money is presented by $Ma = \$100 - 500i$. Find an equation for the demand for money.

Since $Md = Mt + Ma$, the equation in this case is

$$Md = 0.20\,Y + \$100 - 500i$$

14.4. Use the equation for the demand for money in Problem 14.3 to find the quantity of money demanded when (a) the rate of interest is 0.10 and the level of income equals \$500 and (b) the rate of interest is 0.10 and the level of income equals \$600.

(a)
$$Md = 0.20(\$500) + \$100 - 500(0.10)$$
$$Md = \$150$$

(b)
$$Md = 0.20(\$600) + \$100 - 500(0.10)$$
$$Md = \$170$$

14.5. What happens to the quantity of money demanded as the level of income increases?

Problem 14.4 shows that a rising income level increases the quantity of money demanded for transaction-precautionary purposes.

14.6. If the money supply equals \$250, the transaction-precautionary demand for money is $0.20\,Y$ and the speculative demand for money is $\$150 - 500i$, what quantity of money is available for speculative balances if the income level equals (a) \$700? (b) \$800? (c) \$900?

(a) The quantity of money available for speculative balances is $Ma = Ms - Mt$. Therefore, $Ma = \$250 - \$140 = \$110$.

(b) $Ma = \$250 - \$160 = \$90$.

(c) $Ma = \$250 - \$180 = \$70$.

14.7. Use the situations in Problem 14.6 to find the rate of interest where there is equilibrium between the supply of money for speculative balances and the speculative demand for money.

Problem 14.6 established the quantity of money available for speculative balances given a level of income and a quantity of money. The equilibrium rate of interest is found by equating the quantity of money available for speculative balances with the speculative demand for money ($150 − 500i).

(a)
$$\$110 = \$150 - 500i$$
$$\$40 = 500i$$
$$0.08 = i$$

(b)
$$\$90 = \$150 - 500i$$
$$\$60 = 500i$$
$$0.12 = i$$

(c)
$$\$70 = \$150 - 500i$$
$$\$80 = 500i$$
$$0.16 = i$$

14.8. The speculative demand for money is presented in quadrant 1 of Fig. 14.8. A constant money supply is plotted in quadrant 2. (This $200 money supply must be used in its entirety for either speculative or transaction-precautionary balances.) The transaction-precautionary demand for money is presented in quadrant 3. In quadrant 4 derive a schedule of equilibrium between the demand for and supply of money.

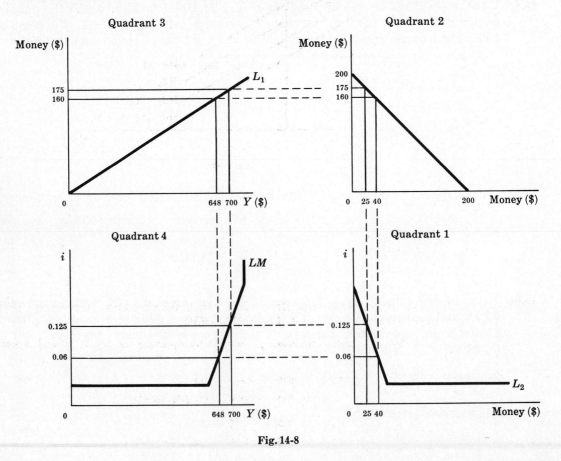

Fig. 14-8

There are various combinations of rates of interest and levels of income where the $200 supply of money is used for either speculative or transaction-precautionary purposes. For example, the entire $200 money supply is demanded if the rate of interest is 0.06 and the level of income is $640 since at these levels $Ma = \$40$ and $Mt = \$160$. The entire $200 money supply is also demanded if the level of income is $700 and the rate of interest is 0.125. By continuous choosing of the level of income, we derive in quadrant 4 a schedule of monetary equilibrium where the demand for money equals the supply of money.

14.9. In monetary equilibrium, why is there a positive relationship between the level of income and the rate of interest?

As the level of income increases, the transaction-precautionary demand for money increases, leaving smaller quantities of money for speculative balances. Equilibrium between a decreasing supply of and a given demand for speculative balances must occur at a higher rate of interest. Thus, there is a positive combination of the level of income and the rate of interest where the demand for money equals a given supply of money.

14.10. Using the schedules in Fig. 14-9, find the rate of interest if the money supply is M_1 and the level of income is (a) Y_1, (b) Y_2 and (c) Y_3.

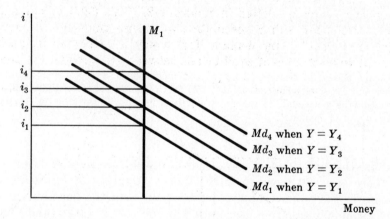

Fig. 14-9

(a) The rate of interest is i_1.

(b) The rate of interest is i_2.

(c) The rate of interest is i_3.

14.11. Derive the LM equation if (a) $Ms = \$200$, $Mt = 0.25\,Y$ and $Ma = \$40 - 500i$ or (b) $Ms = \$180$, $Mt = 0.20\,Y$ and $Ma = \$50 - 200i$.

An equation for monetary equilibrium is derived by equating the supply of and demand for money (i.e., $Ms = Mt + Ma$).

(a)
$$\$200 = 0.25\,Y + \$40 - 500i$$
$$Y = \$640 + 2000i \qquad \text{the } LM \text{ equation}$$

(b)
$$\$180 = 0.20\,Y + \$50 - 200i$$
$$Y = \$650 + 1000i \qquad \text{the } LM \text{ equation}$$

14.12. With reference to Fig. 14-10, which of the following equations represents (*a*) LM_1? (*b*) LM_2?

$$\$160 = 0.25\,Y - 500i \qquad (1)$$
$$\$170 = 0.25\,Y - 500i \qquad (2)$$
$$\$180 = 0.25\,Y - 500i \qquad (3)$$
$$\$190 = 0.25\,Y - 500i \qquad (4)$$

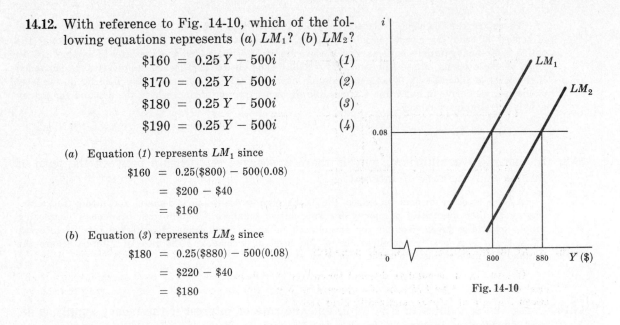

Fig. 14-10

(*a*) Equation (*1*) represents LM_1 since

$$\$160 = 0.25(\$800) - 500(0.08)$$
$$= \$200 - \$40$$
$$= \$160$$

(*b*) Equation (*3*) represents LM_2 since

$$\$180 = 0.25(\$880) - 500(0.08)$$
$$= \$220 - \$40$$
$$= \$180$$

14.13. The LM_1 and LM_2 schedules in Problem 14.12 differ only with respect to the constant of the equation. We shall assume that this represents a difference in the money supply. Thus, schedule (*3*) has a money supply that is \$20 greater than schedule (*1*). Why does monetary equilibrium for a given 0.08 rate of interest differ by \$80 when the money supply changes by only \$20?

It was shown in Section 12.1 that the income level representing equilibrium in the supply of and demand for money changes by $\Delta M(1/k)$ for a given change in the supply of money. Since the LM schedule is a schedule of monetary equilibrium, it will shift by $\Delta M(1/k)$ and not by the change in the supply of money.

14.14. Establish the direction and magnitude of the shift in the LM schedule when (*a*) $k = 0.20$ and there is a \$20 increase in the money supply, (*b*) $k = 0.50$ and there is a \$10 decrease in the money supply, (*c*) $k = 0.20$ and the constant in the speculative demand for money equation decreases \$20 or (*d*) $k = 0.20$ and there is a \$10 increase in the money supply as the constant in the speculative demand for money equation decreases \$20.

(*a*) The LM schedule shifts rightward \$100 since \$20(1/0.20) equals \$100.

(*b*) The LM schedule shifts leftward \$20 since \$10(1/0.50) equals \$20.

(*c*) There is an autonomous decrease in the demand for money. The rightward shift of the LM schedule equals $\Delta D(1/k)$, where D represents the constant of the speculative demand equation. The shift to the right equals \$100.

(*d*) The LM schedule shifts rightward \$150.

14.15. What happens to the LM schedule if there is a decrease in the transaction-precautionary demand for money?

Figure 14-11 shows that a decrease in the transaction-precautionary demand for money from $Mt = 0.50\,Y$ to $Mt = 0.25\,Y$ shifts the LM schedule rightward from LM_1 to LM_2. We see that the shift at a 0.10 rate of interest is \$420 while it is \$370 at a 0.05 rate of interest. Thus, a decrease in the transaction-precautionary demand for money not only shifts the LM schedule rightward but also decreases its slope.

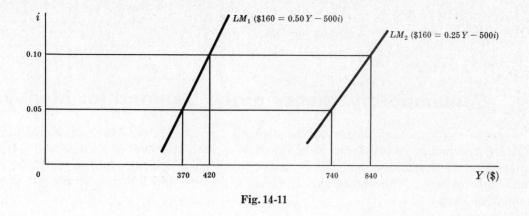

Fig. 14-11

14.16. What is the shape of the *LM* schedule if there is no speculative demand for money?

If there is no speculative demand for money, the demand for money is a function only of the level of income. The *LM* schedule appears as a vertical line when presented as a relationship between the rate of interest and the level of income.

Chapter 15

Contemporary Theory of the Demand for Money

In the contemporary theory of the demand for money, the transaction-precautionary demand for money is presented as a function of both the level of income and the rate of interest. The speculative demand is restructured as a special topic in portfolio theory. Although revised, the theory retains the level of income and the rate of interest as the explanatory variables.

15.1 THE TRANSACTION DEMAND FOR MONEY

There is no return from money. Therefore, owners of idle transaction balances might find it profitable to invest these balances in short-term financial assets, provided that money is recovered in time to allow for planned expenditures. If expenditures are uniform and transaction balances are held in part in short-term bonds, the average quantity of money held for transactions becomes

$$Mt = \frac{1}{2n}\left(\frac{Y}{365}\right)\gamma$$

where Y is the annual level of income, γ is the number of days in a pay period, and n is the total number of bond transactions (assuming one purchase and $n-1$ sales).

EXAMPLE 1. Assuming uniform expenditures and all transaction balances held as money, the average quantity of *money* held for transactions was given in Section 13.2 as

$$Mt = \frac{1}{2}\left(\frac{Y}{365}\right)\gamma$$

Assuming uniform expenditures and all transaction balances invested in short-term bonds, the average quantity of *bonds Bd* held is

$$Bd = \frac{n-1}{2n}\left(\frac{Y}{365}\right)\gamma$$

When expenditures are uniform and transaction balances are held in short-term bonds and money, the average quantity of money held is then

$$Mt = \frac{1}{2}\left(\frac{Y}{365}\right)\gamma - \frac{n-1}{2n}\left(\frac{Y}{365}\right)\gamma$$

which reduces to

$$Mt = \frac{1}{2n}\left(\frac{Y}{365}\right)\gamma$$

Assuming profit maximization, the optimum number of bond transactions occurs where total revenues less total costs are greatest. Suppose that curves C and R in Fig. 15-1 represent the total cost and total revenue associated with the total number of bond transactions. The total cost C of transactions in short-term securities is the product of the fixed cost a per transaction times the number n of transactions, or $C = an$. The total revenue from short-term securities is given by

$$R = i\left(\frac{n-1}{2n}\right)\left(\frac{Y}{365}\right)\gamma$$

where i is the interest earned in each period.   The optimum number of transactions occurs at n_1 where N, the net revenue curve, is at its maximum (i.e., where the difference between total revenue and total cost is greatest).   Algebraically (see Problem 15.5 for derivation), the optimum number of bond transactions occurs where

$$n = \sqrt{\frac{i}{2a}\left(\frac{Y}{365}\right)\gamma}$$

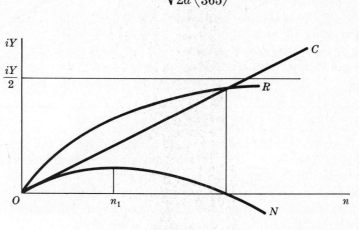

Fig. 15-1

Changes in the interest earned each period, the income received annually, the number of days in a pay period, and the fixed cost per transaction alter the optimum number of bond transactions and the average quantity of money held for transactions.   The optimum number of bond transactions increases when i, Y and/or γ increase and a falls.   The average quantity of money held increases when a, Y and/or γ increase and i falls.

EXAMPLE 2.   Variations in the transaction demand for money are described in the four situations below.

Situation I: If the fixed cost per transaction increases, *ceteris paribus*, the cost curve in Fig. 15-1 pivots to the left and there is a decrease in the optimum number of transactions.   Given no change in the level of income and the number of days in a pay period, a decrease in the number of transactions results in a larger quantity of transaction balances held in the form of money.   (See Problem 15.3.) Thus, the transaction demand for money is positively related to the fixed cost per transaction.

Situation II: If the rate of interest earned each period increases, *ceteris paribus*, the revenue curve in Fig. 15-1 moves upward and there is an increase in the optimum number of bond transactions. Given no change in the level of income and the number of days in a pay period, an increase in the number of bond transactions results in a smaller quantity of transaction balances held in the form of money.   (See Problem 15.3.)   Thus, the transaction demand for money is negatively related to the rate of interest.

Situation III: If the level of income received annually increases, *ceteris paribus*, the revenue curve in Fig. 15-1 moves upward and there is an increase in the optimum number of bond transactions.   The effect that this has upon the quantity of money demanded depends upon the relative change in n and Y. If the relative increase in the optimum number of bond transactions is equal to the relative increase in income, there is no change in the quantity of money demanded as income expands.   (See Problem 15.8.)   If the relative increase in the optimum number of bond transactions is less than the relative increase in income, there is an increase in the quantity of money demanded as income expands.   (See Problem 15.9.)   From $n = \sqrt{(i/2a)(Y/365)\gamma}$ (the formula for the optimum number of bond transactions), we find that the relative increase in n cannot exceed one-half the relative increase in the level of income.   Therefore, the quantity of money held for transaction purposes is positively related to the level of income.

Situation IV: If there is a decrease in the number of days in a pay period, *ceteris paribus*, the revenue curve in Fig. 15-1 moves downward and there is a decrease in the optimum number of bond transactions.   The effect of a change in γ, like that of a change in income, depends upon the relative change in γ and n.   Since the relative change in n is always less than the relative change in γ, money held for transaction balances decreases as the number of days in a pay period falls. That is, the transaction demand for money is positively related to the number of days in a pay period.

The number of days in a pay period and the fixed cost per transaction change only sporadically. Therefore, the transaction demand for money in the short run is presented as a function of the rate of interest and the level of income. In Fig. 15-2, the transaction demand for money appears as a family of curves where Mt_1, Mt_2 and Mt_3 represent the transaction demand for money at increasing levels of income.

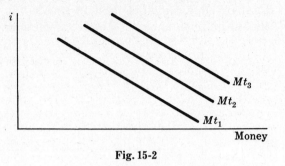

Fig. 15-2

15.2 THE ASSET DEMAND FOR MONEY

According to Keynes' formulation of the speculative demand for money, investors hold either money or bonds depending upon the relationship between the current rate of interest and their expectations about the future rate of interest. James Tobin reformulated the speculative motive into an asset motive. According to Tobin, investors hold a combination of money and bonds, this combination depending upon their willingness to assume the risk associated with uncertainty about the future rate of interest.

Tobin's *asset demand for money theory* assumes that the investor has a choice of holding long-term government bonds and money. In assuming only government bonds, we are able to ignore the possibility of default on interest payments and non-repayment of principal.

The *actual yield from a bond* depends upon (1) the market yield of the bond at the time of purchase and (2) the change in price of the bond upon sale or repayment. For example, a bond's actual yield equals its market yield at time of purchase if the investor recovers his original purchase price upon resale or repayment. However, a bond's actual yield is less than its market yield at purchase if there is a capital loss upon eventual sale or repayment.

EXAMPLE 3. Suppose that the market yield of a bond at purchase is 0.08. If the bond is sold one year later at the original purchase price, the actual yield from holding the bond is 0.08. If the bond is sold one year later at a price that is 0.02 less than the original purchase price, the actual yield from holding the bond is 0.06.

The *actual yield from a portfolio* r_a equals $A(r_b + g_a)$, where A is the proportion of investible funds (proportion of the portfolio) invested in bonds, r_b is the average market yield on bonds at the time of purchase and g_a is the actual gain or loss upon resale or repayment of the bond.

EXAMPLE 4. Portfolio yields are described in the two situations below.

Situation I: The actual yield from a portfolio is 0.06 if the portfolio is invested completely in bonds and the average market yield on bonds r_b is 0.08 and the loss upon sale of bonds g_a is 0.02.

$$r_a = A(r_b + g_a)$$
$$= 1.0(0.08 - 0.02)$$
$$= 0.06$$

Situation II: The actual yield from a portfolio is 0.03 if bonds comprise only 50% of the portfolio while the average market yield on bonds is 0.08 and the loss upon sale of bonds is 0.02.

$$r_a = A(r_b + g_a)$$
$$= 0.50(0.08 - 0.02)$$
$$= 0.03$$

EXAMPLE 5. The actual yield from a portfolio is presented graphically in Fig. 15-3. Suppose that $g_a = 0$ and $r_b = 0.08$. From Fig. 15-3 we see that the actual yield from the portfolio is 0.02 if the portfolio is composed of 25% bonds, is 0.04 if the proportion is 50%, is 0.06 if it is 75%, and is 0.08 if only bonds are held.

Line OA in Fig. 15-3 pivots to the right if the market yield at the time of purchase increases and pivots to the left if it falls. Changes in the value of g_a also cause schedule OA to move, pivoting it to the right when there is a positive change in g_a and to the left when there is a negative change in g_a. Thus, the actual yield from a given portfolio increases as r_b rises and/or g_a has a positive change.

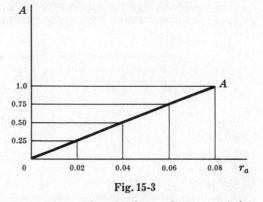

Fig. 15-3

We have assumed thus far certainty about the future price of bonds (i.e., g has a certain value). In the real world, the future price of bonds is uncertain and therefore g has an expected value noted by g_e. Although we might expect the future price of bonds to remain the same as their current price ($g_e = 0$), it is possible that the capital return g_a will be greater or less than 0. Obviously the actual yield from the portfolio is not the sum of r_b and g_e, given $A = 1$, but the sum of r_b and g_a.

EXAMPLE 6. Suppose that a portfolio is composed entirely of bonds, the average market yield is 0.06 and the expected capital return is 0 (although the range of possible capital returns is ± 0.10).

The expected yield from the portfolio $[A(r_b + g_e)]$ is 0.06, but the actual yield from the portfolio $[A(r_b + g_a)]$ is (a) 0.08 if the actual value of g is 0.02, (b) -0.04 if the actual value of g is -0.10 and (c) 0.00 if the actual value of g is -0.06.

There is a larger range of actual yields from a portfolio as the proportion of bonds in the portfolio increases. If the width of this range is a measure of risk, an investor incurs a higher degree of risk the greater the proportion of bonds in his portfolio. Assuming r_b, g_e and the range of g_e are constant, an investor can increase the expected yield from a portfolio only by incurring more risk (i.e., by holding more bonds).

EXAMPLE 7. The expected yields and the actual yields from a portfolio of varying proportions of bonds are computed as follows, given $r_b = 0.06$ and $g_e = 0$ with a range of ± 0.10.

Expected yield from the portfolio when

    (a) $A = 0.25$ is $0.25(r_b + g_e) = 0.25(0.06 + 0) = 0.015$

    (b) $A = 0.50$ is $0.50(r_b + g_e) = 0.50(0.06 + 0) = 0.03$

    (c) $A = 0.75$ is $0.75(r_b + g_e) = 0.75(0.06 + 0) = 0.045$

    (d) $A = 1.00$ is $(r_b + g_e) = 0.06$

Actual yield from the portfolio if $g_a = 0.10$ and

    (a) $A = 0.25$ is $0.25(r_b + g_a) = 0.25(0.06 + 0.10) = 0.04$

    (b) $A = 0.50$ is $0.50(r_b + g_a) = 0.50(0.06 + 0.10) = 0.08$

    (c) $A = 0.75$ is $0.75(r_b + g_a) = 0.75(0.06 + 0.10) = 0.12$

    (d) $A = 1.00$ is $(r_b + g_a) = 0.16$

Actual yield from the portfolio if $g_a = -0.10$ and

    (a) $A = 0.25$ is $0.25(r_b + g_a) = 0.25[0.06 + (-0.10)] = -0.01$

    (b) $A = 0.50$ is $0.50(r_b + g_a) = 0.50[0.06 + (-0.10)] = -0.02$

    (c) $A = 0.75$ is $0.75(r_b + g_a) = 0.75[0.06 + (-0.10)] = -0.03$

    (d) $A = 1.00$ is $(r_b + g_a) = -0.04$

The expected yields and ranges of possible yields are given in Table 1. The range of possible yields widens as the proportion of bonds in the portfolio increases.

Table 1

Bonds in Portfolio	Expected Yields	Ranges of Possible Yields
0.25	0.015	−0.01 to 0.04
0.50	0.030	−0.02 to 0.08
0.75	0.045	−0.03 to 0.12
1.00	0.060	−0.04 to 0.16

EXAMPLE 8. The relationship between expected yield and risk is presented in Fig. 15-4. Given r_b, g_e and a range for g_e, an investor can increase the expected yield from r_1 to r_2 only by holding more bonds and thereby assuming s_2 rather than s_1 risk.

Line OB pivots to the left if there is an increase in r_b or a positive change in g_e and pivots to the right if r_b falls or there is a negative change in g_e. OB pivots to the left if the range for g_e narrows and to the right if it widens. An increase in r_b or a positive change in g_e increases the expected yield for a given level of risk while an increase in the range for g_e increases the level of risk associated with a given expected yield.

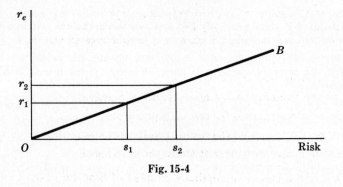

Fig. 15-4

We now theorize about the effect of changes in the current market yield upon the proportion of the portfolio invested in bonds and held as money. Let us initially assume, as presented in Fig. 15-5(a), that a household holds OA_1 bonds and therefore A_1A_n money. The expected yield from the portfolio is r_1 with risk of s_1 in Fig. 15-5(b). If there is an increase in r_b (the current market yield), OA and OB pivot to the left. The expected yield from a portfolio of OA_1 bonds increases to r_2 with no change in risk. It is generally theorized, however, that some investors are more willing to assume risk if there is an increase in the expected yield from a *given* portfolio. Thus, given the increase in r_b, investors are now willing to assume s_2 risk and thereby increase the proportion of bonds held to OA_2 and decrease the proportion of money held to A_2A_n.

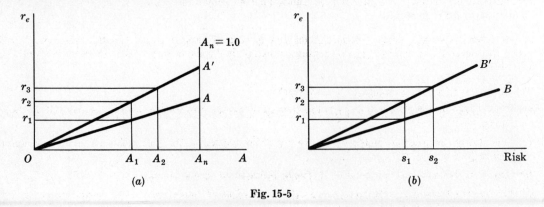

(a)   (b)

Fig. 15-5

If investors are more willing to assume risk as the current market yield increases, it follows that the demand for money is inversely related to the current market yield from bonds. Such a schedule, presented in Fig. 15-6, bears close resemblance to the Keynesian speculative schedule. Unlike the Keynesian theory, however, the asset demand theory views money as an asset that will be held in varying proportions depending upon (1) the expected yield from bonds, (2) the degree of risk associated with holding bonds and (3) investors' willingness to assume risk.

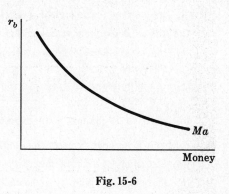

Fig. 15-6

Review Questions

1. Both costs and revenues are associated with the investment of idle balances. The optimum number of bond transactions occurs where (a) revenues equal costs, (b) costs exceed revenues, (c) revenues exceed costs or (d) revenues less costs are at their maximum.

2. If bond yields rise, the optimum number of bond transactions (a) increases and the average money balance held increases, (b) decreases and the average money balance held increases, (c) increases and the average money balance held decreases or (d) decreases and the average money balance held decreases.

3. The average money balance held

   (a) falls as interest rates rise or the cost of transactions increases,

   (b) increases as interest rates rise or the cost of transactions increases,

   (c) increases as interest rates rise or the cost of transactions decreases or

   (d) falls as interest rates rise or the cost of transactions decreases.

4. As the level of income increases, the optimum number of bond transactions (a) decreases and the average money balance held decreases, (b) decreases and the average money balance held increases, (c) increases and the average money balance held increases or (d) increases and the average money balance held decreases.

5. In this chapter, the transaction-precautionary demand for money is

   (a) positively related to the level of income and the rate of interest,

   (b) negatively related to the level of income and the rate of interest,

   (c) positively related to the level of income and negatively related to the rate of interest or

   (d) negatively related to the level of income and positively related to the rate of interest.

6. The expected yield from a portfolio increases as the (a) current market yield increases, (b) expected capital gain decreases, (c) proportion of funds held as money increases or (d) proportion of funds invested in bonds decreases.

7. Bonds have a current market yield of 0.06 and an actual capital gain of 0.02. The actual yield from the portfolio is 0.06 if the percentage invested in bonds is (a) 100%, (b) 90%, (c) 80% or (d) 75%.

8. Which of the following statements is *incorrect*?

   (a) The expected return from a portfolio increases as the proportion of funds invested in bonds increases.

   (b) The range of possible yields from the portfolio widens as the proportion of funds invested in bonds increases.

   (c) Risk increases as the proportion of funds invested in bonds increases.

   (d) The current market yield increases as the proportion of funds invested in bonds increases.

9. As the current market yield increases,

   (a) the expected yield from a given portfolio increases as does the risk associated with the portfolio,

   (b) the expected yield from a given portfolio increases with a reduction in risk associated with the portfolio,

   (c) the expected yield from a given portfolio increases with no change in the risk associated with the portfolio or

   (d) there is no change in the expected yield or the risk associated with the given portfolio.

10. According to Tobin's asset demand for money theory, an increase in the current market yield

   (a) has no effect upon the quantity of bonds or money demanded,

   (b) increases the quantity of bonds demanded and decreases the quantity of money demanded,

   (c) decreases the quantity of bonds demanded and increases the quantity of money demanded or

   (d) increases the quantity of bonds demanded with no change in the quantity of money demanded.

Answers to Review Questions

1. (d) Review Section 15.1.

2. (c) See Example 2, Situation II.

3. (d) See Example 2, Situations I and II.

4. (c) See Example 2, Situation III.

5. (c) See Fig. 15-2 and discussion.

6. (a) See Example 7.

7. (d) See Example 4.

8. (d) See Examples 7 and 8.

9. (c) See Fig. 15-5 and discussion.

10. (b) Review Section 15.2.

Solved Problems

15.1. A household is paid $140 weekly and spends its entire income uniformly over the pay period. What is the average holding of money (a) if all idle transaction balances are held as money? (b) If one-half of the period's income is invested in short-term securities at the beginning of the period and is recovered during mid-period? (c) What happens to the average holding of money if some transaction balances are invested in short-term securities?

   (a) The average holding of money is found by calculating the average of the average daily money balances held.

Table 2

	Money Balance Held ($)		
	Start of Day	End of Day	Average
Monday	140	120	130
Tuesday	120	100	110
Wednesday	100	80	90
Thursday	80	60	70
Friday	60	40	50
Saturday	40	20	30
Sunday	20	0	10
Sum			490

The average holding of money for the seven day period $= 490/7 = \$70$.

   (b) When $70 is invested in short-term securities on Monday, it is converted into cash midday Thursday (see Table 3).

Table 3

	Money Balance Held ($)		
	Start of Day	End of Day	Average
Monday	70	50	60
Tuesday	50	30	40
Wednesday	30	10	20
Thursday	10	60	35
Friday	60	40	50
Saturday	40	20	30
Sunday	20	0	10
Sum			245

The average holding of money for the seven day period = 245/7 = $35.

(c) There is a decrease in the average holding of money if some transaction balances are invested in short-term securities.

15.2. If the expenditures in Problem 15.1 are continuous, show graphically the absolute holding of money at any point in time during the pay period.

If no bonds are held, $140 is held at the beginning of the pay period and 0 at the end. Thus, line AEB in Fig. 15-7 measures the absolute quantity of money held at any time during the pay period. If bonds are held for one-half of the pay period, line $CDEB$ measures the absolute quantity of money held at any time during the pay period.

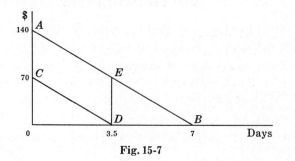

Fig. 15-7

15.3. The average transaction balance held in short-term securities or money is found by the formulas

$$Bd = \frac{n-1}{2n}\left(\frac{Y}{365}\right)\gamma \quad \text{and} \quad Mt = \frac{1}{2n}\left(\frac{Y}{365}\right)\gamma$$

(a) Find the average transaction balance held in money and short-term securities if a household is paid weekly, receives $14,600 annually, and

(1) one-half of the idle transaction balance is invested in short-term securities and sold during mid-period,

(2) two-thirds of the idle transaction balance is invested in short-term securities and one-half of these securities is sold after one-third of the period and the other one-half is sold after two-thirds of the period or

(3) three-quarters of the idle transaction balance is invested in short-term securities and one-third of these securities is sold after one-quarter of the period, one-third is sold after one-half of the period and the last one-third is sold after three-quarters of the period.

(b) What happens to the average quantity of money held as a household elects to increase its number of bond transactions?

(a) The average transaction balances for the specified conditions are

$$(1) \qquad Bd = \frac{n-1}{2n}\left(\frac{Y}{365}\right)\gamma = \frac{1}{4}\left(\frac{\$14{,}600}{365}\right)7 = \$70$$

$$Mt = \frac{1}{2n}\left(\frac{Y}{365}\right)\gamma = \frac{1}{4}\left(\frac{\$14{,}600}{365}\right)7 = \$70$$

$$(2) \qquad Bd = \frac{n-1}{2n}\left(\frac{Y}{365}\right)\gamma = \frac{2}{6}\left(\frac{\$14{,}600}{365}\right)7 = \$93.33$$

$$Mt = \frac{1}{2n}\left(\frac{Y}{365}\right)\gamma = \frac{1}{6}\left(\frac{\$14{,}600}{365}\right)7 = \$46.67$$

$$(3) \qquad Bd = \frac{n-1}{2n}\left(\frac{Y}{365}\right)\gamma = \frac{3}{8}\left(\frac{\$14{,}600}{365}\right)7 = \$105$$

$$Mt = \frac{1}{2n}\left(\frac{Y}{365}\right)\gamma = \frac{1}{8}\left(\frac{\$14{,}600}{365}\right)7 = \$35$$

(b) Given a constant level of income and days in a pay period, the average quantity of transaction balances held in money falls as a household elects to purchase increasingly larger quantities of short-term securities and sell them at more frequent intervals. Thus, holding Y and γ constant, the quantity of money held for transactions is negatively related to the number of bond transactions.

15.4. If there are costs associated with the purchase and sale of short-term bonds, what determines the optimum holding of money and bonds?

We assume that money generates no revenue and incurs no cost. The holding of short-term securities includes both costs and revenues. Costs are related to n, the initial bond purchase plus the number of bond sales. (If a larger volume of bonds is held, *ceteris paribus*, bonds must be sold at more frequent intervals to recover money to allow for a flow of expenditures.) Thus, the decision to invest idle transaction balances in short-term securities rather than money depends upon the revenues and costs associated with the purchase and sale of bonds. In Fig. 15-8, if C is the cost of transactions and R the revenue from transactions, the optimum number of transactions occurs at n_1, where net revenue is maximized.

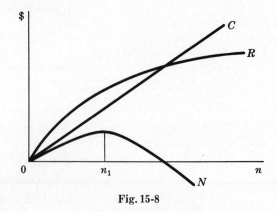

Fig. 15-8

15.5. The optimum number of bond transactions occurs where net revenue N is maximized. If the total cost of bond transactions is $C = an$ and the gross revenue from holding bonds is

$$R = i\left(\frac{n-1}{2n}\right)\left(\frac{Y}{365}\right)\gamma$$

derive a formula for the optimum number of bond transactions.

The optimum number of bond transactions occurs where $R - C = N$ is maximized.

$$N = i\left(\frac{n-1}{2n}\right)\left(\frac{Y}{365}\right)\gamma - an$$

Differentiating with respect to n,

$$\frac{dN}{dn} = \frac{i}{2n^2}\left(\frac{Y}{365}\right)\gamma - a$$

The maximum condition exists where dN/dn equals 0. Thus,

$$0 = \frac{i}{2n^2}\left(\frac{Y}{365}\right)\gamma - a$$

and solving for n,

$$n = \sqrt{\frac{i}{2a}\left(\frac{Y}{365}\right)\gamma}\qquad \text{the formula for the optimum}$$
number of bond transactions

15.6. Using the graph in Fig. 15-9, explain what happens to the optimum number of bond transactions if there is (a) a decrease in the interest earned each period, (b) an increase in the annual level of income or (c) an increase in the fixed cost per transaction.

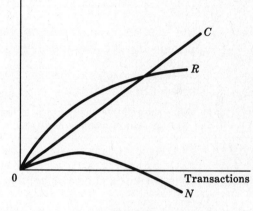

Fig. 15-9

(a) The revenue curve is moving downward. The net revenue curve moves to the left and there is a reduction in the optimum number of bond transactions.

(b) The revenue curve is moving upward. The net revenue curve moves to the right and there is an increase in the optimum number of bond transactions.

(c) The cost curve is pivoting to the left. The net revenue curve moves to the left and there is a decrease in the optimum number of bond transactions. (See Example 2.)

15.7. Using the formula $n = \sqrt{(i/2a)(Y/365)\gamma}$, determine what happens to the optimum number of bond transactions for situations (a), (b) and (c) in Problem 15.6.

Since n is positively related to i, Y and γ and negatively related to a, n decreases for (a), n increases for (b) and n decreases for (c).

15.8. (a) What is the average transaction balance held as money and invested in short-term bonds when income is received weekly, expenditures are uniform and

(1) household income is $7300 while the total number of bond transactions is 2,

(2) household income is $14,600 while the total number of bond transactions is 4 or

(3) household income is $21,900 while the total number of bond transactions is 6?

(b) What happens to average quantity of money held if, as in situations (1) through (3) above, the relative increase in n is equal to the relative increase in Y?

(a) The average holding of bonds is $Bd = [(n-1)/2n](Y/365)\gamma$. The average quantity of money held is $Mt = (1/2n)(Y/365)\gamma$.

(1)
$$Bd = \frac{1}{4}\left(\frac{\$7300}{365}\right)7 = \$35$$

$$Mt = \frac{1}{4}\left(\frac{\$7300}{365}\right)7 = \$35$$

(2)
$$Bd = \frac{3}{8}\left(\frac{\$14{,}600}{365}\right)7 = \$105$$

$$Mt = \frac{1}{8}\left(\frac{\$14{,}600}{365}\right)7 = \$35$$

(3)
$$Bd = \frac{5}{12}\left(\frac{\$21{,}900}{365}\right)7 = \$175$$

$$Mt = \frac{1}{12}\left(\frac{\$21{,}900}{365}\right)7 = \$35$$

(b) There is no change in the quantity of money held for transactions as income increases if the relative increase in the number of bond transactions equals the relative increase in income.

15.9. As the level of income expands, what are the relationships between (a) n and Y and (b) income and the average quantity of money held for transactions?

(a) From the formula $n = \sqrt{(i/2a)(Y/365)\gamma}$ we see that $\Delta n = \sqrt{\Delta Y}$. Thus, if Y doubles, the increase in n equals $1.414\,n$.

(b) Since the relative change in n is less than the relative change in income, the quantity of money held for transactions is positively related to the level of income.

15.10. An investor has a choice of holding long-term bonds or money. Money has no interest return while bonds at the time of purchase have a market yield of r_b. The expected capital gain or loss from holding long-term bonds is g_e and A is the proportion of the portfolio invested in long-term bonds. What is the expected yield from the portfolio if (a) $A = 0.90$, $r_b = 0.06$ and $g_e = 0.02$, (b) $A = 0.50$, $r_b = 0.06$ and $g_e = -0.02$, (c) $A = 0.80$, $r_b = 0.06$, and $g_e = 0$ or (d) $A = 0.60$, $r_b = 0.06$ and $g_e = -0.01$?

The expected yield from a portfolio is $r_e = A(r_b + g_e)$. Therefore, (a) 0.072, (b) 0.02, (c) 0.048 and (d) 0.03.

15.11. Given a portfolio of $100,000 and using the situations in Problem 15.10, find the amount of funds invested in bonds and held as money.

Bond holdings equal $A(\$100{,}000)$. Money holdings equal $100,000 minus $A(\$100{,}000)$. Therefore in (a) bonds held equal $90,000 and money held equals $10,000, in (b) bonds held equal $50,000 and money held equals $50,000, in (c) bonds held equal $80,000 and money held equals $20,000 and in (d) bonds held equal $60,000 and money held equals $40,000.

15.12. Assuming that $A = 1.0$, determine (a) the expected yields for the following combinations of r_b and g_e and (b) the expected yield lines in Fig. 15-10 consistent with these combinations of r_b and g_e.

(1) $r_b = 0.06$ and $g_e = 0.02$

(2) $r_b = 0.06$ and $g_e = -0.02$

(3) $r_b = 0.06$ and $g_e = 0$

(4) $r_b = 0.06$ and $g_e = -0.01$

(a) The expected yields from bonds are (1) 0.08, (2) 0.04, (3) 0.06 and (4) 0.05.

(b) As shown in Fig. 15-10, the applicable expected yield lines are (1) OA_4, (2) OA_1, (3) OA_3 and (4) OA_2.

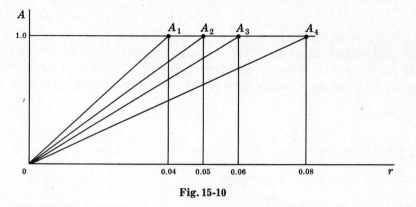

Fig. 15-10

15.13. The expected value of g is 0. It is possible, however, that g will take a value between ±0.08. r_b is 0.05. What are (a) the expected yields and (b) the ranges of possible yields for a portfolio composed of (1) 25% bonds, (2) 50% bonds, (3) 75% bonds and (4) 100% bonds?

(a) The expected yield equals $A(r_b + g_e)$. Therefore, it equals 0.0125 in (1), 0.025 in (2), 0.0375 in (3) and 0.05 in (4).

(b) The range of possible yields equals $A(r_b$ + the possible high and low values for g). Therefore, it equals +0.0325 to −0.0075 in (1), +0.065 to −0.015 in (2), +0.0975 to −0.0225 in (3) and +0.13 to −0.03 in (4).

15.14. What happens to the range of possible yields for a portfolio of increasing proportions of bonds?

Problem 15.13 shows that the range of possible yields widens as a portfolio is composed of an increasing proportion of bonds. Thus, an all-bond portfolio has not only a higher expected yield but carries greater yield variation than a portfolio of fewer bonds.

15.15. What happens to the risk position of a portfolio as (a) the proportion of bonds in the portfolio increases, (b) the range of g_e narrows or (c) there is a negative change in the expected value of g?

Since we are assuming that risk is measured by the width of the range of possible yields, in (a) risk increases, in (b) risk decreases and in (c) there is no change in the risk position of a *given* portfolio although the expected yield falls.

15.16. In Fig. 15-11, why does line OB pivot to the left if (a) r_b increases and (b) the range for g narrows?

(a) As the market yield increases, there is no change in the width of the range of possible yields (risk) although the absolute values for the range increase. Thus, for risk level s_0 the expected yield is greater than r_0 because of the higher value of r_b.

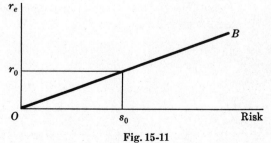

Fig. 15-11

(b) There is a change in the width of the range of possible yields. For a given expected yield such
as r_0, there is a risk level less than s_0.

15.17. An investor has the choice of holding bonds or money. If s_2 in Fig. 15-12 represents
the willingness to assume risk, (a) what proportions of money and bonds should be in
his portfolio? (b) What is the expected yield from his portfolio? (c) What happens
to the proportion of bonds held if the willingness to assume risk falls to s_1?

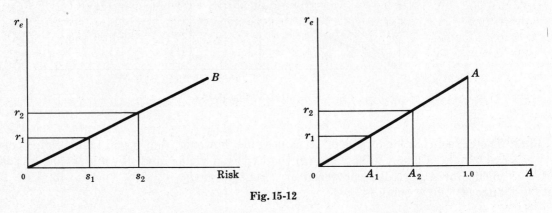

Fig. 15-12

(a) A_2 is the proportion of the portfolio invested in bonds. The distance from A_2 to 1.0 is the
proportion of the portfolio held as money.

(b) The expected yield from this portfolio is r_2.

(c) The proportion of bonds held falls from A_2 to A_1.

15.18. What happens to the quantity of money demanded if (a) investors' willingness to
assume risk is unaffected by changes in expected yields for a given portfolio? (b) If
investors are willing to assume more risk as there is an increase in expected yields
for a given portfolio?

(a) If investors are unwilling to assume more risk as expected yields increase for a given portfolio,
then the bond composition of the portfolio is unaffected by changes in current market yields.
It also follows that changes in market yields have no effect upon the quantity of money demanded.

(b) If investors are willing to assume more risk for a given portfolio as expected yields rise, then
there is an increase in the quantity of bonds held as market yields rise. It therefore follows that
the quantity of money demanded falls as market yields rise and increases as market yields fall.

(See Fig. 15-5 and related discussion.)

Chapter 16

Simultaneous Equilibrium
in the Money and Commodity Markets

Monetary and commodity equilibrium were developed in Chapters 11 and 14 respectively. In this chapter we find that simultaneous equilibrium in the money and commodity markets necessitates that equilibrium in both markets occurs at the same level of income and the same rate of interest. We then trace the effect that shifts in the IS and LM schedules have upon the equilibrium level of income.

16.1 MONETARY AND COMMODITY EQUILIBRIUM

LM_0 and IS_0 in Fig. 16-1 are schedules of monetary and commodity equilibrium. At rate of interest i_1, equilibrium between the supply of and demand for money exists at level of income Y_1, while equilibrium between the demand for and supply of goods exists at level of income Y_2. There is only one rate of interest, i_0, where the money and commodity markets are in equilibrium at the same Y_0 level of income. This rate of interest is determined by the intersection of the IS and LM schedules.

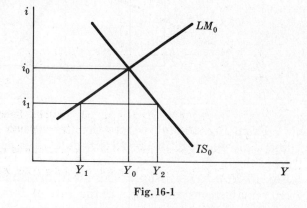

Fig. 16-1

EXAMPLE 1. Equilibrium in the money and commodity markets is found by simultaneous solution of the IS and LM equations.

Given: A two-sector model where $C = \$90 + 0.625\,Yd$, $Yd = Y$, $I = \$150 - 100i$ $Mt = 0.25\,Y$, $Ma = \$50 - 200i$ and $Ms = \$180$.

Monetary equilibrium exists where $Ms = Mt + Ma$ (see Section 14.2).
$$\$180 = 0.25\,Y + \$50 - 200i$$
$$100i = 0.125\,Y - \$65$$

Commodity equilibrium exists where $Y = C + I$ (see Section 11.1).
$$Y = \$90 + 0.625\,Y + \$150 - 100i$$
$$100i = \$240 - 0.375\,Y$$

Simultaneous equilibrium in the money and commodity markets exists where $IS = LM$.

$$100i = \$240 - 0.375\,Y$$
$$\text{(minus)} \quad 100i = -\$65 + 0.125\,Y$$
$$\overline{ \quad 0 = \$305 - 0.50\,Y}$$
$$Y = \$610$$

Substituting into the IS or LM equations, $i = 0.1125$, $I = \$138.75$, $C = \$471.25$, $Mt = \$152.50$ and $Ma = \$27.50$.

There is equilibrium in both the money and commodity markets when the rate of interest is 0.1125 and the income level is \$610. Rates of interest higher or lower than 0.1125 do not represent equilibrium in the two markets since income levels would differ.

16.2 AUTONOMOUS CHANGES IN INVESTMENT DEMAND

Shifts in the IS or LM schedule change the conditions of equilibrium in each market and therefore the economy's equilibrium level of income and rate of interest. For instance, the leftward shift of IS schedule IS_0 in Fig. 16-2 to IS_1 results in a lower level of income and a lower rate of interest. A rightward shift from IS_0 to IS_2 increases the level of income and the rate of interest.

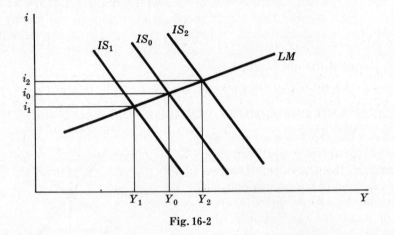

Fig. 16-2

From Fig. 16-3(a), we see that the actual change in the equilibrium level of income is less than the shift in the IS schedule. Let us assume that the leftward shift of the IS schedule in Fig. 16-3(a) is due to an $I_0 - I_1$ decrease in investment demand depicted in Fig. 16-3(b). As a result of this shift, investment volume falls by $I_0 - I_1$ if the rate of interest remains constant at i_0. If the rate of interest declines to i_1 as the investment demand schedule shifts leftward, investment volume falls by $I_0 - I_2$ rather than $I_0 - I_1$. Thus, while an autonomous decrease in investment causes a $k_e \Delta I (Y_0 - Y_1)$ leftward shift of the IS schedule, the decline in the rate of interest offsets part of the initial decline in investment volume and the equilibrium level of income falls to Y_2 rather than Y_1.

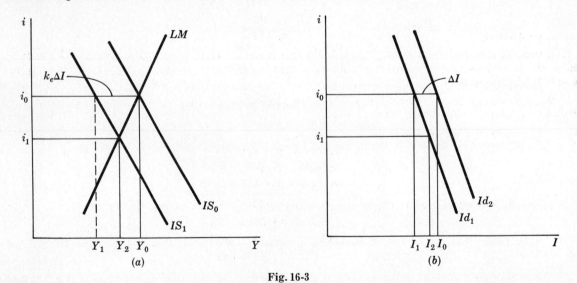

Fig. 16-3

EXAMPLE 2. We can measure the effect that an autonomous decrease in investment has upon the equilibrium level of income by retaining the parameters of Example 1 except for a $10 decrease in autonomous investment. The equation for monetary equilibrium remains $100i = 0.125\,Y - \$65$.

Commodity equilibrium exists where $Y = C + I$.

$$Y = \$90 + 0.625\,Y + \$140 - 100i$$
$$100i = \$230 - 0.375\,Y$$

Simultaneous equilibrium in the money and commodity markets exists where $IS = LM$.

$$100i = \$230 - 0.375\,Y$$
$$\text{(minus)}\ \ \underline{100i = -\$65 + 0.125\,Y}$$
$$0 = \$295 - 0.50\,Y$$
$$Y = \$590$$

Substituting into the IS or LM equations, $i = 0.0875$, $C = \$458.75$, $I = \$131.25$, $Mt = \$147.50$ and $Ma = \$32.50$.

Given rate of interest 0.1125, investment volume was \$138.75 in Example 1 but falls to \$128.75 when autonomous investment decreases \$10. However, in this example, the rate of interest falls to 0.0875 as investment decreases so that the actual decline in investment volume is \$7.50 rather than \$10 and the actual decline in equilibrium income is \$20 instead of \$26.67. Thus, interest rate changes moderate the effect that changes in autonomous investment have upon the equilibrium level of income.

The extent to which autonomous changes in spending are moderated by interest rate changes depends upon the sensitivity of investment demand to the rate of interest. Example 3 shows that the level of income is affected less by autonomous changes in spending when investment demand is more sensitive to changes in the rate of interest.

EXAMPLE 3. The parameters of Example 1 are retained except that the investment demand equation is now $I = \$195 - 500i$. The equation for monetary equilibrium remains $100i = 0.125\,Y - \$65$.

Commodity equilibrium exists where $Y = C + I$.

$$Y = \$90 + 0.625\,Y + \$195 - 500i$$
$$500i = -0.375\,Y + \$285$$
$$100i = -0.075\,Y + \$57$$

Simultaneous equilibrium in the money and commodity markets exists where $IS = LM$.

$$100i = \$57 - 0.075\,Y$$
$$\text{(minus)}\ \ \underline{100i = -\$65 + 0.125\,Y}$$
$$0 = \$122 - 0.20\,Y$$
$$Y = \$610$$

Substituting, $\qquad i = 0.1125$

Although the investment demand equation is changed from $I = \$150 - 100i$ in Example 1 to $I = \$195 - 500i$ here, simultaneous equilibrium in the money and commodity markets remains at a \$610 level of income and a 0.1125 rate of interest.

We now assume, as we did in Example 2, a \$10 autonomous decrease in investment. The investment equation is now $I = \$185 - 500i$.

Commodity equilibrium exists where $Y = C + I$.

$$Y = \$90 + 0.625\,Y + \$185 - 500i$$
$$500i = -0.375\,Y + \$275$$
$$100i = -0.075\,Y + \$55$$

Simultaneous equilibrium in the money and commodity markets exists where $IS = LM$.

$$100i = \$55 - 0.075\,Y$$
$$\text{(minus)}\ \ \underline{100i = -\$65 + 0.125\,Y}$$
$$0 = \$120 - 0.20\,Y$$
$$Y = \$600$$

Substituting into the IS or LM equations, $i = 0.10$, $I = \$135$, $C = \$465$, $Mt = \$150$ and $Ma = \$30$.

Comparing the levels of income in Examples 2 and 3, we find that a \$10 autonomous decrease in investment demand results in a smaller reduction in the level of income in Example 3 than in Example 2 since investment demand in 3 is more responsive to interest rate changes.

16.3 CHANGES IN GOVERNMENT SPENDING AND TAXATION

Changes in government spending or taxes also cause shifts in the IS schedule. For instance, in Fig. 16-4, increased government spending shifts the IS schedule to the right by $k_e \Delta G$. The change in the equilibrium level of income, however, is less than $k_e \Delta G$. As the level of income increases, the amount of money demanded for transactions increases, leaving smaller balances for the speculative motive. This raises the rate of interest, which reduces the volume of investment and thereby offsets part of the stimulative effect of increased government spending.

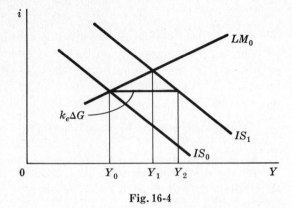

Fig. 16-4

Examples 4 and 5, which are extensions of the private sector model in Example 1, measure the effect that fiscal actions have upon the equilibrium level of income.

EXAMPLE 4. The equilibrium level of income in Example 1 is $610 with a 0.1125 rate of interest. The parameters of Example 1 are retained with the addition of $10 in government spending. The equation for monetary equilibrium remains $100i = 0.125\,Y - \$65$.

Commodity equilibrium exists where $Y = C + I + G$.

$$Y = \$90 + 0.625\,Y + \$150 - 100i + \$10$$
$$100i = \$250 - 0.375\,Y$$

Simultaneous equilibrium in the money and commodity markets exists where $IS = LM$.

$$
\begin{aligned}
100i &= 0.125\,Y - \$65 \\
\text{(minus)}\quad 100i &= -0.375\,Y + \$250 \\
\hline
0 &= 0.50\,Y - \$315 \\
Y &= \$630
\end{aligned}
$$

Substituting into the IS or LM equations, $i = 0.1375$, $C = \$483.75$, $I = \$136.25$, $G = \$10$, $Mt = \$157.50$ and $Ma = \$22.50$.

We see that increased government spending raises the equilibrium level of income from $610 to $630 and the rate of interest from 0.1125 to 0.1375. A higher rate of interest lowers investment volume from $138.75 to $136.25 and thereby partly reduces the stimulative effect of increased government spending.

EXAMPLE 5. The equilibrium level of income in Example 1 is $610 with a 0.1125 rate of interest. The parameters of Example 1 are retained with the addition of $10 in government spending and taxes. The equation for monetary equilibrium remains $100i = 0.125\,Y - \$65$.

Commodity equilibrium exists where $Y = C + I + G$.

$$Y = \$90 + 0.625(Y - \$10) + \$150 - 100i + \$10$$
$$100i = \$243.75 - 0.375\,Y$$

Simultaneous equilibrium in the money and commodity markets exists where $IS = LM$.

$$
\begin{aligned}
100i &= 0.125\,Y - \$65 \\
\text{(minus)}\quad 100i &= -0.375\,Y + \$243.75 \\
\hline
0 &= 0.50\,Y - \$308.75 \\
Y &= \$617.50
\end{aligned}
$$

Substituting into the IS or LM equations, $i = 0.1219$, $C = \$469.69$, $I = \$137.81$, $G = Tx = \$10$, $Mt = \$154.38$ and $Ma = \$25.62$.

A higher rate of interest from the net stimulative effect of an increased balanced budget retards investment and results in an increase in the equilibrium level of income which is less than $k_b \Delta G$.

Examples 1 through 5 show that one cannot predict the effect of autonomous changes in spending without prior knowledge of how these spending changes affect the rate of interest and, in turn, the volume of investment.   Obviously, little reliance can be placed on a model of the economy that excludes the money market.

16.4   CHANGES IN THE QUANTITY OF MONEY

The *LM* schedule shifts as a result of changes in (1) the transaction demand for money, (2) the speculative demand for money and (3) the quantity of money. In this section we investigate shifts in the *LM* schedule caused by changes in the supply of money.

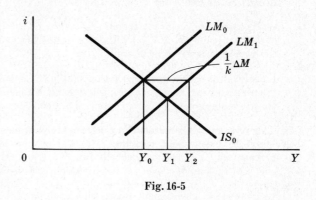

In Fig. 16-5, the *LM* schedule shifts to the right by $\Delta M(1/k)$ as a result of an increase in the money supply. The increase in the income level from Y_0 to Y_1 is less than $Y_2 - Y_0$ (the shift in the *LM* schedule).

Fig. 16-5

EXAMPLE 6.   The equilibrium level of income in Example 5 is \$617.50 and the rate of interest is 0.1219. The parameters of Example 5 are retained except that the money supply is increased from \$180 to \$200. The equation for commodity equilibrium remains $100i = \$243.75 - 0.375\,Y$.

Monetary equilibrium exists where $Ms = Mt + Ma$.

$$\$200 \ = \ 0.25\,Y + \$50 - 200i$$
$$100i \ = \ 0.125\,Y - \$75$$

Simultaneous equilibrium in the money and commodity markets exists where $IS = LM$.

$$
\begin{aligned}
100i \ &= \quad\ \ 0.125\,Y - \$75 \\
\text{(minus)}\quad 100i \ &= \ -0.375\,Y + \$243.75 \\[-4pt]
\hline
0 \ &= \quad\ \ 0.50\,Y \ - \$318.75 \\
Y \ &= \quad\ \$637.50
\end{aligned}
$$

Substituting into the *IS* or *LM* equations, $i = 0.0469$, $C = \$482.19$, $I = \$145.31$, $Mt = \$159.38$ and $Ma = \$40.62$.

The above calculation shows that monetary policy affects the level of income through investment spending. Investment volume increases from \$137.81 in Example 5 to \$145.31 as an increased money supply lowers the rate of interest from 0.1219 to 0.0469.   A larger volume of investment, in turn, has a multiple effect upon the equilibrium level of income.

The \$20 increase in the money supply raises the level of income by less than $\Delta M(1/k)$ since the quantity of money demanded increases as the rate of interest falls.   Note that the money multiplier $(1/k = Y/M)$ decreases from 3.43 to 3.19 as the money supply increases \$20 and the rate of interest falls from 0.1219 to 0.0469.

Review Questions

The following questions assume that investment is a function of the rate of interest and that the demand for money is a function of the level of income and the rate of interest.

1.   An autonomous increase in investment will result in (*a*) a higher level of income and a higher rate of interest, (*b*) a lower level of income and a lower rate of interest, (*c*) a higher level of income and a lower rate of interest or (*d*) a lower level of income and a higher rate of interest.

2.   An increase in taxes will result in (*a*) a higher level of income and a higher rate of interest, (*b*) a lower level of income and a lower rate of interest, (*c*) a higher level of income and a lower rate of interest or (*d*) a lower level of income and a higher rate of interest.

3. An increase in the money supply will result in (a) a higher level of income and a higher rate of interest, (b) a lower level of income and a lower rate of interest, (c) a higher level of income and a lower rate of interest or (d) a lower level of income and a higher rate of interest.

4. An autonomous increase in investment (a) will increase the level of income by $k_e \Delta I$, (b) will increase the level of income by less than $k_e \Delta I$, (c) will increase the level of income by more than $k_e \Delta I$ or (d) will not increase the level of income.

5. A decrease in government spending (a) has no effect upon the level of income, (b) will decrease the level of income by $k_e \Delta G$, (c) will decrease the level of income by less than $k_e \Delta G$ or (d) will decrease the level of income by more than $k_e \Delta G$.

6. A decrease in government spending (a) has no effect upon consumption and investment spending, (b) stimulates investment spending but reduces consumption spending, (c) reduces investment spending but stimulates consumption spending or (d) reduces both investment and consumption spending.

7. If there is an equal decrease in taxes and government spending, (a) the income level will fall by the change in government spending, (b) the income level will fall but the level of consumption will increase, (c) the income level will fall but the level of investment will increase or (d) the income level will fall but the levels of consumption and investment will increase.

8. An increase in government taxes will result in (a) less investment, (b) a higher level of investment, (c) an increase in the marginal propensity to consume or (d) an increase in the money supply.

9. If there is a decrease in the money supply, (a) the level of consumption will remain the same, (b) the' level of investment will remain the same, (c) the level of investment will increase or (d) the level of investment will decrease.

10. An increase in the money supply will result in (a) an increase in the rate of interest and the level of income, (b) an increase in the level of income equal to $\Delta M(1/k)$, (c) an increase in the level of income greater than $\Delta M(1/k)$ or (d) an increase in the level of income less than $\Delta M(1/k)$.

Answers to Review Questions

1. (a) Review Section 16.2.

2. (b) Review Section 16.3.

3. (c) Review Section 16.4.

4. (b) Review Section 16.2.

5. (c) Review Section 16.3.

6. (b) Review Section 16.3.

7. (c) Review Section 16.3.

8. (b) Review Section 16.3.

9. (d) Review Section 16.4.

10. (d) Review Section 16.4.

Solved Problems

16.1. Explain why equilibrium is said to exist only at the rate of interest and the level of income where the *IS* and *LM* schedules intersect.

The rate of interest and the level of income must be the same in the money and commodity markets in order to have equilibrium in both markets. This exists only at the point of intersection of the *IS* and *LM* schedules. This condition does not exist if the same equilibrium rate of interest occurs in both markets at different levels of income or if the same level of income exists in both markets at different rates of interest.

16.2. Given a two-sector model where $C = \$100 + 0.80\,Y$, $I = \$150 - 600i$, $Ms = \$200$, $Mt = 0.20\,Y$ and $Ma = \$50 - 400i$, find (a) the equilibrium level of income and (b) the levels of consumption and investment at the equilibrium level of income.

Given

The *IS* equation	The *LM* equation
$Y = C + I$	$Ms = Mt + Ma$
$Y = \$100 + 0.80\,Y + \$150 - 600i$	$\$200 = 0.20\,Y + \$50 - 400i$
$0.20\,Y = \$250 - 600i$	$0.20\,Y = \$150 + 400i$

(*a*) Equilibrium income occurs where $IS = LM$.

$$0.20\,Y = \$250 - 600i$$
$$0.20\,Y = \$150 + 400i$$
$$\overline{}$$
$$0 = \$100 - 1000i$$
$$i = 0.10$$

Substituting,
$$Y = \$950$$

(*b*)
$$C = \$860 \quad \text{and} \quad I = \$90$$

16.3. If a government sector is added to the private sector model of Problem 16.2 where $G = \$10$ and $Tx = 0$, (*a*) what are the direction and magnitude of the shifts in the *IS* and *LM* schedules? (*b*) Find the new equilibrium level of income and (*c*) explain what has happened to the levels of consumption and investment.

(*a*) There is no change in the *LM* schedule. The *IS* schedule shifts rightward $\$50$ ($k_e\,\Delta G$).

(*b*) The *IS* equation is now $0.20\,Y = \$260 - 600i$. The equilibrium level of income is $\$970$.

(*c*) The level of consumption has increased to $\$876$. Investment has fallen to $\$84$ since the rate of interest has increased from 0.10 to 0.11. Consumption increases because government spending has a net stimulative effect.

16.4. Assume that the investment equation in Problem 16.2 is $I = \$100 - 100i$. Retaining the other parameters of Problem 16.2, the equilibrium level of income remains at $\$950$. Calculate (*a*) the equilibrium level of income if $\$10$ in government spending is added to the model and (*b*) the new consumption and investment levels. (*c*) Why do the income levels in Problems 16.3 and 16.4 differ although there is an equal $\$10$ increase in government spending in both problems?

(*a*) The *IS* equation is $0.20\,Y = \$210 - 100i$ The equilibrium level of income is $\$990$.

(*b*) $C = \$892$ and $I = \$88$.

(*c*) The investment equation in Problem 16.4 is less sensitive to changes in the rate of interest. Thus, investment volume falls $\$2$ (between Problems 16.2 and 16.4) rather than $\$6$ (between Problems 16.2 and 16.3).

16.5. What effect does a highly elastic investment demand schedule have upon autonomous changes in spending?

A highly elastic investment demand schedule means that investment volume is sensitive to interest rate changes. That is, small changes in the rate of interest have large effects upon the volume of investment. If the *IS* schedule shifts to the right and the rate of interest rises, there is a large decline in investment volume. Leftward shifts cause large increases in investment volume. One would conclude, then, that the influence of autonomous changes in spending are largely but not completely offset by opposing changes in the volume of investment if the investment demand schedule is highly elastic.

16.6. (*a*) Calculate the volumes of investment for the following investment equations when the rates of interest are 0.12, 0.10 and 0.08 and (*b*) rank these equations in order of their interest elasticity of investment demand.

$$I = \$90 - 100i \qquad (1)$$
$$I = \$100 - 200i \qquad (2)$$
$$I = \$120 - 400i \qquad (3)$$
$$I = \$160 - 800i \qquad (4)$$

(*a*) The volumes of investment for the four equations are given in Table 1.

Table 1

Rate of Interest	Volume of Investment ($)			
	(*1*)	(*2*)	(*3*)	(*4*)
0.12	78	76	72	64
0.10	80	80	80	80
0.08	82	84	88	96

(*b*) The investment equation for (*4*) is most interest elastic since investment volume is most responsive to interest rate changes. The interest elasticity of the other equations in descending order is (*3*), (*2*) and (*1*).

16.7. Could we have found the interest elasticity of investment demand for the equations in Problem 16.6 without constructing a table of investment volume?

Yes, because the behavioral coefficient of i in the investment demand equation measures the effect of i upon the volume of investment. The larger the behavioral coefficient, the greater the interest elasticity of investment demand.

16.8. Given $C = \$150 + 0.50\,Y$, $I = \$200 - 400i$, $Mt = 0.25\,Y$, $Ma = \$50 - 100i$ and $Ms = \$180$, for the money and commodity markets, calculate (*a*) the equilibrium level of income and (*b*) the levels of consumption and investment.

Given

The *IS* equation	The *LM* equation
$Y = C + I$	$Ms = Mt + Ma$
$Y = \$150 + 0.50\,Y + \$200 - 400i$	$\$180 = 0.25\,Y + \$50 - 100i$
$0.50\,Y = \$350 - 400i$	$0.50\,Y = \$260 + 200i$

(*a*) Equilibrium income occurs where $IS = LM$.

$$0.50\,Y = \$350 - 400i$$
$$\underline{0.50\,Y = \$260 + 200i}$$
$$0 = \$90 - 600i$$
$$i = 0.15$$

Substituting, $Y = \$580$

(*b*) $C = \$440$ and $I = \$140$

16.9. Assume that the money supply in Problem 16.8 is increased $20. (*a*) What are the direction and magnitude of the shifts in the *IS* and *LM* schedules? (*b*) Find the new equilibrium level of income and (*c*) explain what has happened to the level of consumption and the level of investment.

(a) There is no change in the *IS* schedule. At interest rate 0.15 and income level $580, the value of $1/k$ equals 3.22 ($1/k = Y/M$). (See Example 6.) The *LM* schedule shifts rightward $64.44.

(b) The *LM* equation is now $0.50\,Y = \$300 + 200i$. The equilibrium level of income is $633.33.

(c) Consumption has increased to $466.66 and investment has increased to $166.67.

16.10. Given: $C = \$150 + 0.50\,Y$, $I = \$260 - 800i$, $Mt = 0.25\,Y$, $Ma = \$50 - 100i$ and $Ms = \$180$. The equilibrium level of income is $580 with $C = \$440$ and $I = \$140$. (a) Find the new equilibrium level of income and the levels of consumption and investment if there is a $20 increase in the money supply. (b) Contrast the changes in income for Problems 16.9 and 16.10 that result from a $20 increase in the money supply. Explain why it is not the same for these two problems.

(a) Solving for simultaneous equilibrium, $Y = \$644$, $C = \$472$ and $I = \$172$.

(b) The income level increases $53.33 in Problem 16.9 and $64 in Problem 16.10. This difference is due to the greater interest elasticity of investment demand in Problem 16.10.

16.11. How does a change in the money supply affect the level of income?

The model assumes that money supply changes alter the rate of interest, thereby changing the volume of investment and, through the multiplier, the level of consumption.

16.12. Assume that the parameters of Problem 16.8 are retained except that the marginal propensity to consume increases to 0.60. (a) In what direction has the *IS* or *LM* schedule shifted? (b) What is the new equilibrium level of income? (c) Find the new levels of consumption and investment. (d) What must the central bank do to maintain investment at $140, the level established in Problem 16.8? (e) What change in the money supply is needed to keep investment at $140?

(a) The *IS* schedule has shifted to the right.

(b) $Y = \$621.43$.

(c) $C = \$522.86$ and $I = \$98.68$.

(d) The central bank must increase the money supply to maintain a constant rate of interest.

(e) If the rate of interest remains at 0.15, investment volume stays at $140. If $I = \$140$ and $C = \$150 + 0.60\,Y$, the equilibrium level of income is $725. Given $Y = \$725$ and $i = 0.15$, there is equilibrium between the demand for and supply of money if the money supply equals $216.25 since

$$Ms = Mt + Ma$$
$$Ms = 0.25(\$725) + \$50 - 100(0.15)$$
$$Ms = \$216.25$$

Since the money supply was originally $180, the money supply must be increased $36.25.

16.13. What must government do to achieve the full stimulative effect of increased government spending?

Increased government spending increases the rate of interest, thereby reducing the volume of investment. Thus, to achieve the full stimulative effect of increased government spending, the money supply must be increased to keep the interest rate at its current level. Monetary policy must complement fiscal policy.

16.14. Given: $C = \$150 + 0.50\,Y$, $I = \$200 - 400i$, $Mt = 0.25\,Y$, $Ma = \$50 - 100i$ and $Ms = \$180$. The equilibrium level of income is \$580 with $i = 0.15$, $C = \$440$ and $I = \$140$. Assume a \$30 autonomous decrease in investment. (a) In what direction has the IS or LM schedule shifted? (b) Find the new equilibrium level of income. (c) Find the new consumption and investment levels. (d) Explain why investment did not fall \$30.

(a) The IS schedule has shifted leftward \$60.

(b) $Y = \$560$.

(c) $C = \$430$ and $I = \$130$.

(d) The fall in the rate of interest raises the volume of investment. This partially offsets the autonomous decrease in investment.

16.15. Given: $C = \$150 + 0.50\,Y$, $I = \$200 - 800i$, $Mt = 0.25\,Y$, $Ma = \$50 - 100i$ and $Ms = \$180$. The equilibrium level of income is \$556 with $i = 0.09$, $C = \$428$ and $I = \$128$. Assume a \$30 decrease in autonomous investment. (a) Find the new equilibrium level of income. (b) Find the new consumption and investment levels. (c) Why does the fall in investment in Problems 16.14 and 16.15 differ although there is a \$30 decrease in autonomous investment in both instances?

(a) $Y = \$544$.

(b) $I = \$122$ and $C = \$422$.

(c) Investment demand is more interest elastic in Problem 16.15.

16.16. Given: $C = \$100 + 0.80\,Yd$, $I = \$150 - 600i$, $Yd = Y - Tx$, $Tx = 0.25\,Y$, $G = \$100$, $Mt = 0.20\,Y$, $Ma = \$50 - 200i$ and $Ms = \$200$. (a) Find the equilibrium level of income. (b) Is the government sector operating with a deficit or a surplus?

(a) The IS equation is $0.40\,Y = \$350 - 600i$. The LM equation is $0.20\,Y = \$150 + 200i$. $Y = \$800$.

(b) There is a surplus since $Tx = \$200$ and $G = \$100$.

16.17. Government spending in Problem 16.16 is increased \$100. (a) In what direction has the IS or LM schedule shifted? (b) Find the new equilibrium level of income. (c) Has investment increased or decreased? (d) Is the budget now balanced?

(a) The IS schedule has shifted to the right.

(b) $Y = \$900$.

(c) Investment has fallen from \$120 to \$60.

(d) There is still a surplus since $Tx = \$225$ and $G = \$200$.

Chapter 17

The Effectiveness of Monetary and Fiscal Policy

The analysis of monetary and commodity equilibrium in Chapter 16 showed that the change in the equilibrium level of income does not equal the shift of the *IS* or *LM* schedule. In this chapter we find that the *slopes* of the *IS* and *LM* schedules determine the effect of monetary and fiscal policy upon the equilibrium level of income.

17.1 THE SLOPE OF THE *IS* SCHEDULE

The equation for commodity equilibrium is generally presented in the form $Y = \text{constant} - \phi i$, with the slope of the schedule given as $1/\phi$. In a two-sector model of the economy, the value of the behavioral coefficient ϕ in the *IS* equation depends upon (1) the responsiveness of investment to changes in the rate of interest and (2) the value of the marginal propensity to consume.

EXAMPLE 1. *Given*: A two-sector model where consumption spending is $C = \$10 + 0.75\,Y$.

Suppose that investment demand is interest elastic where $I = \$150 - 1000i$; the *IS* equation equals $Y = \$640 - 4000i$. If investment demand is less interest elastic so that $I = \$70 - 200i$, the *IS* equation becomes $Y = \$320 - 800i$. As we can see from plotting the *IS* equations in Fig. 17-1, the slope of the *IS* schedule is greatest when investment demand is least responsive to interest rate changes [i.e., the absolute slope $(1/\phi)$ of *IS* is largest when investment demand is the least interest elastic]. It follows that the *IS* schedule is vertical (has an infinite slope) when investment is completely interest inelastic (investment is unrelated to the rate of interest).

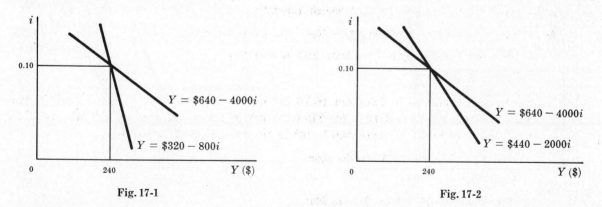

Fig. 17-1   Fig. 17-2

EXAMPLE 2. *Given*: A two-sector model where the investment demand equation is $I = \$150 - 1000i$.

Suppose that the MPC equals 0.50 and the consumption equation is $C = \$70 + 0.50\,Y$; the *IS* equation is $Y = \$440 - 2000i$. If the MPC is larger and the consumption equation reads $C = \$10 + 0.75\,Y$, the *IS* equation becomes $Y = \$640 - 4000i$. Plotting these *IS* equations in Fig. 17-2, we find that the slope of the *IS* schedule is greatest when the MPC is smallest. Thus, the absolute slope $(1/\phi)$ of the *IS* schedule varies inversely with the size of the multiplier, provided that investment demand is responsive to changes in the rate of interest. If the marginal propensity to consume equals zero, the absolute slope of the *IS* schedule is large but not infinite (the curve is not vertical) unless investment demand is completely interest inelastic. If the marginal propensity to consume equals one, the *IS* schedule has a zero slope (is horizontal), provided that investment demand is not completely interest inelastic.

Although both the interest elasticity of investment demand and the marginal propensity to consume determine the slope of the *IS* schedule, the interest elasticity of investment demand takes precedence in explaining the slope of *IS*. As noted in Example 2, a necessary condition for a negatively sloped *IS* schedule is an investment schedule that is responsive to the rate of interest.

When we expand the model to four sectors (household, investment, government and international), the slope of *IS* is then said to depend upon the interest elasticity of spending and the marginal propensities to spend and save. Spending that is responsive to the rate of interest remains a necessary condition for a negatively sloped *IS* schedule.

17.2 THE SLOPE OF THE *LM* SCHEDULE

The equation for monetary equilibrium is generally presented in the form $Y = \text{constant} + \psi i$, with the slope of the schedule given as $1/\psi$. In a two-sector model of the economy, the value of the behavioral coefficient ψ (psi) in the *LM* equation depends upon (1) the responsiveness of the speculative demand for money to changes in the rate of interest and (2) the relationship between the transaction demand for money and the level of income.

EXAMPLE 3. *Given*: A two-sector model where the transaction demand for money is $Mt = 0.25\,Y$ and the money supply equals \$200.

Suppose that the speculative demand for money is responsive to interest rate changes where $Ma = \$100 - 1000i$; the *LM* equation is $Y = \$400 + 4000i$. If the speculative demand for money is less interest elastic such that $Ma = \$50 - 200i$, the *LM* equation is $Y = \$600 + 800i$. We can see from plotting the *LM* equations in Fig. 17-3 that the *LM* schedule has the greatest slope when the speculative demand for money is least interest elastic. Thus, the absolute slope $1/\psi$ of the *LM* schedule falls as the speculative demand for money becomes more responsive to the rate of interest. It therefore follows that the *LM* schedule is horizontal (zero slope) when the speculative demand for money is completely interest elastic and is vertical (infinite slope) when there is no speculative demand.

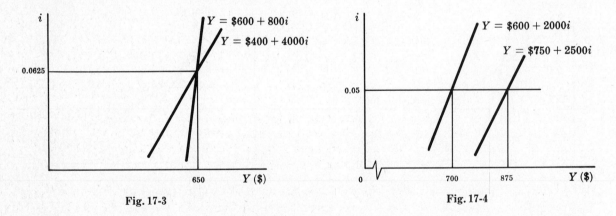

Fig. 17-3   Fig. 17-4

EXAMPLE 4. *Given*: A two-sector model where the money supply equals \$200 and the speculative demand for money is $Ma = \$50 - 500i$.

Suppose that the transaction demand for money is $Mt = 0.25\,Y$; the *LM* equation is $Y = \$600 + 2000i$. If the transaction demand for money is $Mt = 0.20\,Y$, the *LM* equation is $Y = \$750 + 2500i$. We see from plotting the *LM* equations in Fig. 17-4 that the larger the transaction demand for money, the greater the slope of the *LM* schedule. That is, the absolute slope of the *LM* schedule is positively related to the size of the transaction demand for money, given a speculative demand for money. If there is no speculative demand, the *LM* schedule is vertical.

The slope of the *LM* schedule is generally explained in terms of the interest elasticity of the speculative demand for money (the dominating factor) for the same reason that the

IS schedule is explained in terms of the interest elasticity of investment demand. Thus, a positively sloped *LM* schedule requires that the speculative demand for money be negatively related to the rate of interest. If the demand for money is restructured along the line suggested in Chapter 15, a positively sloped *LM* schedule requires that the transaction and/or asset demand for money be related to the rate of interest.

17.3   THE EFFECTIVENESS OF FISCAL POLICY

The slopes of the *IS* and *LM* schedules determine the success of a fiscal action in changing the level of income by the multiplier times the fiscal change. We find that fiscal policy is most effective when there is a large absolute slope for the *IS* schedule and/or a small absolute slope for the *LM* schedule.

EXAMPLE 5. In Fig. 17-5, increased government spending shifts the *IS* schedule from IS_1 to IS_2. The rightward shift of $k_e \Delta G$ equals Y_3 minus Y_1. By inspection, we see that the increase in income from Y_1 to Y_2 is greater in Fig. 17-5(a), where the *IS* schedule has the larger absolute slope. Given a *LM* schedule, the change in income approaches the multiplier times the fiscal change as the *IS* schedule approaches a vertical position.

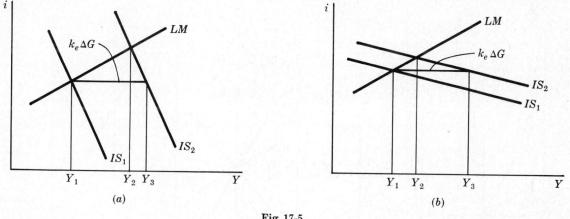

Fig. 17-5

EXAMPLE 6. Figure 17-6 shows that the effect of a fiscal action upon the level of income also depends upon the slope of the *LM* schedule. Again, as in Example 5, Y_3 minus Y_1 equals $k_e \Delta G$, the shift of the *IS* schedule. The greater change in income (Y_1 to Y_2) occurs in Fig. 17-6(a), where the *LM* schedule has the smaller slope. The change in income approaches the multiplier times the fiscal change as the *LM* schedule approaches a horizontal position.

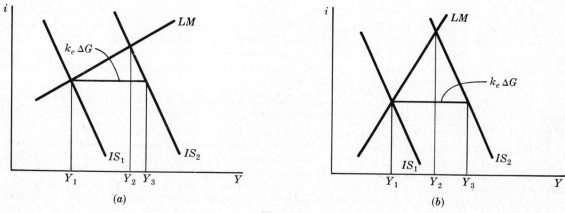

Fig. 17-6

We conclude from Examples 5 and 6 that an increase in government spending increases income by $k_e \Delta G$ only if the LM schedule is horizontal (has a zero slope) or the IS schedule is vertical (has an infinite slope). If the LM schedule has a slope greater than zero and the IS schedule has a finite slope, increased government spending increases income by less than $k_e \Delta G$. An increase in government spending has no effect upon the level of income if the LM schedule is vertical or the IS schedule is horizontal.

The analysis of fiscal policy in Examples 5 and 6 has greater economic meaning, however, if analyzed in terms of the relatedness of commodity and monetary equilibrium to the rate of interest. (The relatedness of commodity equilibrium to the rate of interest depends upon the interest elasticity of spending and the marginal propensities to spend and save, while the relatedness of monetary equilibrium depends upon the interest elasticity of the demand for money and the size of the transaction demand for money.) Example 7 demonstrates that fiscal policy is most effective when spending is least responsive to the rate of interest and/or money balances are readily released from their current use with little change in the rate of interest.

EXAMPLE 7. Figure 17-7 presents monetary and commodity equilibrium schedules that bear diverse relationships to the rate of interest. Fiscal policy is most effective when spending is unrelated to the rate of interest (IS_1) and the speculative demand for money is completely interest elastic (range I).

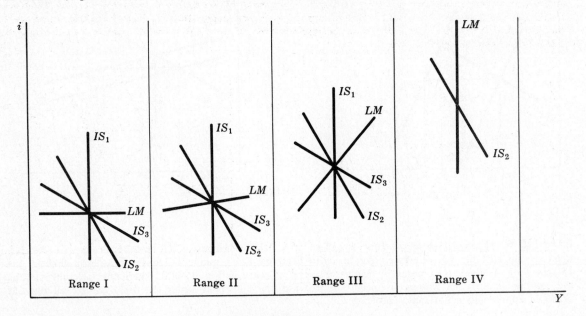

Fig. 17-7

Fiscal Policy in Range I. The schedule of monetary equilibrium in range I indicates that current holders of money readily release idle money balances upon demand without requiring an increase in the rate of interest. Fiscal policy, therefore, is completely effective in range I regardless of the relatedness of spending to the rate of interest since increased government spending does not raise the rate of interest and thereby does not decrease spending in other sectors.

Fiscal Policy in Range II. The schedule of monetary equilibrium in range II indicates that transaction balances, for an expanded income level, can be secured from current holders with only a small increase in the rate of interest.

Fiscal policy is completely effective regardless of the increase in the rate of interest if spending is unrelated to the rate of interest (IS_1). Fiscal policy is largely effective in range II if the rate of interest bears little relationship to spending (IS_2). Fiscal policy is largely ineffective for commodity equilibrium schedule IS_3 since spending is highly related to the rate of interest and only a small increase in the rate of interest from increased government spending results in a largely offsetting decline in spending in other sectors of the economy.

Fiscal Policy in Range III. An expanding level of income necessitates large increases in the rate of interest to release money from its current use to satisfy the increased need for transaction balances.

Fiscal policy is largely or completely effective in range III if spending has little (IS_2) to no (IS_1) relationship to the rate of interest. With schedule IS_3, spending is related to interest rate changes so that the increase in the rate of interest caused by increased government spending results in a nearly equal reduction of spending in other sectors of the economy.

Fiscal Policy in Range IV. Monetary equilibrium is unrelated to the rate of interest. Regardless of the relatedness of spending to the rate of interest, fiscal policy has no effect upon the level of income since no idle money balances are available for an increase in the level of income.

17.4 THE EFFECTIVENESS OF MONETARY POLICY

The effectiveness of monetary policy is also a function of the slopes of the IS and LM schedules. Monetary policy is most effective when the IS schedule has a small absolute slope and/or the LM schedule has a large absolute slope.

EXAMPLE 8. In Fig. 17-8, an increase in the money supply shifts the LM schedule rightward by $\Delta M/k$ or Y_3 minus Y_1. From an inspection of Figs. 17-8(a) and (b), we find that the increase in income from Y_1 to Y_2 is greatest in Fig. 17-8(a), where IS has the smaller slope. In Figs. 17-8(c) and (d), the slope of the LM schedule varies and we find that the distance from Y_1 to Y_2 is greatest in Fig. 17-8(d), where the LM schedule has the largest slope.

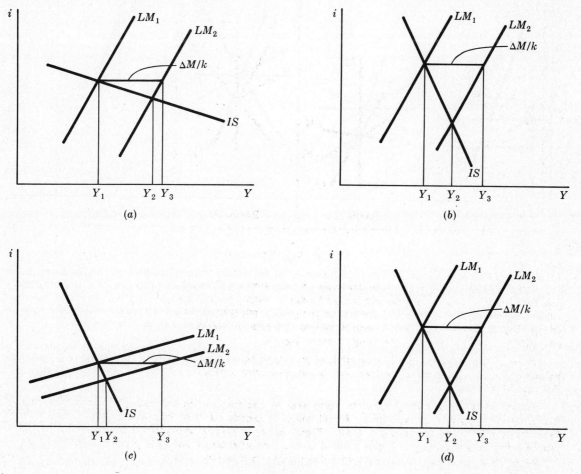

Fig. 17-8

It follows from Example 8 that an increase in the money supply is completely effective when the *IS* schedule is horizontal (has a zero slope) or the *LM* schedule is vertical (has an infinite slope). If the *IS* schedule has a slope greater than zero and the *LM* schedule has a finite slope, increases in the money supply will not change income by $\Delta M/k$. If the *IS* schedule is vertical or the *LM* schedule is horizontal, increases in the money supply have no effect upon the level of income.

As evaluated, the success of a monetary action depends upon the relatedness of monetary and commodity equilibrium to the rate of interest. Monetary policy is obviously ineffective when commodity equilibrium is completely unrelated to the rate of interest and/or changes in the money supply fail to alter the rate of interest. Monetary policy is most effective when spending is highly responsive to the rate of interest and/or a major portion of a money supply change is spent and not held as an idle balance.

EXAMPLE 9. Figure 17-9 presents monetary and commodity equilibrium schedules that bear diverse relationships to the rate of interest. Monetary policy is most effective when spending is responsive to the rate of interest (IS_3) and the demand for money is unrelated to the rate of interest (range IV).

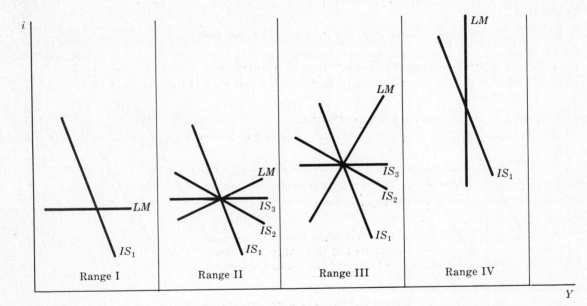

Fig. 17-9

Monetary Policy in Range I. Since all increases in the money supply are held as idle balances, monetary policy does not change the rate of interest and therefore has no effect upon the level of spending.

Monetary Policy in Range II. An increase in the money supply results in only a small decline in the rate of interest since a major portion of the increased money supply is held as an idle balance.

Monetary policy is largely ineffective in range II if spending bears little relationship to the rate of interest (IS_1). Monetary policy is largely or completely effective if spending is highly (IS_2) or completely (IS_3) responsive to small changes in the rate of interest.

Monetary Policy in Range III. An increase in the money supply causes a large decline in the rate of interest since there is little demand for idle money balances. Monetary policy is largely or completely effective if spending is highly (IS_2) or completely (IS_3) responsive to changes in the rate of interest. Monetary policy is less effective if spending (IS_1) is largely unresponsive to the rate of interest.

Monetary Policy in Range IV. Monetary policy is completely effective here since there is no speculative demand for idle money and all money supply changes result in changes in the level of spending.

Review Questions

1. Increased government spending shifts the *IS* schedule to the right by $k_e \Delta G$. This fiscal measure increases the level of income by $k_e \Delta G$ if (*a*) there is no speculative demand for money, (*b*) the *LM* schedule is vertical, (*c*) the *LM* schedule is horizontal or (*d*) the *LM* schedule has a slope greater than zero.

2. An increase in the money supply shifts the *LM* schedule rightward by $\Delta M/k$. The income level increases by $\Delta M/k$ if (*a*) the schedule of monetary equilibrium is unrelated to the rate of interest, (*b*) spending is unrelated to the rate of interest, (*c*) the *LM* schedule has a zero slope or (*d*) the *LM* schedule has a slope greater than zero but less than one.

3. A fiscal measure has no effect upon the level of income if (*a*) the *LM* schedule has a zero slope, (*b*) the *LM* schedule has a slope greater than zero but less than infinity, (*c*) the *LM* schedule has an infinite slope or (*d*) the demand for money is related to the rate of interest.

4. An increase in the money supply has no effect upon the level of income if (*a*) the schedule of monetary equilibrium is unrelated to the rate of interest, (*b*) spending is completely unrelated to the rate of interest, (*c*) the *IS* schedule has a zero slope or (*d*) the LM schedule is positively sloped.

5. In which situation is monetary policy most effective?

   (*a*) The *IS* schedule has an infinite slope; the *LM* schedule has a slope greater than zero but less than infinity.

   (*b*) The *IS* schedule has a slope greater than zero but less than infinity; the *LM* schedule has a zero slope.

   (*c*) The *IS* schedule has an infinite slope; the *LM* schedule has a zero slope.

   (*d*) The *IS* schedule has a slope greater than zero but less than infinity; the *LM* schedule has an infinite slope.

6. In which situation is fiscal policy most effective?

   (*a*) The *IS* schedule has a zero slope; the *LM* schedule has a slope greater than zero but less than infinity.

   (*b*) The *IS* schedule has a zero slope; the *LM* schedule has an infinite slope.

   (*c*) The *IS* and *LM* schedules have slopes greater than zero but less than infinity.

   (*d*) The *IS* schedule has a slope greater than zero but less than infinity; the *LM* schedule has a zero slope.

7. The slope of the *IS* schedule is largest when investment demand is (*a*) interest inelastic and the multiplier is large, (*b*) interest elastic and the multiplier is small, (*c*) interest elastic and the multiplier is large or (*d*) interest inelastic and the multiplier is small.

8. The slope of the *LM* schedule is smallest when

   (*a*) there is no speculative demand for money and the transaction demand for money is completely interest inelastic,

   (*b*) the speculative and transaction demands for money are interest inelastic,

   (*c*) there is a small transaction demand for money and the speculative demand for money is interest inelastic or

   (*d*) the demand for money is highly interest elastic.

9. Which of the following *IS* schedules is least steeply sloped?

   (*a*) $Y = \$640 - 2000i$.

   (*b*) $Y = \$640 - 1000i$.

   (*c*) $0.50\,Y = \$320 - 800i$.

   (*d*) $0.25\,Y = \$160 - 800i$.

10. In which set of equations is monetary policy most effective?

    (*a*) The *IS* equation is $Y = \$500 - 2000i$; the *LM* equation is $Y = \$400 + 4000i$.

    (*b*) The *IS* equation is $Y = \$500 - 2000i$; the *LM* equation is $Y = \$400 + 2000i$.

    (*c*) The *IS* equation is $0.25\,Y = \$160 - 800i$; the *LM* equation is $0.50\,Y = \$200 + 1000i$.

    (*d*) The *IS* equation is $0.50\,Y = \$320 - 1600i$; the *LM* equation is $0.25\,Y = \$100 + 100i$.

11. In which set of equations is fiscal policy most effective?

   (a) The IS equation is $0.25\,Y = \$160 - 800i$; the LM equation is $0.25\,Y = \$100 + 100i$.

   (b) The IS equation is $Y = \$640 - 3200i$; the LM equation is $Y = \$400 + 400i$.

   (c) The IS equation is $0.25\,Y = \$160 - 500i$; the LM equation is $Y = \$400 + 4000i$.

   (d) The IS equation is $Y = \$160 - 500i$; the LM equation is $0.25\,Y = \$125 + 1000i$.

12. Which of the following statements is *not* true?

   (a) Fiscal policy is effective if the demand for money is completely interest elastic.

   (b) Fiscal policy is largely effective if the demand for money is interest inelastic and spending is highly related to the rate of interest.

   (c) Monetary policy is largely effective if spending is highly related to the rate of interest and the activation of idle money balances requires large changes in the rate of interest.

   (d) Monetary policy is completely effective if the demand for money is unrelated to the rate of interest and spending is highly related to the rate of interest.

Answers to Review Questions

1. (c)   Review Section 17.3.

2. (a)   Review Section 17.4.

3. (c)   Review Section 17.3.

4. (b)   Review Section 17.4.

5. (d)   Review Section 17.4.

6. (d)   Review Section 17.3.

7. (d)   See Examples 1 and 2.

8. (d)   See Examples 3 and 4.

9. (d)   Review Section 17.1.

10. (d)   Review Sections 17.1, 17.2 and 17.4.

11. (d)   Review Sections 17.1, 17.2 and 17.3.

12. (b)   Review Sections 17.3 and 17.4.

Solved Problems

17.1. What determines the slope of the IS schedule?

   The slope of the IS schedule is a function of the value of the multiplier and the interest elasticity of spending. If the schedule of commodity equilibrium is unrelated to the rate of interest, there is no relationship between spending and the rate of interest and the IS schedule is vertical. If a spending sector, such as the investment sector, is responsive to interest rate changes, the IS schedule is negatively sloped. The magnitude of this slope depends upon the interest elasticity of spending and the multiplying effect that spending changes have upon the equilibrium level of income.

17.2. What determines the slope of the LM schedule?

   The LM schedule is a schedule of equilibrium between the demand for and supply of money. If there is no relationship between the rate of interest and the supply of and demand for money, the LM schedule is vertical. If either the supply of or the demand for money is influenced by interest rate changes, the LM schedule is positively sloped. The magnitude of this slope depends upon the interest elasticity of the supply of and demand for money and the size of the transaction demand for money.

17.3. Given below are three equations of consumption and investment spending for a two-sector model of the economy. (a) Derive the IS equations and (b) rank them in descending order of their relationships to the rate of interest.

   (1) $C = \$50 + 0.80\,Y$ and $I = \$60 - 200i$

   (2) $C = \$50 + 0.80\,Y$ and $I = \$70 - 100i$

   (3) $C = \$50 + 0.80\,Y$ and $I = \$100 - 1000i$

(a) The IS equation is $Y = C + I$.

(1) $Y = \$50 + 0.80\,Y + \$60 - 200i$ or $Y = \$550 - 1000i$.

(2) $Y = \$50 + 0.80\,Y + \$70 - 100i$ or $Y = \$600 - 500i$.

(3) $Y = \$50 + 0.80\,Y + \$100 - 1000i$ or $Y = \$750 - 5000i$.

(b) Ranking in descending order of relationships to the rate of interest: (3), (1), (2).

17.4. For the three equations of consumption and investment spending for a two-sector model of the economy given below, (a) derive the IS equations and (b) rank them in descending order of their relationships to the rate of interest.

(1) $C = \$50 + 0.80\,Y$ and $I = \$60 - 200i$

(2) $C = \$120 + 0.50\,Y$ and $I = \$60 - 200i$

(3) $C = \$80 + 0.75\,Y$ and $I = \$60 - 200i$

(a) The IS equation is $Y = C + I$.

(1) $Y = \$50 + 0.80\,Y + \$60 - 200i$ or $Y = \$550 - 1000i$.

(2) $Y = \$120 + 0.50\,Y + \$60 - 200i$ or $Y = \$360 - 400i$.

(3) $Y = \$80 + 0.75\,Y + \$60 - 200i$ or $Y = \$560 - 800i$.

(b) Ranking in descending order of relationships to the rate of interest: (1), (3), (2).

17.5. Explain the rankings in Problems 17.3 and 17.4.

The coefficient of i in the IS equation measures the relatedness of spending to changes in the rate of interest. The larger the coefficient of i, the greater the relationship between spending and the rate of interest. The coefficient of i in the IS equation is determined by the size of the multiplier and the interest elasticity of investment demand (the coefficient of i in the investment demand equation). In Problem 17.3, the multiplier is constant so that the value of the coefficient of i in the IS equation depends upon the interest elasticity of investment demand. In Problem 17.4, the interest elasticity of investment demand is constant, with the value for the coefficient of i dependent upon the size of the multiplier.

17.6. Listed below are equations for the supply of and demand for money. (a) Derive the LM equations and (b) rank them in descending order of their relationships to the rate of interest.

(1) $Ms = \$200,\ Mt = 0.20\,Y$ and $Ma = \$80 - 1000i$

(2) $Ms = \$200,\ Mt = 0.20\,Y$ and $Ma = \$80 - 500i$

(3) $Ms = \$200,\ Mt = 0.20\,Y$ and $Ma = \$80 - 2000i$

(a) The LM equation is $Ms = Mt + Ma$.

(1) $\$200 = 0.20\,Y + \$80 - 1000i$ or $Y = \$600 + 5000i$.

(2) $\$200 = 0.20\,Y + \$80 - 500i$ or $Y = \$600 + 2500i$.

(3) $\$200 = 0.20\,Y + \$80 - 2000i$ or $Y = \$600 + 10{,}000i$.

(b) Ranking in descending order of relationships to the rate of interest: (3), (1), (2).

17.7. Listed below are equations for the supply of and demand for money. (a) Derive the LM equations and (b) rank them in descending order of their relationships to the rate of interest.

(1) $Ms = \$200,\ Mt = 0.20\,Y$ and $Ma = \$80 - 1000i$

(2) $Ms = \$200,\ Mt = 0.10\,Y$ and $Ma = \$80 - 1000i$

(3) $Ms = \$200,\ Mt = 0.25\,Y$ and $Ma = \$80 - 1000i$

(a) The *LM* equation is $Ms = Mt + Ma$.

    (1) $\$200 = 0.20\,Y + \$80 - 1000i$ or $Y = \$600 + 5000i$.

    (2) $\$200 = 0.10\,Y + \$80 - 1000i$ or $Y = \$1200 + 10{,}000i$.

    (3) $\$200 = 0.25\,Y + \$80 - 1000i$ or $Y = \$480 + 4000i$.

(b) Ranking in descending order of relationships to the rate of interest: (2), (1), (3).

17.8. Explain the relationship between the coefficient of i in the schedule of monetary and commodity equilibrium and the slopes of the *LM* and *IS* schedules.

    The slope of a straight line equals the coefficient of the variable on the horizontal axis divided by the coefficient of the variable on the vertical axis. Since convention has i on the vertical axis and Y on the horizontal axis, the slopes of the *IS* and *LM* schedules equal the coefficient of Y divided by the coefficient of i. As the coefficient of i approaches zero, the slope approaches an infinite value with the *IS* and *LM* schedules becoming vertical. As the value of the coefficient of i increases, the absolute value of the slope falls and takes as a limit a zero value when the coefficient of i has an infinite value.

17.9. Given: A two-sector model of the economy where $C = \$10 + 0.75\,Y$ and $I = \$150 - 1000i$. The *IS* equation $Y = \$640 - 4000i$ is plotted in Fig. 17-10 below. What happens to the *IS* schedule if the coefficient of i in the investment demand equation assumes a zero value?

    The *IS* schedule pivots rightward, becoming a vertical line at the \$640 level of income.

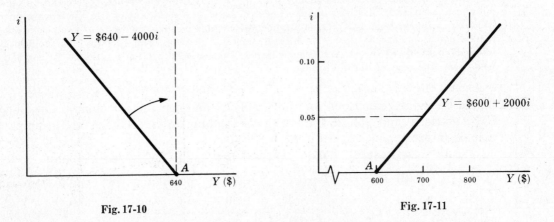

Fig. 17-10   Fig. 17-11

17.10. Suppose that (1) the money supply equals \$200, (2) the transaction demand for money is $0.25\,Y$ and (3) the speculative demand for money is $\$50 - 500i$. The *LM* equation $Y = \$600 + 2000i$ is plotted in Fig. 17-11 above. Explain what happens to the *LM* schedule if (a) there is no speculative demand for money above a 0.10 rate of interest, (b) there is an infinite speculative demand for money at a 0.05 rate of interest and (c) the coefficient of i approaches zero.

(a) When there is no speculative demand for money, the *LM* schedule bears no relationship to the rate of interest. Thus, the *LM* schedule is vertical for rates of interest equal to and greater than 0.10.

(b) When there is an infinite speculative demand for money, the *LM* schedule is horizontal. Thus, the *LM* schedule is horizontal at a 0.05 rate of interest.

(c) If the value of the coefficient for i goes to zero, the LM schedule pivots from A leftward and becomes a vertical line at the $600 level of income.

17.11. Identify and explain which of the LM schedules in Fig. 17-12 is the best graphic presentation of (1) a completely interest inelastic demand for money, (2) a completely interest elastic demand for money, (3) a highly interest elastic demand for money and (4) a highly interest inelastic demand for money.

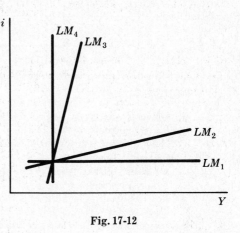

Fig. 17-12

The more inelastic the demand for money, *ceteris paribus*, the greater the slope of the LM schedule. Thus, (1) vertical schedule LM_4 must represent a completely interest inelastic demand for money schedule, (2) LM_1 must represent a completely interest elastic one, (3) LM_2 must represent a highly interest elastic one and (4) LM_3 must represent a highly interest inelastic demand for money schedule.

17.12. Using Fig. 17-12, establish which LM schedule is necessary for an effective (a) monetary policy and (b) fiscal policy.

(a) LM_3 and LM_4 are necessary for an effective monetary policy.

(b) LM_1 and LM_2 are necessary for an effective fiscal policy.

(See Examples 7 and 9.)

17.13. Identify and explain which IS schedule in Fig. 17-13 best represents sector spending which is (1) completely interest inelastic, (2) completely interest elastic, (3) highly interest inelastic and (4) highly interest elastic.

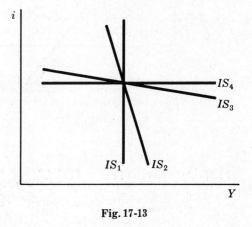

Fig. 17-13

The slope of the IS schedule increases as spending becomes less responsive to the rate of interest. Thus, (1) vertical schedule IS_1 represents sector spending that is unrelated to the rate of interest, (2) IS_4 represents sector spending that is completely interest elastic, (3) IS_2 represents sector spending that is highly interest inelastic and (4) IS_3 represents sector spending that is highly interest elastic.

17.14. Using Fig. 17-13, establish which IS schedule is necessary for an effective (a) monetary policy and (b) fiscal policy.

(a) IS_3 and IS_4 are necessary for a highly effective monetary policy.

(b) IS_1 and IS_2 are necessary for a highly effective fiscal policy.

(See Examples 7 and 9.)

17.15. Table 1 gives three sets of *IS* and *LM* equations. (*a*) Rank these sets in terms of the effectiveness of a given fiscal policy. (*b*) Explain your ranking.

Table 1

	Set 1	Set 2	Set 3
IS	$Y = \$650 - 1000i$	$Y = \$650 - 1000i$	$Y = \$650 - 1000i$
LM	$Y = \$500 + 500i$	$Y = \$550$	$Y = \$540 + 100i$

(*a*) 1, 3, 2.

(*b*) Given a negatively sloped *IS* schedule, the effectiveness of a given fiscal policy depends upon the magnitude of the increase in the rate of interest needed to release money balances from their current use for an increased volume of transactions that accompanies a higher level of income. That is, the effectiveness of a given fiscal policy depends upon the slope of the *LM* schedule. Fiscal policy is completely ineffective if the slope of *LM* is infinite (vertical) since no money balances are released by a change in the rate of interest and therefore there can be no net change in spending and the level of income. Fiscal policy is completely effective if the slope of *LM* is zero (horizontal) since money balances are readily available for an increased volume of transactions as income expands without a change in the rate of interest. Thus, fiscal policy is completely ineffective in set 2 where the *LM* schedule has an infinite slope. Fiscal policy is more effective for set 1 than 3 because of the smaller slope for *LM* schedule 1.

17.16. Table 2 gives three sets of *IS* and *LM* equations. (*a*) Rank these sets in terms of the effectiveness of a given fiscal policy. (*b*) Explain your ranking.

Table 2

	Set 1	Set 2	Set 3
IS	$Y = \$550$	$Y = \$600 - 500i$	$Y = \$700 - 1500i$
LM	$Y = \$450 + 1000i$	$Y = \$450 + 1000i$	$Y = \$450 + 1000i$

(*a*) 1, 2, 3.

(*b*) Given a positively sloped *LM* schedule, the effectiveness of a given fiscal policy is dependent upon the relationship of spending to the rate of interest. If spending bears no relationship to the rate of interest (the slope of the *IS* schedule is infinite), fiscal policy is fully effective since a rise in the rate of interest as income expands has no effect upon any sector's spending. If spending bears a strong relationship to the rate of interest (the slope of the *IS* schedule is small), sector spending falls as fiscal policy expands income and raises the rate of interest. In this latter situation, fiscal policy is less effective. Thus, fiscal policy is completely effective for set 1 since spending is unaffected by interest rate changes. Fiscal policy is more effective for set 2 than 3 because in set 2 spending is less affected by interest rate changes.

17.17. Explain the effectiveness of monetary policy for the sets in (*a*) Problem 17.15 and (*b*) Problem 17.16.

(*a*) Given a negatively sloped *IS* schedule, the effectiveness of a given monetary policy depends upon the amount of money balances held idle as changes in the supply of money alter the rate of interest. If the holding of money is unrelated to the rate of interest (the *LM* schedule is vertical), monetary policy is completely effective since an increased money supply lowers the rate of interest and affects spending rather than the holding of idle money balances. If an increase in the money supply is held idle (the *LM* schedule is horizontal), monetary policy is completely ineffective. Thus, monetary policy for set 2 is completely effective since the increased money supply results in increased spending. Monetary policy is least effective for set 1 since an increase in the money supply has a larger impact upon the quantity of money balances held idle than it does for set 3.

(b) Given a positively sloped *LM* schedule, monetary policy is more effective the greater the relationship of spending to the rate of interest. Monetary policy is completely ineffective for set 1 since spending is unrelated to the rate of interest. Monetary policy is more effective for set 3 than set 2 because spending has a greater relationship with the rate of interest in 3.

Chapter 18

Equilibrium Output with a Market for Labor Services

By adding a market for labor services to the model, the equilibrium level of income requires simultaneous equilibrium in the money, commodity and labor services markets. In this and the following chapters, small letters denote real values while capital letters continue to represent nominal money values.

18.1 THE SHORT-RUN SUPPLY OF OUTPUT

The supply of output depends upon the quantity and productivity of factor inputs (i.e., land, labor and capital).

In the short run, land and capital are assumed constant so that output depends upon the quantity of labor inputs. This is noted by $y = f(N)$, where y is the supply of real output and N is the quantity of labor inputs. The positive relationship between labor inputs and short-run output is presented in Fig. 18-1, where we see that by increasing the quantity of labor inputs from N_1 to N_2, output increases from y_1 to y_2.

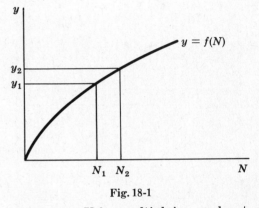

Fig. 18-1

Real output is transformed into the money value of output Y by multiplying real output y by the index of prices p. We shall analyze the labor services market in terms of the money value of output which, as explained in Section 1.6, is synonymous with the money level of income. In this chapter, we shall assume that the index of prices is constant so that changes in Y represent changes in the real level of output.

18.2 THE DEMAND FOR LABOR INPUTS

To facilitate our analysis, we shall assume that (1) labor inputs are homogeneous (of uniform quality) and mobile, (2) the demand for labor inputs for the economy can be derived from firms' demand schedules and (3) competition exists in the buying and selling of labor as well as in the buying and selling of goods.

The incremental revenue associated with an increase in the use of labor inputs, called the marginal revenue product of labor MRP_N in microeconomic theory, depends upon the price p at which goods are sold and the marginal physical product of labor MPP_N. The marginal physical product of labor, the incremental output associated with an increase in the quantity of labor inputs, is derived from the short-run supply of output schedule (see Problem 18.3). According to the law of diminishing returns, the marginal physical product of labor falls as the quantity of labor inputs increases. Thus, the marginal revenue product of labor is negatively related to the quantity of labor inputs.

EXAMPLE 1.   Suppose that the price level is 1 and the marginal physical product of labor is given by $750 - 20N$. Incremental revenue is $\text{MPP} \times p = 1(750 - 20N) = \$750 - 20N$. A schedule of incremental revenue from increasing quantities of labor inputs is given in Table 1.

Table 1

Labor Inputs	10	12	14	16	18	20
Marginal Revenue (\$)	550	510	470	430	390	350

Assuming profit maximization, labor inputs are added as long as the incremental revenue $(\text{MPP} \cdot p)$ per unit of labor input exceeds per unit incremental cost. That is, additional units of labor are demanded until $\text{MPP} \cdot p = W$, where W is the dollar cost per unit of labor input, or until $\text{MPP} = W/p$ (see Problem 18.5). This last equation states that labor inputs are added until the real value of their incremental output is equal to their real wage. The inverse relationship between the quantity of labor inputs demanded and the real wage is presented in Fig. 18-2 and is labeled Nd, the aggregate demand for labor inputs.

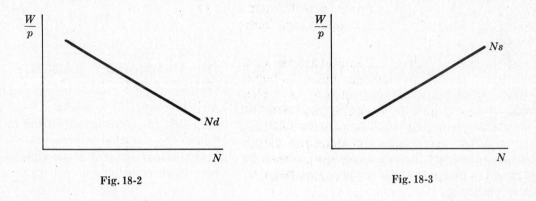

Fig. 18-2   Fig. 18-3

18.3   THE SUPPLY OF LABOR INPUTS

Work competes with leisure. If workers attach a positive value to leisure, there is increasing disutility associated with each additional hour of labor input. We shall assume that the increasing disutility of work can be overcome by increased material reward. This assumed behavior is presented in Fig. 18-3 as a positively sloped aggregate supply schedule where higher real wages are necessary for an increase in the quantity of labor inputs.

18.4   EQUILIBRIUM IN THE MARKET FOR LABOR SERVICES

Equilibrium in the market for labor services occurs where the quantity of labor inputs supplied equals the quantity of labor inputs demanded. We shall assume that the level of output determined by the equilibrium condition in the market for labor services represents the full-employment level of output.

EXAMPLE 2.   Given labor market supply and demand schedules Ns and Nd in Fig. 18-4 (page 166), equilibrium in the market for labor services occurs at real wage $(W/p)_0$. If the real wage is above $(W/p)_0$, for instance $(W/p)_1$, the quantity of labor supplied exceeds that demanded and there is involuntary unemployment of N_2 minus N_1. When such a condition exists, given a constant price level, equilibrium is achieved only by a sufficient decrease in the level of money wages.

EXAMPLE 3.   Given labor market supply and demand schedules Ns and Nd in Fig. 18-5 (page 166), equilibrium occurs at real wage $(W/p)_0$. N_0 labor units are employed at this real wage with Y_0 supplied. Thus, output Y_0 in Fig. 18-5 represents the equilibrium condition in the market for labor services and therefore the full-employment level of output.

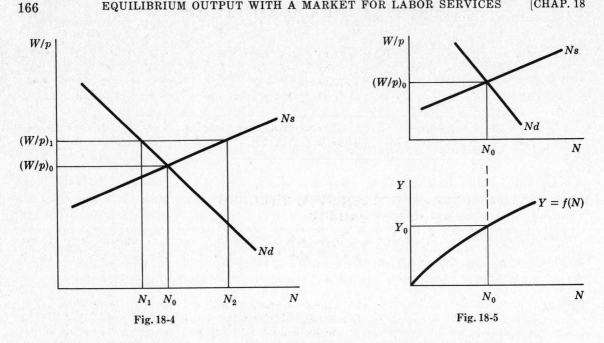

Fig. 18-4   Fig. 18-5

18.5 EQUILIBRIUM IN THE LABOR, MONEY AND COMMODITY MARKETS

With a market for labor services, a condition of full-employment equilibrium requires simultaneous equilibrium in the money, commodity and labor services markets. If the sale of output is a necessary condition for producing, it is possible for equilibrium in the money and commodity markets to occur at an income level below the one that represents equilibrium in the market for labor services. Thus, involuntary unemployment is possible if the real wage is above the equilibrium real wage or if there is an equilibrium real wage but a lack of spending.

EXAMPLE 4.   Suppose that income level Y_0 in Fig. 18-6(a) represents equilibrium in the market for labor services. Given monetary and commodity equilibrium schedules LM_0 and IS_0 and income level Y_1 in Fig. 18-6(a), there are, in Fig. 18-6(b) at income level Y_1, N_0 minus N_1 labor inputs that are involuntarily unemployed. Thus, insufficient spending can cause involuntary unemployment.

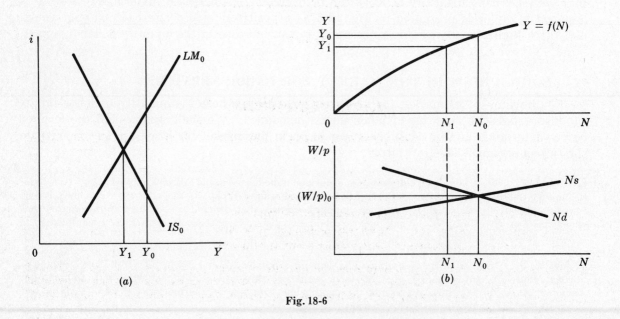

(a)   (b)

Fig. 18-6

EXAMPLE 5.   Suppose that   (1) $C = \$40 + 0.80\, Yd$, $I = \$150 - 1000i$, $Tx = \$20$ and $G = \$20$ with the equation for commodity equilibrium $Y = \$970 - 5000i$ and that (2) $Mt = 0.25\, Y$, $Ma = \$102.50 - 200i$ and $Ms = \$200$ with the equation for monetary equilibrium $Y = \$390 + 800i$. Furthermore, suppose that equilibrium in the market for labor services exists at a $2 real wage and a $500 level of output with the employment of 300 units of labor.

Solving for simultaneous equilibrium in the money and commodity markets, we obtain a $470 level of income. Since a $470 level of income employs less than 300 units of labor, there must be unemployed labor units.

18.6   FULL-EMPLOYMENT EQUILIBRIUM THROUGH MONETARY AND FISCAL POLICY

Involuntary unemployment, caused by a lack of spending, can be eliminated through an expansive monetary and/or fiscal policy if the IS and LM schedules have slopes greater than zero but less than infinity.

EXAMPLE 6.   Suppose that Y_0 in Fig. 18-7 represents equilibrium in the market for labor services and that the initial IS and LM schedules are IS_0 and LM_0. Either monetary or fiscal policy can establish full employment (i.e., simultaneous equilibrium in the three markets). Increased government spending or decreased taxes could shift the IS schedule from IS_0 to IS_1 or an increase in the stock of money could shift the LM schedule from LM_0 to LM_1. Obviously, full-employment equilibrium can be achieved by various combinations of monetary and fiscal measures.

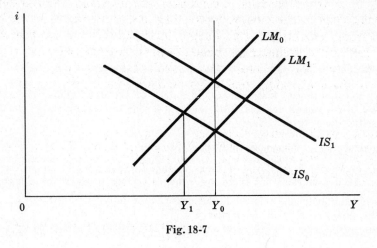

Fig. 18-7

Review Questions

In answering the following questions, assume that there is perfect competition in the buying and selling of labor.

1. The short-run labor supply function is
    (a) positively sloped because of the increasing disutility of work,
    (b) negatively sloped because of the decreasing disutility of work,
    (c) positively sloped because of the decreasing disutility of leisure   or
    (d) negatively sloped because of the increasing disutility of leisure.

2. The demand for labor   (a) is derived from the quantity of goods produced by labor, (b) is derived from the price of goods produced by labor, (c) is derived from the incremental cost and incremental revenue generated by the employment of labor   or   (d) depends upon the firm's ability to sell goods produced by labor.

3. If the marginal physical product of labor is $800 - 2N$, the price of goods is \$2 and the cost of labor is \$4 per unit, the quantity of labor employed is (a) 20 units, (b) 399 units, (c) 800 units or (d) 80 units.

4. An increase in money wages will (a) shift the demand for labor schedule to the right, (b) shift the demand for labor schedule to the left, (c) increase the quantity of labor demanded or (d) decrease the quantity of labor demanded.

5. Given a demand for labor schedule, the units of labor demanded (a) fall as the price level rises, (b) increase as the price level rises, (c) increase if there is a proportionate increase in prices and money wages or (d) decrease if there is a proportionate increase in prices and money wages.

6. If money wages increase and there is no change in the price level, the real wage (a) increases and the employment of labor decreases, (b) increases and the employment of labor increases, (c) decreases and the employment of labor decreases or (d) decreases and the employment of labor increases.

7. Labor inputs are involuntarily unemployed if

   (a) the quantity of labor demanded exceeds the quantity of labor supplied at the existing real wage,

   (b) the quantity of labor demanded equals the quantity of labor supplied at the existing real wage,

   (c) the quantity of labor supplied exceeds the quantity of labor demanded at the existing real wage or

   (d) workers willing to work at a higher real wage are currently unemployed.

8. Which of the following statements is *true*?

   (a) Full-employment equilibrium exists if there is simultaneous equilibrium in the money, commodity and labor services markets.

   (b) There is involuntary unemployment if equilibrium in the money and commodity markets occurs at an income level higher than the one representing equilibrium in the labor services markets.

   (c) The only cause of involuntary unemployment is too high a real wage.

   (d) None of the above.

9. If involuntary unemployment exists because of a lack of spending, full-employment equilibrium can be achieved by (a) lowering the real wage, (b) lowering the money wage, (c) lowering taxes or (d) decreasing the quantity of money.

10. Which of the following statements is *not* true?

   (a) Labor is voluntarily unemployed if there is simultaneous equilibrium in the money, commodity and labor services markets but there are workers willing to work for a higher real wage.

   (b) Labor is involuntarily unemployed if the quantity of labor supplied at the existing real wage exceeds the quantity of labor demanded.

   (c) Labor is involuntarily unemployed if the supply of goods exceeds the demand for goods.

   (d) Labor is involuntarily unemployed if there is simultaneous equilibrium in the money, commodity and labor services markets but there are workers willing to work for a lower real wage.

Answers to Review Questions

1. (a) Review Section 18.3.

2. (c) Review Section 18.2.

3. (b) Review Section 18.2.

4. (d) Review Section 18.2.

5. (b) Review Section 18.2.

6. (a) Review Section 18.2.

7. (c) See Example 2.

8. (a) Review Sections 18.4 and 18.5.

9. (c) Review Section 18.6.

10. (d) Review Sections 18.4 and 18.5.

Solved Problems

18.1. Why is the labor supply function positively sloped?

Work competes with leisure. It is generally postulated that the labor population prefers leisure to work and thereby will supply additional hours of labor input only if paid a higher real wage. Thus, the supply of labor inputs is positively related to the level of real wages.

18.2. What happens to the supply of labor schedule if the (a) disutility of work falls, (b) disutility of work increases or (c) the labor population increases?

(a) If there is a decrease in the disutility of work, the labor supply schedule shifts to the right, indicating labor's willingness to offer more services for a given real wage.

(b) If the disutility of work increases, the labor supply schedule shifts to the left, indicating labor's willingness to offer less services for a given real wage.

(c) If the labor population increases, the labor supply schedule shifts to the right since there are more workers willing to offer their services at a given real wage.

18.3. From the short-run schedule of aggregate output in Table 2, find the incremental output attributed to each additional unit of labor input.

Table 2

Quantity of Labor Inputs	100	101	102	103	104	105	106
Aggregate Output	950	1000	1040	1075	1105	1125	1140

In adding the 101st labor input, aggregate output increases 50. Thus, the incremental output for the 101st labor input is 50, for the 102nd labor input is 40, for the 103rd labor input is 35, for the 104th labor input is 30, for the 105th labor input is 20 and for the 106th labor input is 15.

18.4. Using the data in Problem 18.3, find the incremental revenue from each additional unit of labor input if the price level is 1.

Incremental revenue from each additional labor input equals $MPP \cdot p$, where MPP (marginal physical product) is the incremental output and p is the price level. Thus, the incremental revenue of the 101st labor input is $50, the 102nd is $40, the 103rd is $35, the 104th is $30, the 105th is $20 and the 106th is $15.

18.5. The marginal physical product of labor equals $1500 - 8N$, where N is the quantity of labor inputs. What quantity of labor is demanded if (a) wages are $4 a unit and the price level is 2, (b) wages are $4 a unit and the price level is 1 or (c) wages are $6 a unit and the price level is 1.5?

In a competitive market, workers are hired until the incremental revenue from their service equals the incremental cost of each additional unit employed. Incremental revenue equals $p(1500 - 8N)$. Incremental cost equals W. Since the quantity of labor units employed is $p(1500 - 8N) = W$ or $1500 - 8N = W/p$ (see Example 1),

(a) $1500 - 8N = 2$ and $N = 187.25$ units.

(b) $1500 - 8N = 4$ and $N = 187$ units.

(c) $1500 - 8N = 4$ and $N = 187$ units.

18.6. Given a demand for labor services schedule, what happens to the quantity of labor demanded if (a) the money wage per labor input decreases, (b) the price level falls or (c) there is a proportionate decrease in the money wage per labor input and the price level?

   (a) If there is a decrease in the money wage with no change in the price level, there is a reduction in the real wage and thereby an increase in the quantity of labor demanded.

   (b) If there is a fall in the price level, *ceteris paribus*, the real wage increases and the quantity of labor demanded decreases.

   (c) A proportionate change in the money wage and prices does not affect the quantity of labor demanded since there is no change in the real wage.

18.7. Given a demand for labor schedule, explain the relationships between the quantity of labor demanded and (a) the price level, and (b) the money wage per unit of input.

   (a) Assuming no change in the money wage, there is a negative relationship between the price level and the real wage. The higher the price level, the lower the real wage and therefore the greater the quantity of labor inputs demanded.

   (b) Assuming no change in the price level, there is a positive relationship between the money wage per unit of input and the real wage. The higher the money wage, the greater the real wage, and therefore the smaller the quantity of labor inputs demanded.

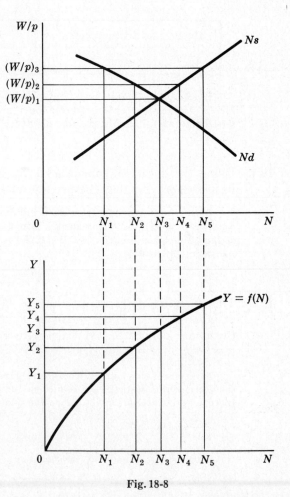

Fig. 18-8

18.8. With reference to Fig. 18-8, find the level of involuntary unemployment if the real wage is (a) $(W/p)_1$, (b) $(W/p)_2$ and (c) $(W/p)_3$.

   (a) There is no involuntary unemployment for real wage $(W/p)_1$ since the quantity of labor demanded equals the quantity of labor supplied.

   (b) At real wage $(W/p)_2$, the quantity of labor supplied exceeds the quantity of labor demanded. $N_4 - N_2$ labor units are involuntarily unemployed.

   (c) At real wage $(W/p)_3$, the quantity of labor supplied exceeds the quantity of labor demanded. $N_5 - N_1$ labor units are involuntarily unemployed.

18.9. Using Fig. 18-8 as your point of reference, explain what happens to involuntary unemployment as the real wage falls from $(W/p)_3$ to $(W/p)_1$.

   As the real wage falls, labor units that were involuntarily unemployed become either employed or voluntarily unemployed. As the real wage falls from $(W/p)_3$ to $(W/p)_1$, $N_3 - N_1$ of the involuntarily unemployed become employed while $N_5 - N_3$ become voluntarily unemployed. This latter group of labor units is not employed because it is unwilling to work for the lower real wage.

18.10. In Fig. 18-9, the real wage is $(W/p)_1$. What happens to the level of involuntary unemployment if (a) the disutility of work decreases or (b) the marginal physical productivity of labor increases?

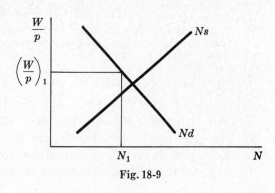
Fig. 18-9

(a) A decrease in the disutility of work shifts the labor supply schedule to the right, increasing involuntary unemployment.

(b) An increase in the productivity of labor shifts the demand for labor schedule to the right, reducing involuntary unemployment.

18.11. The demand for labor Nd equals $175 - 12.5\,w$, where w represents the real wage. The supply of labor Ns equals $140 + 5\,w$. (a) Is there equilibrium in the market for labor services if the real wage is \$3? (b) What is the equilibrium real wage?

(a) There is disequilibrium in the market for labor services at a \$3 real wage since 17.5 units of labor are involuntarily unemployed. Solution: Substituting \$3 into the supply and demand equations, we have $Nd = 175 - 12.5(3)$, with 137.5 units of labor demanded and $Ns = 140 + 5(3)$, with 155 units of labor supplied.

(b) There is equilibrium in the market for labor services when $Nd = Ns$. Solving $175 - 12.5\,w = 140 + 5w$, we find that the equilibrium real wage is \$2.

18.12. Can involuntary unemployment persist if it is caused by too high a real wage?

If there is competition in the supply of and demand for labor, involuntary unemployment due to too high a real wage is only a temporary phenomenon. In a competitive situation, involuntary unemployment should result in a decrease in money wages. Through such reductions, equilibrium will evolve by means of a lower real wage.

18.13. In Fig. 18-10, Y_f represents equilibrium between the supply of and demand for labor services. Y_1 represents equilibrium in the money and commodity markets. Is there full employment of the labor force?

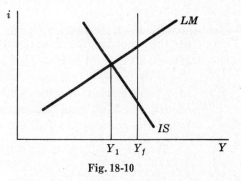
Fig. 18-10

Full employment of the labor force requires (1) that output be sold and (2) that there be equilibrium between the demand for and supply of labor. Since Y_1 spending is less than Y_f (full-employment output), there is involuntary unemployment.

18.14. Will changes in the real wage eliminate the involuntary unemployment characterized in Problem 18.13?

Since Y_f represents equilibrium in the labor services market, any change in the real wage creates disequilibrium in this market. Thus, when insufficient demand is the cause of involuntary unemployment, there must be increased spending to overcome such unemployment.

18.15. Will involuntary unemployment persist when it is due to insufficient demand?

In the absence of a price effect upon the level of spending, involuntary unemployment will persist until remedied by an expansive economic policy. Chapter 19 investigates how price changes affect the *IS* and *LM* schedules and therefore spending.

18.16. Suppose that $C = \$60 + 0.75\,Yd$, $Yd = Y - Tx$, $I = \$250 - 2000i$, $Tx = G = \$24$, $Mt = 0.25\,Y$, $Ma = \$134 - 500i$, $Ms = \$250$ and equilibrium between the demand for and supply of labor occurs when 375 labor units are employed and the level of output is \$624. Establish whether there is simultaneous equilibrium in the commodity, money and labor services markets.

The schedule for commodity equilibrium (Section 11.3) is

$$Y = C + I + G$$

$$Y = \$60 + 0.75(Y - \$24) + \$250 - 2000i + \$24$$

$$Y = \$1264 - 8000i$$

The schedule for monetary equilibrium (Section 14.2) is

$$Ms = Mt + Ma$$

$$\$250 = 0.25\,Y + \$134 - 500i$$

$$Y = \$464 + 2000i$$

Equilibrium in the money and commodity markets is

IS equation:	$Y = \$1264 - 8000i$
LM equation:	$Y = \$464 + 2000i$
	$0 = \$800 - 10{,}000i$
	$i = 0.08$
	$Y = \$624$

There is simultaneous equilibrium in all three markets since the \$624 level of income in the commodity markets is equal to a full-employment level of output.

18.17. Given: (1) $C = \$40 + 0.80\,Yd$, $Yd = Y - Tx$, $I = \$150 - 500i$ and $Tx = G = \$20$, (2) the equation for commodity equilibrium is $Y = \$970 - 2500i$, (3) $Ms = \$250$, $Mt = 0.20\,Y$ and $Ma = \$146 - 400i$, (4) the equation for monetary equilibrium is $Y = \$520 + 2000i$, (5) equilibrium between the demand for and supply of labor occurs at a \$750 level of income and (6) equilibrium in the money and commodity market occurs at a \$720 level of income. What change in government spending or taxes will bring the economy to full employment?

Through fiscal policy, the *IS* schedule shifts rightward, intersecting the *LM* schedule at the \$750 full-employment level of income. Substituting \$750 into the *LM* equation we have

$$\$750 = \$520 + 2000i$$

$$i = 0.115$$

Through the stimulative fiscal action (and thereby rightward shift of the *IS* schedule), there is simultaneous equilibrium in the three markets at a 0.115 rate of interest. However, investment spending falls as the rate of interest increases from 0.10 to 0.115. Fiscal policy must therefore negate the \$17.50 decline in investment spending as well as increase income \$30. The possible alternative fiscal policies are (1) increased government spending $(k_e\,\Delta G - k_e\,\Delta I = \Delta Y)$ and (2) decreased taxes $(k_{tx}\,\Delta Tx - k_e\,\Delta I = \Delta Y)$.

If government spending is used to achieve full employment, there must be a \$23.50 increase in government spending.

$$k_e \Delta G - k_e \Delta I = \Delta Y$$

$$5\Delta G - \$87.50 = \$30$$

$$\Delta G = \$23.50$$

If a decrease in taxes is used as the policy tool, there must be a \$29.375 decrease in taxes.

$$k_{tx} \Delta Tx - k_e \Delta I = \Delta Y$$

$$4\Delta Tx - \$87.50 = \$30$$

$$\Delta Tx = \$29.375$$

Chapter 19

The Price Level and Equilibrium Income

In this chapter we continue the analysis of simultaneous equilibrium in the money, commodity and labor services markets, analyzing the effect that price changes and wage rigidities have upon a simultaneous solution for the three markets.

19.1 THE PRICE LEVEL AND EQUILIBRIUM IN THE MONEY MARKET

The real money supply m equals the nominal money supply M divided by price level p. It follows that when the price level falls, the real money supply increases and the LM schedule, plotted with respect to real income, shifts to the right. When the price level increases, the real money supply falls, shifting the LM schedule leftward. It therefore follows that price changes can move the three markets toward simultaneous equilibrium if prices rise when equilibrium income in the money and commodity markets exceeds the full-employment level of output and prices fall when this income level falls short of the full-employment level of output.

EXAMPLE 1. Suppose that real income level y_0 in Fig. 19-1 represents full employment in the market for labor services and that the relevant monetary and commodity equilibrium schedules are LM_0 and IS_0. With equilibrium in the money and commodity markets occurring at y_1, there are unemployed labor inputs. If prices and money wages fall proportionately when there is unemployment, the real wage is unchanged and equilibrium in the market for labor services remains at the y_0 level of real income. A decline in prices, however, increases the real money supply, shifting the LM schedule rightward. Prices and money wages stop falling when schedule LM_1 is reached and there is simultaneous equilibrium in the money, commodity and labor services markets at real income y_0.

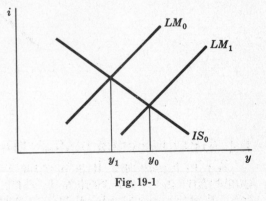

Fig. 19-1

19.2 THE PRICE LEVEL AND EQUILIBRIUM IN THE COMMODITY MARKET

Changes in the price level affect the real value of financial wealth, with the real value of debt owned by creditors and owed by borrowers increasing as the price level falls and decreasing as the price level rises. Changes in the price level also affect the real value of the nominal money supply, with the real value of money increasing as prices fall and decreasing as prices increase. If all debt is issued by the government sector and is owned by the household sector and the credit money supply is also issued by government and owned by households, it follows that households' holding of real debt plus real money (the sum of which we shall call real balances) increases as the price level falls and decreases as the price level increases.

EXAMPLE 2. Suppose that the household sector owns $200 of the nominal money supply and $250 of the debt issued by the government sector.

When the price level is 2, households' real balances (holdings of nominal money plus debt issued by the government divided by the price level) equal ($200 + $250)/2 = $225. When the price level is 1.50, households' real balances are $300 while they equal $200 when the price level is 2.25. Thus, real balances increase from $225 to $300 if the price level falls from 2 to 1.50 and decrease from $225 to $200 if the price level increases from 2 to 2.25.

If household spending is positively related to changes in its holding of real balances while spending by the government sector is unaffected by such changes, a fall in the price level will increase aggregate spending. Thus, if there is credit money and/or government debt outstanding, the *IS* schedule shifts to the left when the price level rises and shifts to the right when the price level falls.

EXAMPLE 3. Suppose that there is equilibrium in the market for labor services at real income y_0 and that schedules IS_0 and LM_0 in Fig. 19-2 establish equilibrium in the commodity and money markets at real income y_1. We continue our assumptions that (1) goods and services are supplied only when there is a demand for them and (2) wages and prices fall proportionately when there is unemployment.

Unemployment exists at income level y_1 in Fig. 19-2. Prices should therefore fall, causing increases in the real money supply and real balances (assuming credit money and government debt). There are continuous declines in the price level, shifting *IS* and *LM* rightward, until there is simultaneous equilibrium in the money, commodity and labor services markets at real income y_0.

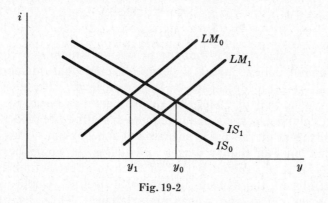

Fig. 19-2

19.3 SIMULTANEOUS EQUILIBRIUM: PRICE CHANGES vs. ECONOMIC POLICY

We have seen that it is possible to achieve simultaneous equilibrium in the money, commodity and labor services markets through price changes (Sections 19.1 and 19.2) or through monetary and fiscal policy (Section 18.6). The success and viability of these alternatives depend upon the slopes of the *IS* and *LM* schedules, the volume of real balances and their effect upon household spending, and the duration of unemployment with a price adjustment mechanism.

EXAMPLE 4. Suppose, as depicted in Fig. 19-3, there is a deflationary condition where y_0 is the full-employment level of income. Furthermore, assume that the marginal propensity to consume real balances and the volume of real balances are small.

The steeply sloped *IS* schedule and the nearly horizontal *LM* schedule in Fig. 19-3 indicate that a rightward shift of *LM* from an increased money supply has little effect upon the level of income. (See Section 17.4 and Problems 19.5-19.6.) In addition, a weak real balance effect causes small rightward shifts of the *IS* schedule as the price level falls. Thus, to increase the level of aggregate spending, there would have to be a substantial fall in the price level to reach full employment.

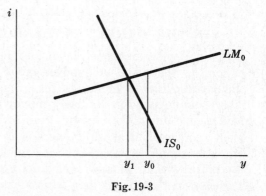

Fig. 19-3

EXAMPLE 5.   Suppose, as depicted in Fig. 19-4, there is a deflationary condition where y_0 is the full-employment level of income.   Furthermore, assume that the marginal propensity to consume real balances and the volume of real balances are large.

The steeply sloped LM schedule and negatively sloped IS schedule in Fig. 19-4 indicate that a rightward shift of LM from an increased real money supply has a large effect upon the rate of interest and the level of aggregate spending.   (See Section 17.4 and Problems 19.5-19.6.)   In addition, a strong real balance effect is supportive of price declines as a means of increasing household spending.   Thus, it is possible to move the economy to full-employment equilibrium with a relatively small decline in the price level.

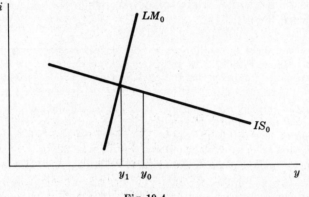

Fig. 19-4

It follows from Examples 4 and 5 that the price mechanism is a viable alternative to an interventionist economic policy during a period of inadequate demand, although in some cases it may necessitate large decreases in the price level.   However, we find that, as a result of the Employment Act of 1946, the government has elected to commit itself to an interventionist policy during periods of inadequate spending because of the possible greater depth and longer duration of the price adjustment mechanism.   For example, since there is a downward inflexibility of money wages and prices, it would be necessary for unemployment to persist for a protracted period of time to effect actual declines in prices and money wages.   In addition, the expectation of price declines would cause a postponement of spending until lower prices and wages materialized.   Thus, by its social commitment to the Employment Act of 1946 to maximize employment, the government has viewed price and wage declines as an unacceptable alternative to a flexible economic policy.

During periods of excessive spending, however, there has been a reliance upon the price adjustment mechanism.   In adhering to a policy of maximum employment, policy makers have in many situations been tardy in initiating a restrictive economic policy for fear that the decline in spending would be excessive and result in unemployment. Thus, during periods of excessive spending, price increases have reduced real balances and the real money supply and thereby have helped eliminate excessive demand.

19.4   MONEY ILLUSION AND A MONEY WAGE FLOOR IN THE MARKET FOR LABOR SERVICES

In a Keynesian model, labor supplies its services for a money rather than a real wage as long as there are unemployed labor inputs.   Furthermore, workers resist reductions in the current level of money wages.   Such behavior is presented in Fig. 19-5(a) where (1) the labor supply function Ns has a money wage floor W_0 (indicating that labor is unreceptive to a reduction in the current level of money wages) and (2) N_0 represents full employment and the point at which there is an end to money illusion.   In Fig. 19-5(b), money wage W_0 is presented in real terms and we find that the real wage falls from W_0/p_0 to W_0/p_1 as the price level increases from p_0 to p_1.   Such a reduction in the real wage through price increases is possible as long as less than N_0 labor inputs are employed.

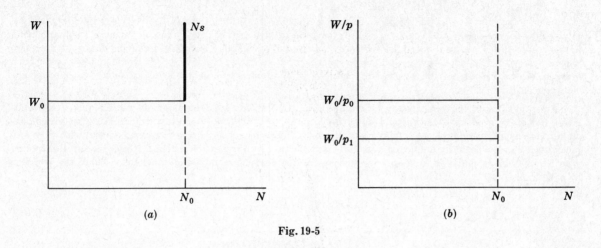

Fig. 19-5

With labor supplying its services for a money wage, it is possible that simultaneous equilibrium in the money, commodity and labor services markets may occur although too high a real wage results in involuntary unemployment. Such a condition of unemployment equilibrium is stable (see Example 6) if there is no expansionary economic policy and no change in the money wage. Thus, when a money wage floor exists, the price mechanism is not even theoretically an alternative to an interventionist economic policy.

EXAMPLE 6. Suppose that in Fig. 19-6(a) the money wage is W_0, the price level is p_1, full employment is N_0 and, in Fig. 19-6(b), money and commodity equilibriums are represented by LM_1 and IS_1. Given the demand for labor services schedule Nd_1, N_1 labor inputs are demanded and y_1 are supplied. Output level y_1 is also the equilibrium level in the money and commodity markets so that y_1 is a position of simultaneous equilibrium in the three markets although there are $N_0 - N_1$ unemployed labor units.

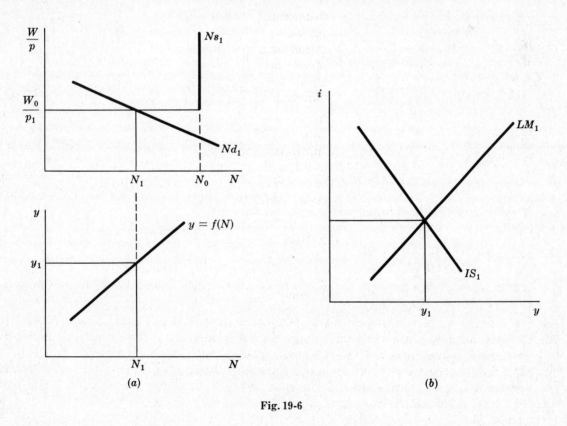

Fig. 19-6

Income level y_1 is a stable position and represents a condition of unemployment equilibrium. A fall in prices would increase the real wage and create additional involuntary unemployment. An increase in prices would lower the real wage and increase the quantity of labor inputs demanded. Given involuntary unemployment and simultaneous equilibrium in the three markets, market forces would not generate such price increases. Thus, in the absence of changes in market forces or the level of money wages, output would remain at y_1.

An expansionist economic policy is required for a condition of unemployment equilibrium. A stimulative monetary or fiscal policy would shift LM_1 or IS_1 in Fig. 19-6(b) rightward, creating an excess demand for output y_1 and prices would rise. Through price increases and a lowering of the real wage, N_0 labor inputs are eventually employed and full-employment equilibrium is reached. Success for this policy requires that labor continue to supply its services at the current money wage and not react to the increase in prices.

Review Questions

1. If the nominal money stock equals $600 and the price level is 3, the real money supply equals (a) $100, ($b$) $200, ($c$) $300 or ($d$) $600.

2. Which one of the following statements is *not* true?
    (a) If the relative increase in the price level is greater than the relative increase in the nominal stock of money, the real money supply decreases.
    (b) If the relative increase in the nominal stock of money is greater than the relative increase in the price level, the real money supply increases.
    (c) If the price level decreases, *ceteris paribus*, the real money supply decreases.
    (d) If the price level increases, *ceteris paribus*, the real money supply decreases.

3. An increase in the price level
    (a) reduces the real money supply and shifts the LM schedule to the right,
    (b) reduces the real money supply and shifts the LM schedule to the left,
    (c) increases the real money supply and shifts the LM schedule to the right or
    (d) increases the real money supply and shifts the LM schedule to the left.

4. A reduction in the price level increases the real money supply but not the level of income (a) if the LM schedule has an infinite slope, (b) if the LM schedule has a slope greater than zero but less than infinity, (c) if the LM schedule has a zero slope or (d) none of the above.

5. Price changes result in a change in real balances if all debt (a) originates in the private sector, (b) is owned by the private sector, (c) originates in and is owned by the private sector or (d) is privately owned and some debt originates in the public sector.

6. Changes in real balances affect aggregate spending if
    (a) the public sector's marginal propensity to consume wealth is zero and the private sector's marginal propensity to consume wealth is greater than zero,
    (b) the private sector's marginal propensity to consume wealth is zero,
    (c) the private sector's marginal propensity to consume wealth is less than the public sector's or
    (d) the private sector's marginal propensity to consume wealth is the same as the public sector's.

7. A gross debt of $800 is owned by the private sector. $400 of this debt is owed by the private sector, $200 is interest-bearing public debt and $200 is credit money issued by the federal government. If the price level is 1, real balances equal (a) $200, ($b$) $400, ($c$) $600 or ($d$) $800.

8. Falling prices increase the real money supply and real balances,
    (a) shifting the IS schedule to the right and the LM schedule to the left,
    (b) shifting the IS schedule to the left and the LM schedule to the right,
    (c) shifting the IS and LM schedules to the right or
    (d) shifting the IS and LM schedules to the left.

9. If the full-employment equilibrium level of income is greater than the equilibrium level of income in the money and commodity markets,

   (a) falling prices will shift the *IS* and *LM* schedules to the right, bringing about simultaneous equilibrium in all markets,

   (b) falling prices will shift the *IS* and *LM* schedules to the left, bringing about simultaneous equilibrium in all markets,

   (c) rising prices will shift the *IS* and *LM* schedules to the left, bringing about simultaneous equilibrium in all markets or

   (d) rising prices will shift the *IS* and *LM* schedules to the right, bringing about simultaneous equilibrium in all markets.

10. The Keynesian labor supply function theorizes that workers (a) accept a decrease in money wages as long as these cuts bring about full employment, (b) accept money wage cuts as long as real wages do not fall, (c) resist any decrease in their real wages or (d) resist any decrease in their money wages.

11. If there is a money wage floor and disequilibrium in the labor markets,

   (a) an increase in the money wage will bring about simultaneous equilibrium in all markets,

   (b) a decrease in the price level will bring about simultaneous equilibrium in all markets,

   (c) price adjustments cannot bring the economy to a position of full employment or

   (d) economic policy cannot bring the economy to a position of full employment.

12. Which of the following statements is *not* true?

   (a) If the price level is falling, expectations prolong and deepen a contraction.

   (b) If the price level is falling, expectations along with increases in real balances and the money supply hasten recovery from a contraction.

   (c) If the price level is falling, adverse expectations might outweigh the positive effect of increased real balances and an increased real supply of money.

   (d) Falling prices are no longer a viable alternative to economic policy during a deflationary period.

Answers to Review Questions

1. (b) Review Section 19.1.

2. (c) Review Section 19.1.

3. (b) Review Section 19.1.

4. (c) See Example 4 and Problem 19.5.

5. (d) See Example 2.

6. (a) Review Section 19.2.

7. (b) See Example 2.

8. (c) See Example 3.

9. (a) See Example 3.

10. (d) Review Section 19.4.

11. (c) See Example 6.

12. (b) Review Section 19.3.

Solved Problems

19.1. The nominal stock of money is $450. What is the real stock of money if the price level is (a) 1, (b) 1.5 or (c) 2?

The real money supply equals the nominal stock of money divided by the price level. The real money supply is

(a) $450.

(b) $300.

(c) $225.

19.2. Explain the negative relationship between the price level and the real money supply.

A given nominal stock of money can be viewed as a stock of spending power. The spending power of this nominal money increases as prices fall and decreases as prices rise. Thus, the spending power of a nominal stock of money (that is, the real money supply) is inversely related to the price level.

19.3. The equation for equilibrium in the commodity markets is $y = \$850 - 2500i$; $y = -\$500 + 5m + 1000i$ is the equation for equilibrium in the money markets. Full-employment equilibrium exists at a $650 real level of income. If the nominal money supply is $200 and the price level is 1, (a) does an inflationary or deflationary condition exist? (b) At what price level will there be simultaneous equilibrium in all markets?

(a) The real money supply m equals $200. Substituting $m = \$200$ into the LM equation, we have $y = \$500 + 1000i$. Simultaneous equilibrium in the money and commodity markets occurs where $IS = LM$.

IS equation:	$y = \$850 - 2500i$
LM equation:	$y = \$500 + 1000i$
	$0 = \$350 - 3500i$

Solving,

$$i = 0.10$$
$$y = \$600$$

Since a $650 income level represents full employment, a deflationary condition exists in the economy.

(b) Substituting $y = \$650$ into the IS equation, we find that a $650 income level is consistent with an 0.08 rate of interest. Substituting $y = \$650$ and $i = 0.08$ into the LM equation, we find the real quantity of money consistent with full-employment equilibrium.

LM equation:	$y = -\$500 + 5m + 1000i$
	$\$650 = -\$500 + 5m + 80$
	$m = \$214$

Given a $200 nominal money supply, the price level must fall from 1.0 to 0.934 to increase the real money supply to $214 and thereby bring about equilibrium in all markets.

19.4. What change in the nominal stock of money in Problem 19.3 would bring about full-employment equilibrium?

In the answer to Problem 19.3(b) we found that the real stock of money must increase from $200 to $214 to effect a condition of full-employment equilibrium. Assuming that the price level remains at 1, there must be a $14 increase in the nominal stock of money.

19.5. If there is a condition of unemployment, will an increase in the real money supply through a fall in prices always bring about a full-employment level of income?

An increase in the real money supply through a fall in prices will bring about full employment if the slope of the LM schedule is greater than zero. If the LM schedule is horizontal, an increase in the real money supply through a price decline has no effect upon the real level of income (see Sections 19.3 and 17.4).

19.6. Assume that only monetary equilibrium is affected by price changes. Which of the following situations would necessitate the largest decline in prices to achieve a given increase in the level of income?

(1) The demand for money is highly interest elastic.

(2) The demand for money is interest inelastic.

(3) The demand for money is completely interest inelastic.

Monetary policy is most effective when the demand for money is highly interest inelastic, i.e., when the *LM* schedule has the largest slope. Thus, situation (1), where the slope of *LM* is smallest, requires the largest decline in the price level to achieve a given increase in the level of income.

19.7. Private debt equals $750. Public debt totals $350 and there is a $200 supply of commodity-backed money. All debt and money is owned by the private sector. What is the private sector's real balances if the price level is 2?

When money is backed by a commodity, money is issued to the private sector upon receipt of an equally valued quantity of commodities from the private sector. Thus, the existence and creation of commodity money has no effect upon the private sector's net wealth. The private sector's real balances, then, equal its nominal holding of public debt divided by the price level. In this problem, the private sector's real balances equal $175 (see Section 19.2).

19.8. If the money supply in Problem 19.7 is credit money, what are the private sector's real balances?

The private sector does not give up wealth to receive credit money. Therefore, given a credit money supply, real balances of the private sector equal its holding of credit money plus public debt divided by the price level. If the money supply in Problem 19.7 is credit money, the private sector's real balances would then equal $275.

19.9. Assuming that the private sector owns the entire quantity of money and public debt outstanding, in which of the following situations would price level changes have the greatest real balance effect?

(1) Interest-bearing public debt totals $250 and the commodity money supply is $100.

(2) Interest-bearing public debt totals $250 and the credit money supply is $100.

(3) Interest-bearing public debt is zero and the commodity money supply is $100.

There are no real balances in situation (3). Real balances are larger in (2) than (1). Therefore, price level changes will have the greatest real balance effect in (2).

19.10. In which of the following situations will the real balance effect have the greatest impact upon the level of income?

(1) Aggregate spending is completely interest inelastic.

(2) Aggregate spending is interest inelastic.

(3) Aggregate spending is interest elastic.

A change in real balances causes a parallel shift of the *IS* schedule. Like fiscal measures, real balance changes are most effective when aggregate spending is least responsive to the rate of interest. The real balance effect is most effective in situation (1).

19.11. In Fig. 19-7, y_f represents the level of income where there is equilibrium in the market for labor services; simultaneous equilibrium in the money and commodity markets occurs at y_1. How is simultaneous equilibrium in all markets achieved?

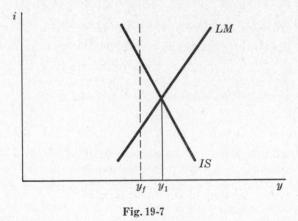

Fig. 19-7

We can see from the figure that there is excessive spending in the economy. In the absence of economic policy, prices will increase, reducing real balances and the real money supply. Prices will rise until the fall in real balances and the real money supply reduce spending through a leftward shift of the IS and LM schedules to income level y_f. The government, through a restrictive monetary and/or fiscal policy, could also shift the LM and/or IS schedules leftward to income level y_f.

19.12. Suppose that the equation for commodity equilibrium in real terms is $y = \$640 + 0.40\,rb - 4000i$, the equation for monetary equilibrium in real terms is $y = -\$410 + 5m + 1000i$ and equilibrium in the labor services market exists at a \$600 real income level. (a) At what real income level is there equilibrium in the commodity and money markets if the nominal money supply is \$200, the price level is 1, and the household sector's nominal real balances are \$500? (b) At what price level is there simultaneous equilibrium in all markets?

(a) If the price level is 1, the real money supply is \$200 and real balances equal \$500. Substituting $m = \$200$ and $rb = \$500$ into the IS and LM equations respectively,

$$y = \$840 - 4000i$$
$$y = \$590 + 1000i$$

Solving,
$$y = \$640$$
$$i = 0.05$$

There is excessive spending in the economy since full employment occurs at a \$600 level of income.

(b) There is simultaneous equilibrium in all markets at a \$600 real income level. Therefore, substituting $y = \$600$, $rb = \$500/p$ and $m = \$200/p$ into the IS and LM equations respectively,

$$\$600 = \$640 + \frac{\$200}{p} - 4000i$$

$$\$600 = -\$410 + \frac{\$1000}{p} + 1000i$$

Solving,
$$i = 0.0576$$
$$p = 1.05$$

The price level must increase from 1 to 1.05 to eliminate the excessive spending in the economy.

19.13. What is meant by money illusion in the supply of labor services?

There is money illusion in the supply of labor services if labor specifies its willingness to work in terms of money wages and the supply schedule is unaffected by changes in the price level.

19.14. With reference to Fig. 19-8, Nd_1 is the demand for labor services and N_0 is the position of full employment of labor services. (*a*) If W_0/p_0 is the current real wage, what must happen to the real wage to achieve full employment? (*b*) What will cause such a change in the real wage? (*c*) What options remain if W_0 is a money wage floor?

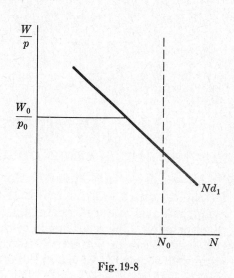

Fig. 19-8

   (*a*) The real wage must fall.

   (*b*) The real wage will fall if (1) given a price level, money wages fall, (2) given a constant level of money wages, the price level increases, (3) money wages fall and the price level increases or (4) money wages fall faster than the price level.

   (*c*) If the money wage will not decline, an increase in the price level is the only way of decreasing the real wage.

19.15. In Fig. 19-9, (1) N_f and y_f represent full employment in the market for labor services, (2) the money wage floor is W_0, (3) the price level is p_0 and (4) LM_0 and IS_0, represent money and commodity equilibrium. Will price changes bring the economy to full-employment equilibrium?

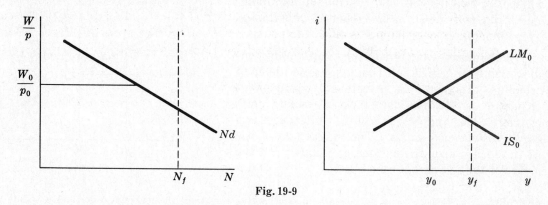

Fig. 19-9

   Given a money wage floor, y_f cannot be achieved through changes in the price level. A price decline is required to shift money and commodity equilibrium to y_f, whereas an increase in the price level is necessary to lower the real wage so that N_f labor units are employed. A stimulative monetary and/or fiscal policy is needed to achieve full-employment equilibrium.

Chapter 20

Determinants of the Price Level

20.1 THE SCHEDULE OF AGGREGATE DEMAND

It was shown in Sections 19.1 and 19.2 that a fall in the price level increases the real money supply and real balances, raising the level of aggregate spending. The relationship between price and real income can be formalized into a schedule of aggregate demand. As prices fall from p_0 to p_1 in Fig. 20-1, there are shifts in the schedules of monetary and commodity equilibriums from LM_0 and IS_0 to LM_1 and IS_1 and an increase in the level of real income from y_0 to y_1. Thus, price level p_0 is consistent with a y_0 level of real income while the lower price level p_1 is consistent with the higher y_1 level of real income. By continuous manipulation of the price level, we are able to derive the aggregate demand schedule in Fig. 20-1.

Changes in parameters of the IS and LM schedules result in shifts of the aggregate demand schedule. Increases in investment, government spending or the nominal stock of money shift aggregate demand to the right, while decreases result in leftward shifts. The magnitude of the shift depends upon the parameter changes and the slopes of the IS and LM schedules.

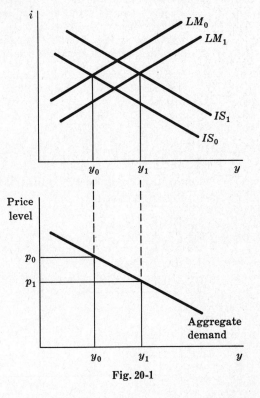

Fig. 20-1

EXAMPLE 1. When there is an increase in *government spending*, the aggregate demand schedule shifts rightward by $k_e \Delta G$ if the LM schedule is horizontal and/or the IS schedule is vertical. If the slope of the IS schedule is less than infinite and the slope of the LM schedule is greater than zero, the rightward shift is less than $k_e \Delta G$.

Alternatively, when there is an increase in the *nominal money supply*, the aggregate demand schedule shifts rightward by $\Delta M/k$ if the IS schedule is horizontal or the LM schedule is vertical. If the slope of the IS schedule is greater than zero and the LM schedule is less than infinity, the rightward shift is less than $\Delta M/k$.

20.2 A CLASSICAL AGGREGATE SUPPLY SCHEDULE

The classical approach to markets presumes perfect competition. Thus, money wages and prices are perfectly flexible and, by assumption, the real wage is *always* at the full-employment level of output. As a result, changes in money wages and prices are proportional, keeping the real wage at w_f in Figs. 20-2(a) and (b), and aggregate supply [Fig. 20-2(c)] is a vertical line at y_f, the full-employment level of output.

184

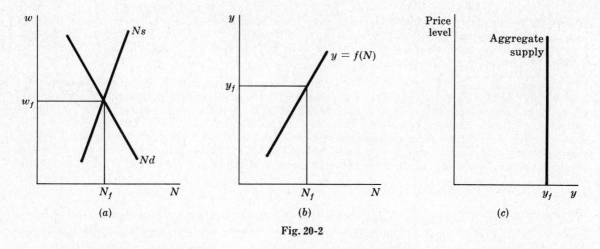

Fig. 20-2

The classical aggregate supply schedule shifts to the right if the productivity of labor increases and/or there is a rightward shift in the supply schedule for labor services.

20.3 AGGREGATE SUPPLY WITH A KEYNESIAN LABOR SUPPLY FUNCTION

In the traditional Keynesian analysis of the market for labor services, money illusion and a money wage floor are included in the labor supply function. As a result of this assumed behavior, aggregate supply is positively related to the price level until the full-employment level of output is reached [see Fig. 20-3(b)].

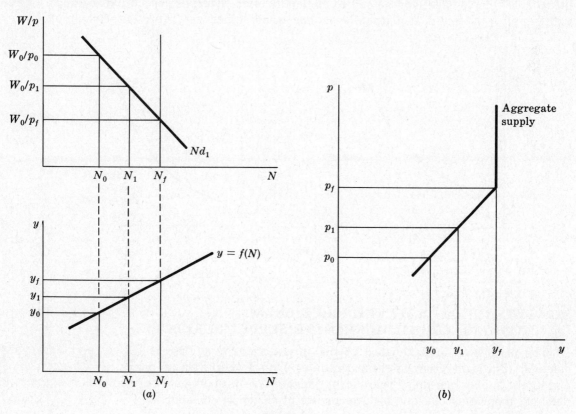

Fig. 20-3

EXAMPLE 2. Suppose that, regardless of the price level, labor supplies its services for money wage W_0 and that this money illusion persists until there is full employment of N_f labor units [see Fig. 20-3(a)]. Furthermore, assume no illusion in the demand for labor units so that with schedule Nd_1, the quantity of labor units demanded depends upon the real wage.

With price level p_0 and money wage W_0 in Fig. 20-3(a), the real wage is W_0/p_0 and business firms hire N_0 labor inputs and supply y_0 output. An increase in the price level to p_1 lowers the real wage to W_0/p_1, increasing the quantity of labor inputs demanded to N_1 and the supply of output to y_1. Output continues to increase until price level p_f, where real wages W_0/p_f results in the full employment of N_f workers. Thus, in Fig. 20-3(b), increases in the price level are positively related to business firms' willingness to supply output until price level p_f, where there is full employment of labor units and an end to money illusion. The aggregate supply schedule becomes vertical once there is full employment of the labor force.

The Keynesian aggregate supply schedule shifts as a result of changes in the productivity of labor and changes in the money wage floor. Productivity increases shift the entire aggregate supply schedule rightward while increases in the money wage floor shift only the positively sloped portion of the aggregate supply schedule leftward.

20.4 AGGREGATE SUPPLY WITH A MONEY WAGE LABOR SUPPLY FUNCTION

We now drop the assumption of a money wage floor but continue to assume that there is money illusion in the supply of labor inputs. Given the money wage labor supply schedule Ns in Fig. 20-4, larger quantities of labor inputs are demanded as the price level increases so that firms' willingness to supply output is positively related to the price level. Unlike the aggregate supply schedule in Example 2, there is no vertical range where, by definition, there is full employment and an end to money illusion. Thus, as conceptualized here, aggregate supply can exceed an output level that would otherwise represent full employment.

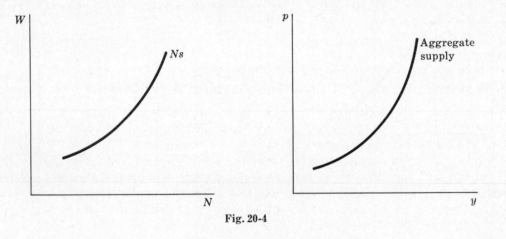

Fig. 20-4

20.5 DETERMINANTS OF THE PRICE LEVEL WITH A CLASSICAL AGGREGATE SUPPLY SCHEDULE

The price level is established at the intersection of aggregate supply and aggregate demand. Shifts in either of these schedules change the levels of prices. With a classical aggregate supply schedule, price level changes are proportional to changes in aggregate demand, the supply of labor services or the productivity of labor.

EXAMPLE 3.   In Fig. 20-5, we trace the effect of increased demand upon the level of prices. The price level is initially p_0, given schedules D_0 and S_0. An increase in the money supply shifts aggregate demand to D_1, causing excessive demand of $y_1 - y_0$ at price level p_0. An increase in prices to p_1 eliminates this excessive demand through a decrease in real balances and the real money supply. Since there is no change in real output y_0, the increase in prices is proportional to the increase in aggregate demand.

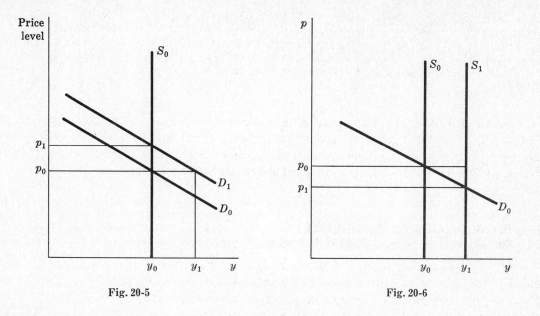

Fig. 20-5   Fig. 20-6

EXAMPLE 4.   Figure 20-6 shows the effect on prices of an increase in the supply of labor services. Additions to the supply of labor services reduce the real wage, increase the quantity of labor units employed and increase the full-employment level of output. Thus, aggregate supply shifts from S_0 to S_1 and inadequate demand of $y_1 - y_0$ develops at price level p_0. As the price level falls to p_1, real balances and the real money supply increase, thereby raising the volume of spending to real income level y_1. The change in price is proportional to the change in the full-employment level of output.

20.6 DETERMINANTS OF THE PRICE LEVEL
WITH A KEYNESIAN AGGREGATE SUPPLY SCHEDULE

With a Keynesian labor supply function, it is possible for aggregate supply and aggregate demand to intersect at a price level below the full-employment level of output. If it does, an increase in aggregate demand not only increases the level of output, thereby reducing the level of unemployment, but increases the price level as well. When unemployment exists in this Keynesian model, changes in aggregate demand are not proportional to changes in the level of output or the price level. Once full employment is reached and money illusion ceases, increases in aggregate demand cause proportional changes in the price level and no change in the level of output.

EXAMPLE 5.   Suppose that output levels below y_f in Fig. 20-7(a) (page 188) represent unemployment and are due to labor's demand for a W_0 level of money wages. Suppose also that there is no money illusion in the supply of labor services at or beyond output level y_f.

Given D_0 and S_0 in Fig. 20-7, there are unemployed labor inputs of $N_f - N_0$ at real output y_0. If, through an expansionist economic policy, aggregate demand increases to D_1, there is excess demand of $y_2 - y_0$ at price level p_0. This excess demand increases prices to p_1, lowering the real wage in Fig. 20-7(b) to W_0/p_1. Then, N_1 rather than N_0 labor inputs are employed and the quantity of output supplied increases to y_1. The increase in output and employment, though, is less than proportional to the increase in aggregate demand since additional labor inputs are employed only if an increase in the price level lowers the real wage.

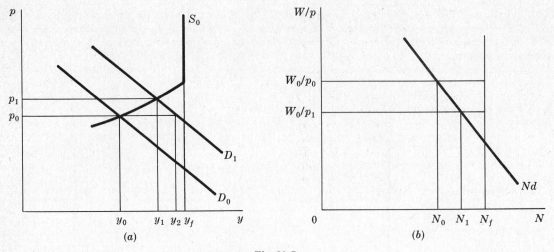

Fig. 20-7

EXAMPLE 6. In Fig. 20-8 we trace the effect of an increase in the money wage floor upon output and prices. Initially we assume aggregate demand and supply schedules D_0 and S_0 with prices at p_0 and output at y_0. An increase in the money wage floor from W_0 to W_1 raises the real wage from W_0/p_0 to W_1/p_0 and shifts the positively sloped portion of the aggregate supply schedule leftward to S_1. At the original price level p_0, there is now excess demand of $y_0 - y_2$. A price increase to p_1 lowers the real wage to W_1/p_1. Simultaneous equilibrium in the supply of and demand for goods occurs at real income y_1. Thus, an increase in the money wage floor results in higher prices, a reduction in the employment of labor inputs and a lower level of output.

If the relative increase in money wages is met by an equal relative increase in the productivity of labor, there is no leftward shift in the aggregate supply schedule and therefore no change in prices or the level of output.

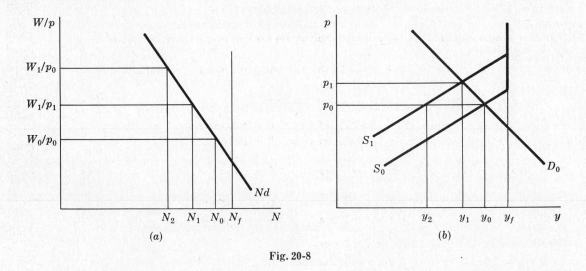

Fig. 20-8

20.7 DETERMINANTS OF THE PRICE LEVEL WITH A MONEY WAGE AGGREGATE SUPPLY SCHEDULE

The analysis of price determination in this section is similar to that in Section 20.6. The price level depends upon the level of aggregate spending and the money wage level. Unlike the Keynesian aggregate supply schedule, however, there is no vertical portion to the schedule since we no longer assume that money illusion ends at full employment. Thus, increases in aggregate demand always result in increases in the levels of price and output.

EXAMPLE 7. In Fig. 20-9, we specify y_0 as the level of output where there is full employment in the market for labor services. Aggregate supply is positively sloped beyond y_0, however, since labor continues to offer its services for a money wage and the increase in money wages is less than the increase in the price level. The extent to which demand increases result in increases in the levels of price and output depends upon the economy's nearness to full employment. An increase in aggregate demand, if initiated in the vicinity of D_1, has a smaller effect upon the price level and a larger effect upon output than would one initiated in the vicinity of D_2, where the economy is at full employment.

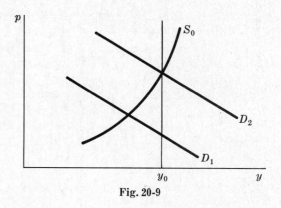

Fig. 20-9

Review Questions

1. Aggregate demand is
   - (a) negatively related to the price level because a fall in prices has a negative effect upon the demand for output,
   - (b) negatively related to the price level because a fall in prices has a positive effect upon the demand for output,
   - (c) positively related to the price level because a fall in prices has a negative effect upon the demand for output   or
   - (d) positively related to the price level because a fall in prices has a positive effect upon the demand for output.

2. Aggregate demand shifts
   - (a) to the right if there is increased government spending and the demand for money is interest elastic,
   - (b) to the right if there is increased government spending and the demand for money is completely interest inelastic,
   - (c) to the left if there is a decrease in the nominal stock of money and the demand for money is completely interest elastic   or
   - (d) to the left if there is an increase in the price level.

3. If there is perfect competition in the market for labor services, aggregate supply is
   - (a) positively related to the price level because a fall in prices has a positive effect upon the employment of labor,
   - (b) positively related to the price level because a fall in prices has a negative effect upon the employment of labor,
   - (c) unrelated to the price level because the real wage is unaffected by changes in the price level   or
   - (d) negatively related to the price level because workers will not work for lower money wages.

4. The classical aggregate supply schedule shifts
   - (a) to the right if there is an increase in the price level,
   - (b) to the left if there is an increase in aggregate demand,
   - (c) to the right if there is an increase in the productivity of labor   or
   - (d) to the left if there is an increase in the supply of labor.

5. Assuming a classical aggregate supply schedule, if there is a rightward shift of aggregate demand,
   - (a) price increases are proportional to the increase in aggregate demand,
   - (b) price increases are more than proportional to the increase in aggregate demand,
   - (c) price increases are less than proportional to the increase in aggregate demand   or
   - (d) there is no increase in prices since the aggregate supply schedule is vertical.

6. Given a classical aggregate supply schedule and a negatively sloped aggregate demand schedule, which of the following statements is *false*?

(*a*) There is a decrease in prices and an increase in the real level of income if there is an increase in the productivity of labor.

(*b*) There is no change in prices and output if government expenditures increase and the demand for money is completely interest inelastic.

(*c*) Price increases are proportional to the increase in the nominal stock of money if the demand for money is completely interest inelastic.

(*d*) There is an increase in prices and a decrease in the real level of income if there is an increase in the supply of labor.

7. If labor units are unemployed and there is a Keynesian money wage floor, an increase in aggregate demand

(*a*) results in an increase in prices proportional to the increase in aggregate demand,

(*b*) results in an increase in prices less than proportional to the increase in aggregate demand,

(*c*) results in an increase in prices more than proportional to the increase in aggregate demand   or

(*d*) has no effect upon prices since there is unemployment.

8. According to Keynesian analysis of the market for labor services, a rise in the money wage floor shifts (*a*) the entire aggregate supply schedule to the left, (*b*) the entire aggregate supply schedule to the right, (*c*) the nonvertical portion of the aggregate supply schedule to the right   or   (*d*) the nonvertical portion of the aggregate supply schedule to the left.

9. Assuming a Keynesian aggregate supply schedule, if there is an increase in the money wage floor, (*a*) both output and prices rise, (*b*) both output and prices fall, (*c*) output increases and prices fall   or   (*d*) output falls and prices rise.

10. If there is a positively sloped money wage labor supply function, aggregate supply (*a*) is vertical, (*b*) is vertical and then has a positive slope, (*c*) has a positive slope and is then vertical   or   (*d*) has a positive slope.

11. Given that aggregate supply and aggregate demand intersect in the positively sloped portion of the aggregate supply schedule, which of the following statements is *false*?

(*a*) If there is an interest elastic demand for money, a decrease in government spending decreases prices and output.

(*b*) If commodity demand is interest elastic, an increase in the nominal stock of money increases prices and output.

(*c*) An increase in the productivity of labor decreases prices and increases output.

(*d*) An increase in money wages decreases prices and output.

12. If there is a positively sloped money wage labor supply function, demand changes (*a*) always result in price and output changes, (*b*) affect prices but not necessarily output, (*c*) affect output but not necessarily prices   or   (*d*) have no effect upon prices or output.

Answers to Review Questions

1. (*b*) Review Section 20.1.

2. (*a*) See Example 1.

3. (*c*) Review Section 20.2.

4. (*c*) Review Section 20.2.

5. (*a*) See Example 3.

6. (*d*) Review Section 20.5.

7. (*b*) See Example 5.

8. (*d*) See Example 6.

9. (*d*) Review Section 20.6.

10. (*d*) Review Section 20.4.

11. (*d*) Review Section 20.6.

12. (*a*) Review Section 20.7.

Solved Problems

20.1. Define the aggregate demand schedule.

The aggregate demand schedule shows the equilibrium levels of real income in the money and commodity markets which are consistent with different price levels. It is derived from the change in simultaneous equilibrium in the money and commodity markets brought about by changes in the price level. For example, a decrease in the price level increases real balances and the real money supply, shifting the *IS* and *LM* schedules to the right. At this lower price level, there is a higher real level of income where there is simultaneous equilibrium in the money and commodity markets.

20.2. What determines the slope of the aggregate demand schedule?

The slope of the aggregate demand schedule measures the effect of price changes upon the level of real income representative of simultaneous equilibrium in the money and commodity markets. A steeply sloped aggregate demand schedule indicates that there is a weak real balance effect and that the demand for money is highly interest elastic. Aggregate demand is less steeply sloped when changes in real balances and the real money supply substantially alter the level of real income where there is simultaneous equilibrium in the money and commodity markets.

20.3. In which of the following situations is the slope of aggregate demand greater?

(1) There is no real balance effect; the demand for money is completely interest elastic.

(2) There is a weak real balance effect; the demand for money is completely interest inelastic.

In situation (1), there is no shift of the *IS* schedule as a result of price changes and the rightward shift of the *LM* schedule has no effect upon real income since it is horizontal. Aggregate demand in situation (1) is unrelated to price (is vertical) and therefore has the greater slope.

20.4. What is the magnitude of the shift of aggregate demand (*a*) when there is an increase in the nominal stock of money, the *LM* schedule is positively sloped and the *IS* schedule is negatively sloped? (*b*) When there is an increase in taxes, the *LM* schedule is positively sloped and the *IS* schedule is negatively sloped? (*c*) When there is an increase in government spending, the *LM* schedule has an infinite slope and the *IS* schedule is negatively sloped?

(*a*) Aggregate demand shifts rightward by less than $\Delta M/k$.

(*b*) Aggregate demand shifts leftward by less than $k_{tx} \Delta Tx$.

(*c*) There is no shift in aggregate demand since increased government spending has no effect upon the level of income when the *LM* schedule is vertical.

20.5. Define the aggregate supply schedule.

The aggregate supply schedule shows the effect that price changes have upon the level of output that represents equilibrium in the market for labor services. If the real wage is lowered by a price increase and more labor units are, in turn, employed, the level of output that represents equilibrium in the market for labor services becomes a positive function of the price level. If the real wage is unaffected by price level changes, then the level of output that represents equilibrium in the market for labor services bears no relationship to the price level.

20.6. Which of the aggregate supply schedules in Fig. 20-10 below best represents (a) the supply of labor which is inelastic with respect to the level of money wages? (b) A money wage floor and money illusion in the supply of labor until full employment is realized? (c) The supply of labor which is elastic with respect to the level of money wages?

(a) S_3 shows that since the money wage level has little effect upon the quantity of labor supplied, price changes, which alter the real wage, have little effect upon the supply of output.

(b) S_1 is eventually vertical, indicating that money illusion no longer exists at some level of employment.

(c) S_2 shows that there are large changes in output from small changes in price, indicating an elastic labor supply function.

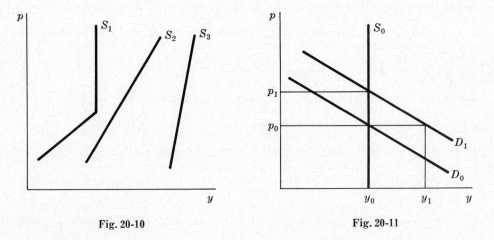

Fig. 20-10　　　　　　　　　　　　　Fig. 20-11

20.7. With reference to Fig. 20-11 above, (a) what happens to the level of prices and output if aggregate demand increases from D_0 to D_1 and (b) how does a price increase eliminate excess demand?

(a) Increased demand results in excess demand of $y_1 - y_0$ at price level p_0. Since supply is not influenced by the price level, there is no change in output and excess demand is eliminated once the price level increases to p_1.

(b) Real balances fall as the price level increases, thereby reducing consumption spending. Investment spending also falls as the reduction in the real money supply increases the rate of interest.

20.8. Given: (1) D_0 and S_0 in Fig. 20-12 (the initial aggregate supply and aggregate demand schedules), (2) a negatively sloped *IS* schedule and (3) a positively sloped *LM* schedule. What happens to aggregate supply, aggregate demand, the price level and real output if there is an increase in (a) the nominal stock of money, (b) government spending, (c) exogenous investment or (d) the size of the labor force?

In situations (a) through (c), D_0 shifts to the right; the price level increases and there is no change in the level of output. In situation (d), S_0 shifts to the right, causing an increase in output and a decline in the price level.

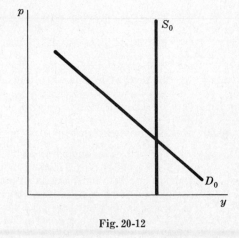

Fig. 20-12

20.9. In what way or ways are the answers to Problem 20.8 altered if (1) the *IS* schedule is vertical *or* (2) the *LM* schedule is vertical?

> The slopes of the *IS* and *LM* schedules affect the answers to situations (*a*) through (*c*) in Problem 20.8.

(1) If the *IS* schedule is vertical, changes in the nominal stock of money have no effect upon the aggregate demand schedule and therefore no effect upon the price level. Situations (*b*) and (*c*) continue to cause a rightward shift of aggregate demand and an increase in the price level.

(2) If the *LM* schedule is vertical, situations (*b*) and (*c*) would not result in a rightward shift of aggregate demand. When the *LM* schedule is vertical, excessive demand can be caused only by an increase in the nominal stock of money.

20.10. Given a classical aggregate supply schedule and a downward sloping aggregate demand schedule, in which of the following situations (*a*) does an exogenous increase in aggregate demand result in the larger increase in the price level and (*b*) is the slope of aggregate demand larger?

(1) Spending is highly interest inelastic, the demand for money is interest elastic and the marginal propensity to consume a change in real balances is 0.05.

(2) Spending is interest elastic, the demand for money is interest inelastic, and the marginal propensity to consume a change in real balances is 0.15.

(*a*) The interest elasticity of spending and the interest elasticity of the demand for money determine the effect of changes in the real money supply upon aggregate spending. The marginal propensity to consume a change in real balances measures the effect of price changes upon household consumption spending. The larger increase in the price level occurs in situation (1), where changes in the real money supply have the smaller effect upon aggregate spending and the real balance effect upon consumption is smaller. That is, price changes have the smaller effect upon aggregate spending in situation (1) and as a result there must be a greater increase in the price level to deter a given volume of excess demand.

(*b*) Since price changes have the smaller effect upon aggregate spending in situation (1), the aggregate demand schedule in situation (1) has the larger slope.

20.11. Given a classical aggregate supply schedule and a negatively sloped aggregate demand schedule, what happens to the price level, the money wage and the real wage if there is an increase in (*a*) the supply of labor services, (*b*) the productivity of labor or (*c*) aggregate demand.

(*a*) There is a decrease in the price level. Since there has been a rightward shift in the supply of labor services, the real wage must fall. The decline in the money wage must exceed the decline in the price level.

(*b*) There is a decrease in the price level. Since there is a rightward shift of the demand for labor, the real wage must rise. The money wage need not fall if the price decline is sufficient to bring the real wage to its new equilibrium level.

(*c*) There is an increase in the price level. Since there is no change in the condition of labor market equilibrium, there is no change in the real wage. The increase in the money wage is proportional to the increase in the price level.

20.12. With reference to Fig. 20-13 (page 194), (*a*) what happens to the level of prices and output if aggregate demand increases from D_0 to D_1 and (*b*) how is excess demand eliminated?

(a) There is excess demand of $y_2 - y_0$ at price level p_0. An upward sloping aggregate supply schedule indicates money illusion in the supply of labor services. Excess demand causes prices to increase to p_1 and real output to increase to y_1.

(b) Excess demand is eliminated by a decrease in aggregate spending and an increase in real output. Spending is reduced by a negative real balance effect and a decrease in the real money supply. Firms' willingness to supply output increases with a reduction in the real wage.

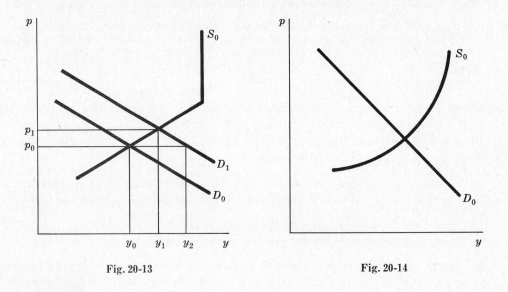

Fig. 20-13   Fig. 20-14

20.13. Suppose that (1) D_0 and S_0 in Fig. 20-14 are the initial aggregate supply and demand schedules, (2) the *IS* schedule is negatively sloped and (3) the *LM* schedule is vertical. What happens to aggregate supply and demand, the level of prices and real output, and the real wage if (a) workers demand higher money wages? (b) There is an increase in taxes? (c) Technological change increases the productivity of labor? (d) There is an increase in the nominal stock of money?

(a) S_0 shifts to the left. The price level increases and output falls. There is an increase in the real wage.

(b) There is no shift in the aggregate demand schedule since the *LM* schedule is vertical. Prices, output and the real wage are unchanged.

(c) S_0 shifts to the right. Prices fall. Output and the real wage increase.

(d) D_0 shifts to the right. The price level and output increase. The real wage falls.

(See Examples 1 and 7.)

20.14. Under what circumstances would a change in the nominal stock of money have its greatest impact upon (a) real output and (b) the price level?

(a) A change in the nominal stock of money has its greatest impact upon output if the demand for money is completely interest inelastic and the supply of labor is highly elastic with respect to the money wage.

(b) In this case, the greatest impact upon the price level occurs when the demand for money is completely interest inelastic and the demand for and supply of labor are both functions of the real wage.

20.15. Is the nominal money supply the sole determinant of the price level?

The nominal money supply is the sole determinant of the price level only if (1) spending is not completely interest inelastic, (2) the demand for money is completely interest inelastic, (3) the supply of and demand for labor are both functions of the real wage and (4) there is no change in the schedules comprising (1) through (3).

Chapter 21

Aggregate Spending and Equilibrium Growth

In this chapter our focus changes from short-run analysis of employment, prices and output to long-run analysis of equilibrium growth. We now address ourselves to the need for adequate growth of aggregate spending to meet an increasingly productive capacity.

The notation yp is used to denote the potential level of output (potential supply) while y continues to represent the actual level of output established by the level of spending.

21.1 THE POTENTIAL LEVEL OF OUTPUT

An economy's potential level of output is a function of the quantity and productivity of natural resources R, labor services N and capital K. In the short-run analysis of earlier chapters, R and K were assumed constant (see Section 18.1) so that $y = f(N)$. In the long run, however, all inputs are variable. We assume, in our analysis of the long run, that (1) there is no money illusion, (2) the increase in all inputs is proportional, and (3) there is no change in the productivity of factor inputs. Thus, we assume that potential output doubles if the quantities of R, N and K double. Such a relationship is presented in Fig. 21-1, where an increase in the stock of capital from K_0 to $2K_0$ increases potential output from yp_0 to $2yp_0$. While not included in Fig. 21-1, the quantities of N and R have also, by assumption, doubled.

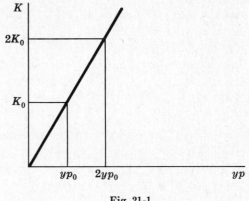

Fig. 21-1

EXAMPLE 1. Suppose that the stock of capital in period 1 is $400, potential output is $100 and there is a $40 increase in the stock of capital in each successive period. We see from Table 1 that the increase in potential output is in direct proportion to net investment, the increase in the stock of capital.

Table 1

Period	Net Investment ($)	Stock of Capital ($)	Potential Output ($)
1	40	400	100
2	40	440	110
3	40	480	120
4	40	520	130

When there are constant returns to scale and proportional growth of factor inputs, the relationship between potential output and the stock of inputs can be presented by $yp = \sigma K$, where σ (sigma) represents the average productivity of capital. Since we have assumed a linear relationship between potential output and the stock of capital, σ also represents the marginal productivity of capital. Thus, $\Delta yp = \sigma \Delta K$. By definition, net investment I is the net addition to an economy's stock of capital so that $\Delta yp = \sigma I$.

21.2 AGGREGATE SPENDING AND INCREASES IN THE POTENTIAL LEVEL OF OUTPUT

In this section, aggregate spending is represented by the private sector $(C + I)$ model of Chapter 2, with the addition of the long-run statistical consumption function discussed in Chapter 8.

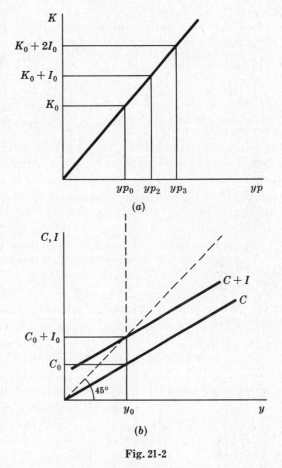

Fig. 21-2

Figure 21-2(a) presents the relationship between potential output and the stock of capital while Fig. 21-2(b) presents the actual level of output determined by the equality of the value of output and aggregate spending. The analysis starts in period 1, where the stock of capital is K_0 and potential output is yp_0; aggregate spending is $C_0 + I_0$ with actual output at y_0. Thus, in period 1 there is full utilization of productive capacity since yp_0 equals y_0.

If there is no autonomous change in investment spending in period 2, actual output remains at y_0. Potential output in period 2, however, has increased to yp_2 as a result of the I_0 volume of net investment during period 1. Thus, excess capacity of $yp_2 - yp_0$ develops in period 2. Excess capacity increases to $yp_3 - yp_0$ in period 3 if there is no increase in aggregate spending.

If there is insufficient growth of autonomous investment spending, an increasing gap between potential and actual output over successive periods develops.

EXAMPLE 2. Suppose that the stock of capital in period 1 is $200 and potential output is $100, $C = 0.90\,y$ and $I_0 = \$10$. If investment remains at $10 in successive periods, there is an increasing difference between actual and potential output, as shown in Table 2.

Table 2

Period	K ($)	yp ($)	I_0 ($)	C ($)	y ($)	$yp - y$ ($)
1	200	100	10	90	100	0
2	210	105	10	90	100	5
3	220	110	10	90	100	10
4	230	115	10	90	100	15
5	240	120	10	90	100	20

The increasing difference of $yp - y$ is due to the rise in capacity from a continuous net investment of $10 while there is no increase in aggregate spending.

21.3 INVESTMENT SPENDING AND EQUILIBRIUM GROWTH

In a private sector model with a long-run consumption function, investment is the source of autonomous spending and therefore growth in actual output. Thus, investment spending must increase at a rate whereby the growth in aggregate spending is equal to the increase in productive capacity.

Increased aggregate spending and therefore increased actual output in a private sector model equal $\Delta y = \Delta I/\alpha$, where α (alpha) is the marginal propensity to save and ΔI is the one-period increase in investment spending. Increased potential output equals $\Delta yp = \sigma I$, where I represents actual net investment of the previous period. In equilibrium growth, incremental spending equals the increase in potential output. Thus,

$$\frac{\Delta I}{\alpha} = \sigma I$$

so that

$$\frac{\Delta I}{I} = \alpha\sigma$$

For equilibrium growth, then, net investment must increase at a rate equal to $\alpha\sigma$. If net investment increases at this rate, the growth of actual output also equals $\alpha\sigma$ (see Problem 21.9).

EXAMPLE 3. A deficiency in aggregate spending, even if eventually corrected, reduces the economy's growth of capacity. Thus, to maximize economic growth, net investment must increase each period at the rate of $\alpha\sigma$.

Situation I: In Table 3, the stock of capital is $800 in period 1, $\sigma = 0.25$ and $\alpha = 0.20$. Net investment is $40 in period 1 and increases in successive periods at a 0.05 rate.

Table 3

Period	K ($)	yp ($)	I ($)	C ($)	y ($)	yp − y ($)
1	800.00	200.00	40.00	160.00	200.00	0
2	840.00	210.00	42.00	168.00	210.00	0
3	882.00	220.50	44.10	176.40	220.50	0
4	926.10	231.53	46.30	185.23	231.53	0
5	972.40	243.10	48.62	194.48	243.10	0
6	1021.02	255.26	51.05	204.21	255.26	0
7	1072.07	268.02	53.61	214.41	268.02	0
8	1125.68	281.42	56.28	225.14	281.42	0
9	1181.96	295.47	59.09	236.38	295.47	0
10	1241.06	310.25	62.05	248.20	310.25	0

Situation II: In Table 4, the stock of capital is $800 in period 1, $\sigma = 0.25$ and $\alpha = 0.20$. Net investment is $40 in periods 1 through 5. Net investment increases to $50 in period 6 to eliminate the difference between potential output and actual output and increases at a 0.05 rate beginning in period 7.

Table 4

Period	K ($)	yp ($)	I ($)	C ($)	y ($)	yp − y ($)
1	800.00	200.00	40.00	160.00	200.00	0
2	840.00	210.00	40.00	160.00	200.00	10.00
3	880.00	220.00	40.00	160.00	200.00	20.00
4	920.00	230.00	40.00	160.00	200.00	30.00
5	960.00	240.00	40.00	160.00	200.00	40.00
6	1000.00	250.00	50.00	200.00	250.00	0
7	1050.00	262.50	52.50	210.00	262.50	0
8	1102.50	275.62	55.12	220.50	275.62	0
9	1157.62	289.40	57.88	231.52	289.40	0
10	1215.50	303.87	60.77	243.10	303.87	0

Contrasting periods 6 through 10, where there is equilibrium growth in both situations, we see that the increase in potential output is larger in each successive period in situation I. Here there is continuous equilibrium growth, while in situation II, there is a deficiency in aggregate spending in the initial periods.

21.4 MONETARY AND FISCAL POLICY AND THE RATE OF ECONOMIC GROWTH

Equilibrium growth can be secured through the use of both monetary and fiscal policy. The choice of policy instruments, however, can effect the economy's rate of economic growth.

EXAMPLE 4. The following situations show that a monetary policy that increases investment at a rate of $\alpha\sigma$ achieves maximum growth while a fiscal policy of consumptive government spending lowers the rate of economic growth.

Given: The stock of capital in period 1 is $800, $\sigma = 0.25$, $\alpha = 0.20$ and $Tx = 0$.

Situation I: Suppose that government spending is zero in all periods and net investment is $40 in period 1. An expansive monetary policy secures a 5% growth of net investment in each successive period to maintain equilibrium growth (see Table 5).

Table 5

Period	K ($)	yp ($)	I ($)	C ($)	G ($)	y ($)
1	800.00	200.00	40.00	160.00	0	200.00
2	840.00	210.00	42.00	168.00	0	210.00
3	882.00	220.50	44.10	176.40	0	220.50
4	926.10	231.53	46.30	185.23	0	231.53

Situation II: Suppose that net investment is $40 in all periods. Consumptive government spending is zero in period 1 but increases $2 a period in each successive period to maintain equilibrium growth (see Table 6).

Table 6

Period	K ($)	yp ($)	I ($)	C ($)	G ($)	y ($)
1	800	200	40	160	0	200
2	840	210	40	168	2	210
3	880	220	40	176	4	220
4	920	230	40	184	6	230

Potential output after four periods is less in situation II, where consumptive government expenditures rather than net investment is the source of exogenous spending.

A fiscal measure of increased consumptive government spending results in a rate of growth of $\alpha\sigma - \sigma G/y$ while increased government spending of the investment type causes a growth of $\alpha\sigma$ provided that public and private investment are equally productive (see Problem 21.12). Tax reductions, an alternative fiscal measure, represent a decrease in the rate of aggregate saving and therefore have the same effect upon economic growth as consumptive government spending (see Problem 21.13).

Review Questions

1. The analysis of potential output in this chapter assumes that the increase in potential output is due to
    (a) proportional increases in the quantity of the factors of production,
    (b) increases in the stock of capital,
    (c) an increase in the productivity of capital or
    (d) an increase in the stock and productivity of capital.

2. The capacity effect of a $50 net investment is
    (a) $50 if the average productivity of capital is 0.20,
    (b) $40 if the average productivity of capital is 0.25,
    (c) $25 if the average productivity of capital is 0.50   or
    (d) $10 if the average productivity of capital is 1.0.

3. The capacity effect of net investment is
    (a) negatively related to the average productivity of capital,
    (b) positively related to the marginal propensity to save,
    (c) positively related to the average productivity of capital   or
    (d) negatively related to the marginal propensity to save.

4. Which of the following statements is *incorrect*?
    (a) There is a gap between potential and actual output if aggregate spending increases at a slower rate than capacity.
    (b) There is equilibrium growth if spending increases at the same rate as capacity.
    (c) There is no growth in capacity if net investment does not increase over time.
    (d) Growth in capacity is a function of net investment and the average productivity of capital.

5. To achieve equilibrium growth, net investment must increase
    (a) 4% each period if the average productivity of capital is 0.50 and the marginal propensity to save is 0.10.
    (b) 4% each period if the average productivity of capital is 0.25 and the marginal propensity to save is 0.20.
    (c) 5% each period if the average productivity of capital is 0.50 and the marginal propensity to save is 0.10.
    (d) 5% each period if the average productivity of capital is 0.50 and the marginal propensity to save is 0.20.

6. If the marginal propensity to save is 0.10, the average and marginal productivity of capital is 0.25 and investment demand is growing 3% each period, then (a) aggregate spending is growing faster than capacity, (b) capacity is growing faster than aggregate spending, (c) there is equilibrium growth or   (d) fiscal or monetary policy must be used to stimulate aggregate spending.

7. If a country wishes to increase its rate of equilibrium growth, it should
    (a) increase the rate of saving and increase the average productivity of capital,
    (b) increase the rate of saving and decrease the average productivity of capital,
    (c) decrease the rate of saving and increase the average productivity of capital   or
    (d) decrease the rate of saving and decrease the average productivity of capital.

8. A deficiency in aggregate spending
    (a) has no effect upon an economy's rate of growth of potential output,
    (b) has no effect upon an economy's rate of growth of potential output if the deficiency is replaced by consumptive government spending,
    (c) may be needed to increase the economy's rate of growth of potential output   or
    (d) reduces the economy's rate of growth of potential output.

9. If government spending is the source of increased autonomous spending over time, the rate of growth of potential output is
    (a) greater than $\alpha\sigma$ if government spending is consumptive,
    (b) less than $\alpha\sigma$ if government spending is consumptive,
    (c) greater than $\alpha\sigma$ if government spending represents public investment which has the same average productivity as private investment   or
    (d) less than $\alpha\sigma$ if government spending represents public investment which has the same average productivity as private investment.

10. A reduction in personal income taxes, *ceteris paribus*,
    (a) increases the rate of equilibrium growth since the economy's rate of saving is falling,
    (b) increases the rate of equilibrium growth since the economy's rate of saving is increasing,
    (c) decreases the rate of equilibrium growth since the economy's rate of saving is increasing   or
    (d) decreases the rate of equilibrium growth since the economy's rate of saving is falling.

Answers to Review Questions

1. (a) Review Section 21.1.
2. (c) Review Section 21.1.
3. (c) Review Section 21.1.
4. (c) Review Section 21.2.
5. (c) Review Section 21.3.

6. (a) Review Section 21.3.
7. (a) Review Section 21.3.
8. (d) See Example 3.
9. (b) See Example 4.
10. (d) Review Section 21.4.

Solved Problems

21.1. What is an economy's potential level of output if the average productivity of capital is 0.50 and the stock of capital is (*a*) \$400, (*b*) \$450, (*c*) \$500 or (*d*) \$550?

Since $yp = \sigma K$, the potential level of output is

(*a*) \$200.

(*b*) \$225.

(*c*) \$250.

(*d*) \$275.

21.2. What happens to the economy's potential level of output it net investment is \$40 per period and the marginal productivity of capital is 0.20?

Since $\Delta yp = \sigma I$, the economy's potential level of output increases \$8 per period.

21.3. What happens to the economy's potential level of output if net investment is \$50 per period and the marginal productivity of capital is (*a*) 0.20, (*b*) 0.25, (*c*) 0.50 or (*d*) 1.0?

The increase in potential output per period is

(*a*) \$10.

(*b*) \$12.50.

(*c*) \$25.

(*d*) \$50.

21.4. Suppose that (1) the stock of capital in period 1 is \$400, (2) the average and marginal productivity of capital equals 0.25, (3) $C = 0.80\,y$ and (4) net investment is \$20 each period.   Find actual and potential outputs for periods 1 through 4.

Potential output for each period equals σK while actual output equals I/α (see Table 7).

Table 7

Period	K (\$)	yp (\$)	C (\$)	I (\$)	y (\$)
1	400	100	80	20	100
2	420	105	80	20	100
3	440	110	80	20	100
4	460	115	80	20	100

21.5. Why is potential output greater than actual output for period 4 in Table 7?

There is no exogenous increase in spending and therefore no increase in aggregate spending. Potential output, however, is increasing \$5 each period from the constant \$20 in net investment per period.

21.6. Would there be equilibrium growth in Problem 21.4 if investment increased \$1 each period?

The figures in Table 8 (page 202) show that potential output exceeds actual output in periods 3 and 4. For equilibrium growth (see Section 21.3), net investment must increase by the constant percent $\alpha\sigma$ rather than by a constant amount.

Table 8

Period	K (\$)	yp (\$)	C (\$)	I (\$)	y (\$)
1	400	100.00	80	20	100
2	420	105.00	84	21	105
3	441	110.25	88	22	110
4	463	115.75	92	25	115

21.7. To achieve equilibrium growth in a two-sector model, what is the required rate of growth of net investment if (a) $\alpha = 0.10$ and $\sigma = 0.50$, (b) $\alpha = 0.20$ and $\sigma = 0.25$ and (c) $\alpha = 0.50$ while $\sigma = 0.20$?

Since, for equilibrium growth, net investment must increase at a rate equal to $\alpha\sigma$, it is

(a) 5%.

(b) 5%.

(c) 10%.

21.8. Assume that $\alpha = 0.20$, $\sigma = 0.50$ and there is full utilization of productive capacity in period 1. If net investment is \$50 in period 1, what volume of net investment is required to achieve equilibrium growth in periods 2, 3 and 4?

Investment must increase 10% each period. Thus, net investment must equal \$50(1.10) = \$55 in period 2, \$50(1.10)² = \$60.50 in period 3 and \$50(1.10)³ = \$66.55 in period 4.

21.9. What is an economy's rate of equilibrium growth if net investment increases at a rate of $\alpha\sigma$?

In a two-sector model,

$$y = \frac{I}{\alpha} \quad \text{and} \quad \Delta y = \frac{\Delta I}{\alpha}$$

Since y is proportional to I and Δy is proportional to ΔI, then $\Delta Y/y$ must be proportional to $\Delta I/I$. Thus, if $\Delta I/I$ increases at a rate of $\alpha\sigma$, then $\Delta y/y$ must also increase at this same rate (see Section 21.3).

21.10. Figure 21-3 depicts full utilization of capacity y_0 in period 1, given the saving function S and net investment I_0. Potential output increases $y_1 - y_0$ each period as a result of net investment I_0 per period. Can the economy achieve equilibrium growth through increased consumption rather than increased net investment?

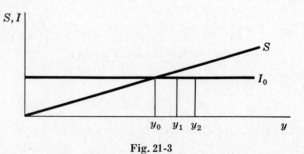

Fig. 21-3

The saving and investment schedules can intersect at income levels y_1, y_2, etc. if there is decreased saving in each successive period. Such a continuous rightward shift of the saving function lowers α and thereby reduces the economy's rate of economic growth.

21.11. Are the terms *equilibrium growth* and *maximum growth* synonymous?

Equilibrium growth signifies that there is full utilization of an increasing capacity (i.e., that the increase in potential output is met by an equal increase in aggregate spending). In a two-sector model, equilibrium growth can be achieved by continuous increases in net investment and/or continuous decreases in saving. The rate of growth is maximized only if the source of incremental spending is an exogenous increase in net investment.

21.12. What is the economy's rate of equilibrium growth for a three-sector model where there is a stable volume of net investment and exogenous government spending is the source of incremental spending?

When the source of incremental spending is consumptive government spending, the increase in potential output y_p equals σI and actual output y equals $I + G/\alpha$. For equilibrium growth, $\Delta y = \Delta y_p$ or $\Delta y_p = \sigma I = \Delta y$. The equation $y = I + G/\alpha$ can be written as $I = \alpha y - G$. Substituting, $I = \alpha y - G$ into $\Delta y = \sigma I$, we have $\Delta y = \alpha \sigma y - \sigma G$, or

$$\frac{\Delta y}{y} = \alpha \sigma - \frac{\sigma G}{y}$$

the rate of growth in actual output when consumptive government spending is the source of incremental spending.

When the source of incremental spending is public investment, the increase in potential output y_p equals $\sigma(I + G)$ and actual output y equals $I + G/\alpha$. For equilibrium growth, $\Delta y = \Delta y_p$ or $\Delta y_p = \sigma(I + G) = \Delta y$. The equation $y = I + G/\alpha$ can be written as $I + G = \alpha y$. Substituting $I + G = \sigma y$ into $\Delta y = \sigma(I + G)$, we have $\Delta y = \alpha \sigma y$, or

$$\frac{\Delta y}{y} = \alpha \sigma$$

the rate of growth in actual output when public investment is the source of incremental spending. (See Section 21.4.)

21.13. What determines an economy's rate of aggregate saving?

There is saving when income is received and not used to purchase domestic output. Thus, aggregate saving is a function of saving leakages originating from household saving, government taxes, corporate retained earnings and imports. There is an increase in the rate of aggregate saving if there is an increase in the tax rate or the propensities to import and retain earnings and a decrease in the propensity to consume.

21.14. What happens to the economy's rate of growth if the source of incremental spending is (1) an increase in consumptive government spending? (2) A reduction in the rate of taxation? (3) A reduction in the propensity to save?

The rate of growth depends upon the rate of aggregate saving, the average productivity of capital and the volume of consumptive government spending (see Problem 21.12). An increase in consumptive government spending (1) and a decline in the rate of aggregate saving [(2) plus (3)] reduce the economy's rate of growth.

INDEX

The letter p following a page number refers to a Problem.